Justin M

LIQUID CRYSTAL ORACLE

BLUE ANGEL®
PUBLISHING

Liquid Crystal Oracle

This printing 2016

Published by Blue Angel Publishing ®
80 Glen Tower Drive, Glen Waverley,
Victoria, Australia 3150
Phone: +61 3 9574 7776
Fax: +61 3 9574 7772
E-mail: info@blueangelonline.com
Website: www.blueangelonline.com

Edited by Catherine Smith

ISBN: 978-0-9805550-7-3

Editor's note: The author frequently capitalizes words that would normally appear in lower case. This is part of his writing style and is designed to emphasize important words and concepts. Out of respect for the author's work and his intention in this text, we have left these words as they were in the original manuscript.

For the Children of Light.
May your Boundless Love,
Eternal Wisdom and Patient Power
Deliver the New Earth into Peace.
Forgive Us our Ignorance of your Greatness.

Contents

Open your heart Great Solar Angel,
Bless the Sun that carries your Light.
Ignite the Flame of you incarnate.
As eyes open, the shadow will be free.

Reach not out or up, but in.
Your eternal fire may not burn its Creator.
The blessing of limitlessness is clouded only in realization.
Will you light the world and open the pathways hidden by search?

The Halls of Wisdom await,
Memories of Earth, only footprints to follow.
To each their own path by birth.
11 Great Temples, 22 Great Guardians that seek to guide.
Dare you walk the path of the ancients?
Be sure to wear the Silent blessing of Wisdom's light, True Fearless action.

I am the open door to Earth Embrace,
Hold tight the serpent's tail and ride its shadow through the Halls of Light.
Watch vigilant the empty and endless Skies.
In their abyss understood, hides the Lightning Strike of completion.

I am the night sky, Peaceful and Endless,
I am the Ocean, Vast and Flowing,
I am the Fire of mind, Focused and Inward,
I am the completion of Earth, within me all is born.

Priestess of the Silver Star,
I wear the crown of Isis and breathe the light of Sirius.
In me all polarities unite, I sit at your feet.
Bless me with a path across the Abyss,
Light my home in the Hidden walls of Shamballa,
I Serve all that ask.

Let the Children of Light rejoice,
We are the Ordained of Planet Earth.
Stand with me and together we will light the Path home,
Reborn Priests and Priestesses of the Atlantian Way of Oneness.

Introduction

Arise great Children of Light; in your hands you hold the rebirth of our Earth, A dawning of a New Age.

Upon the visible horizon sits the Earth of old, the land we walked and named Atlantis is soon to live, nurture and guide us again. The start of 2013 saw the beginning of a new age – heralding a return to the crystalline ways of unity, oneness and truth with the rising of the Goddess into the heavens and the return of the sacred masculine to the Earth's physical embrace. This is a great event that as a race we have never witnessed and one that has been in the making for 15,372 years since the Atlantian planet ascended without many of us.

This oracle will help open the doors and aid in a smooth transition back onto the masculine Earth that once was Atlantis by opening us to the Mineral kingdom's creators, the Master Crystal Devas. These great beings and the holistic energies of the crystals we love were taken from us at the fall of Atlantis as a precaution. We have worked with elementals and minor crystal Devas, but communication with these higher beings was impossible. The crystals have been reunited and the Devic paths are now active, these cards are your keys, walk gently, for with each step you kiss your finest creation.

The ancient wisdom in the book you now read and the accompanying 77 cards can function as a powerful crystal healing system individually, be applied to physical crystals or embraced as part of the holistic Atlantian Liquid Crystals healing system. Whichever you choose, the Earth's Master Crystalline Devas will rise by your side, enclose you in an octahedron of light and lovingly embrace you through the open doorways that the cards offer as you walk your healing path.

I remember the Atlantian world, though like many of us, I too was once confused by the small fragments that have ridden the waves of time better than the whole, leaving conflicting information and complexity. Ten years ago as a new millennium dawned, that changed for me. A Ruby, the Spirit of Geburah, entered my life as a gift for Twelve years from a Tibetan monastery where it resides. They told me that every 200 years since Atlantis I have come to Earth to reunite man, the crystals and their creators, the Devic Kingdom. Since then Atlantis and her ways have filled my life. Now its foundation, the holistic Minerals, Crystals and Metals of our world can come to life for you.

This is Crystal Healing the Atlantian Way, a way of Love, Wisdom and Power combined in balance as a glorious White Rose, within whose petals lies a new world, Man, Angel and Deva as one.

Blessings and Aloha,
Justin

Understanding the Crystal Information in this Guidebook

In this guidebook you will find information on each of the 77 Liquid Crystal Oracle cards. This information has been divided into numerous sections which offer a variety of different perspectives and some suggestions about how to work with each card. Below you will find a brief explanation of what you will find under each subheading to help bring you a greater understanding of each Crystal's message.

Crystal Name and Simple Purpose

The Crystal's name is at the top of this information and the Crystal's Simple Purpose with humanity follows it. The Simple purpose is what the Crystal sees its role with humanity to be in the simplest of terms. Once understood the Simple Purposes can be expanded into volumes of personal information; an art which we will expand upon later and one that empowers readings and healing sessions with the Cards, Devas and even your physical Crystals.

The Message from the Master Crystal Deva

These are channeled messages from the Master Crystal Devas, great beings who exist in the Devic Kingdom. They are the big brothers and sisters of the elementals, who are better known as Gnomes, Fairies, Sylphs and Nymphs. Each crystal has an associated Master Crystal Deva which could be thought of as a Spirit of the Crystal or an Angel of the Earth. Although much of the Devic world has been long forgotten (due to the lessons of Atlantis), your cards and the Liquid Crystals represent its rebirth and a path to explore their world. Usually you will find that the Deva's message expands the Crystal's Simple Purpose and offers a much deeper, more spiritual side to that information. Within many of the messages, you can discover meditations, activations and ancient Atlantian pathways of spiritual growth. Read these messages carefully; profound esoteric information has been deliberately hidden within them.

The Crystal in Healing

In this section you will find a description of each crystal, a little about its history, including important Atlantian information, as well as all the effects that it has in healing from the spiritual to the physical. Often you will also find basic information regarding Ascended Masters, Lords, Ladies and Deities to whom the stone is sacred.

A note on Crystal Healing - It should be noted where crystal healing is concerned that you do not need to actively have all the symptoms found in this section for each Crystal for it to be a healing support. Due to the progressive nature of dis-ease and healing, the physical symptoms should be viewed as the end result of a long pathway with a spiritual seed that may still need to be embraced. Dis-ease travels from the Loving Spiritual self, to the Mental, on to the Emotional and finally into the Etheric body where, if unrealized, it soon becomes physical. At any time we can reverse this process through realization of the loving seed on any level of self. A crystal is a powerful tool to help in this process as it serves one Simple Purpose that has expression on all levels. As the Simple purpose of a crystal and its spiritual qualities re-appear in life and are held within you, Healing will be completed in a step-by-step, permanent and holistic manner. From this we can see, that All Healing is Spiritual, All in our world stems from Love and the pathway to healing and health is Truthfulness with the self, leading to Realization. Thus a single word can change your life, to understand it, is to be Human, to allow it, is to be at One with all and honour your divinity: there is only Love.

Your Healing Journey Today

Under this title you will discover why that crystal has come into your life and what you can do to walk its healing path. If you open yourself, the crystals will speak volumes of personal truth and blessed you will be in their glorious presence fostering a relationship with the Master Devas.

The Affirmation

The Affirmations found throughout this book are intended to empower you, the Liquid Crystals and your healing ability with each crystal. They can be Spoken, Sung, Written or Listened to and will help reprogram the subconscious mind thus moving you in a certain direction or towards your Goals. An affirmation can be used anytime and anywhere but is best when you can focus on it. Although repeating the affirmation for a few minutes twice a day for a week is usually enough to allow it to have an effect on you, a twenty-one day commitment is ideal for lasting healing and growth.

Keywords to help in reading the cards

This section covers the most important aspects of a Crystal's healing pathways and correspondences. If a card is not really making sense to you, this is the first place you should come. These words will help you to read the cards by offering you an alternative understanding of a Crystal's action and will help you to open all the available pathways of information and healing that otherwise may have remained hidden.

Body Card Placement

The information found here relates to the 'Crystal Healing with your Cards' section of this book. It is here that you will find information regarding where on the body a crystal and/or the Card can be placed in order to do its best work and allow healing to result. You will also find many Trinities of Crystals which you may have never encountered. A Trinity of Crystals in healing is a sacred sequence of three stones that complement each other and result in a healing outcome that is not achievable to the same degree by working with the individual stones. This is an ancient Atlantian practice and is an art that qualified Liquid Crystal Practitioners are skilled in. There are over 150 Sacred Trinities throughout this work, and there are many more that you will discover as you work with your cards. Be creative and the cards will work their magic.

Chemical Composition

Nutritionists, Naturopaths and others that understand the body and its processes based on minerals will find this information interesting; this is the actual composition of the crystals you love. Some crystal properties are a direct result of the crystal's composition and its effects on the Bodies.

Color Rays

Here you can discover which of the 13 color rays are found in each crystal. All things in creation are composed of the colored rays and in varied percentages they give rise to many of a crystal's properties and healing abilities. The 13 color rays are Black, Red, Orange, Yellow, Green, Rose (Pink), Blue, Indigo, Violet, White, Gold, Silver and Clear. In Atlantian times when one was actively working with a crystal, a string that matched the color of its most present ray was worn as a reminder on the wrist of the receiving hand. As a general rule the hand you write with directs energy and the other receives it; this makes the receiving hand for most people their Left hand. The wearing of this string works in a similar way to an affirmation, empowering healing, and is one of the many ways to use this information.

The Animal Totems and Essential Oils

The Planet Earth has three kingdoms, the Plant, Animal and Mineral Kingdoms. This is the first time they have been corresponded and united in the one place since Atlantis. The Animals and Essential oils that are included here are energetic matches to the crystals thus delivering a similar message. You will find that you are familiar with most of them, but, I have given the exact matches as they were on the Atlantian Earth, so some may seem a little unusual until you explore them further. It is also worth noting that similar oils and animals have similar messages and roles with humanity. In Atlantian times the Animal and Plant Kingdoms were divided into areas of wisdom, with the result that the message of the Rabbit is similar to that of the Mouse and thus its path of realization is accessible through the same crystal.

The Oils and Animals work well to empower a crystal's healing purpose, which is as simple as wearing or burning the Oil as you meditate with the card, and/or calling the Animal to be with you as you work.

Often the Devas of the Crystals will use the Animal Kingdom to direct you to a certain crystal you should be working with. Keep your eyes open; there are no coincidences, at worst you may be wrong, at best you may change your life. Placing a Crystal card under a candle of the matching color, anointed with its oil, will fill the room with its Simple Purpose and Frequency; a beautiful gift to the home.

Note - Magically anointing a candle with oil is always done from the top of the candle to the middle and then from the base to the middle. This ensures the energy will be there for the whole time the candle burns as the middle is always there no matter how short the candle gets.

How to work with your Liquid Crystal Oracle cards

Aligning with the Crystal Devas and Activating your Cards in their World

As with any new magical or spiritual tool, a brief ritual of dedication is helpful in setting up a link between the item, you and your energy field. This is especially important with your Liquid Crystal cards as the Crystal Devas exist at a refined frequency that few people visit regularly or have experienced for extended periods. The Atlantian Octahedron of Light activation below will powerfully aid this and open Devic communication so you may clearly hear the crystals sing their song.

The Octahedron of Light

In Atlantian times it was recognized that geometric light bodies surrounded the physical human. These shapes of light are worked with as vehicles to activate, change and align a person into various frequencies or realities. The most sacred of these in Atlantis was the Octahedron of Light as it opens direct alignment to the Lords of Nature, the Devic Kingdom, keepers of the Flame of Wisdom, in which it surrounds you. Fragments of this wisdom are responsible for the great Pyramids of Egypt and our fascination with them, an octahedron is formed when two pyramids are joined base to base. This powerful tool still exists around you, it just needs the gentle push of realization, and in fact, just reading this should be enough to start the activation process. Below you will find two options, a simple option and the full ancient activation process, I have incorporated the cards into the process to open a powerful bridge – the choice is yours. Before beginning either please examine the below diagram so you know what everything looks like and can recognize that an Octahedron is two pyramids joined at their base.

Simple Octahedron Activation

Sit quietly and visualize an Octahedron spinning around you, hold your cards to your heart and see them also enclosed in a small spinning Octahedron. Take the Octahedron from around the cards into your heart and out through your feet into the Earth. Link both the Octahedrons together with a ray of light and allow them to spin in opposite directions.

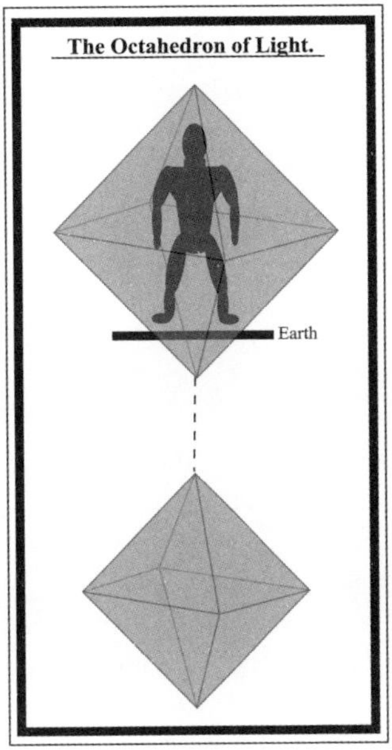

The Full Atlantian Octahedron of Light Activation and Devic Alignment

1) Sit quietly with your cards held to your Heart Chakra (Center of your chest). Visualize a Silver pyramid above your head pointing up and a Gold pyramid below your feet pointing down. Now visualize the same thing much smaller around your cards, just above and below your hands.

2) See two colored rays of light that are individual to you, one from above and one from below, pass through the points of the pyramids then connect at the Heart Chakra (Center of your chest) forming a small white star. Allow the same thing to occur with the cards, then merge the star from within the cards into the one in your heart.

3) Now using your in-breath, draw all the pyramids together, the large ones around your body and the small ones around your cards. They should all meet at the level of your Heart. Often, as they meet and lock together, you may hear a sound or experience a jolt. Once joined, the Octahedrons will spin slowly at first then faster and faster, one should go left and the other right, just let them spin.

4) You are now inside a spinning octahedron of light and at the level of your Heart where you hold your cards they are also enclosed in one. Now draw the octahedron from around the cards into your body and let it move down and out through your feet, coming to rest in the Earth connected to the larger octahedron by a ray of light. (See diagram)

5) Sit quietly, feel and see the octahedrons spin in opposite directions, they are now activated and your cards are powerfully aligned to you. The Master Crystal Devas can now more easily offer guidance.

To work with your Octahedron of Light, just let your attention go to it briefly, let it spin and then invite the Devas into the one below your feet to offer guidance. When communication is active the octahedrons will join together point to point.

A similar activation is completed with a Star Tetrahedron for Angelic Communication where one exists around the body and one above your head. These three geometries, if we include the Physical body, represent the light vehicles of Power, Love and Wisdom and are important in the balance of the Three Fold Flame and Integrated Ascension process.

Understanding the Liquid Crystal Cards

Drawing the Images

Possibly my greatest gift in this life is my spiritual vision, I see many things that others as yet have not allowed themselves to see. Often spirit and physicality for me look the same. As a spiritual healer this gift has always been very powerful allowing me to diagnose, locate and find cure pathways for disease in the physical and energy bodies. Unfortunately in this life, I am not much of an artist, so sharing my gift has been limited to the voice, but when it came to the crystals, that was not going to be enough. The colors, movement, geometry and doorways of the crystals and the Devas that I encountered needed to be shared. I decided that I would channel the art, bring the Crystal Devas into my body and let them draw themselves. They asked me to provide them with a crystalline tool through which they could work more easily, which confused me at first and then I realized that Computers are just that. So I purchased some drawing programs, understanding that I would thankfully not need to operate them, the Devas would. The 77 images that are now your cards are not only almost exactly what I see when working with the Master Crystal Devas, but are also what the Devas want us to see when we are in their glorious presence. I still cannot operate the programs and certainly cannot reproduce the images without their help. In all, drawing the 77 Master Crystal Devas took a period of 6 months, at the close of which I was recognized as a living High Priest of the Atlantian Way. This was mainly due to the channeling process, in which I had to sit as the crystal, meaning that all of its lessons and sacred wisdoms had to be embraced, dealt with and integrated on all levels. This was a quickening of sorts, a time of great healing and a path I now pass to you. Enjoy your crystalline journey, your ascension into light and liberation from rebirth, should you wish it, rests in your hands as you hold the cards.

The Devas in the Images

Looking at the cards you will see the actual Master Crystal Deva as a similar structure and shape in the card, triangular and geometric sitting behind the Symbol Doorway, that is the structure that they wish us to see them as. The other shapes and geometrics on the cards represent energy movements. The Devic, like Angels who are really spherical in form when you really see them, are not humanoid. Angels are Spheres of light, appearing in and as vortices and curved light and Devas are more Cubic, Angular and Geometric, appearing in moving linear light. The Human body is a masterful combination of both these geometrics which is where we get the term, "made in the image of God," we are the ultimate Vessel, a structure of Love. One of the conditions given to me in offering an image of the Devas as beings to the world, was that they would not be made human, as it interferes with their purpose, energy and ability to function. We made that mistake with the Angels many years ago. It should also be noted that the images are of the holistic Master Crystal Devas. This means that for example, the Clear Quartz image can only be seen by reuniting 16,854 individual Quartz Crystals, each from different locations around the Earth into one space or vessel, in this case a Liquid Crystal. We refer to this endeavor in the Liquid Crystals as, "The reuniting of the Stones". This is an ongoing immense project spanning three personal generations, 15 dedicated years of my life and the potent guiding hands of the Druids, Essenes and the Brotherhood of Light.

The colors on the cards are also a direct match to that crystal's Color Ray percentage make up, making them useful in healing, a path that is also enhanced by the symbol, geometry and Deva's direct presence, but more on that later.

The Crystal Symbols (Center of the Card)

Not since Atlantis have the Master Devas been directly interacted with, so it stands to reason that we will be a little rusty at locating their frequencies and remaining within them. To aid us in achieving correct attunement, the Master Devas, once their crystals were reunited, gave us their Atlantian sound, which we would call a name and their ancient Atlantian or Lemurian doorway Symbol. These can aid us in communication and other contact via meditation, but the symbol also forms a direct link to the united master crystalline energy grid and calls forth the Deva. With a little practice this can be seen as a small vortex of colored light over the symbol. When interacted with, this vortex of light becomes more geometric, can grow, surround and be integrated into the self for healing, communication and guidance, thus following the same energy pathway as a physical stone. For that reason the cards can be placed on the body for Crystal Healing with great results. The symbols can also be drawn on the skin for healing and even placed on or under candles to fill a room with a crystal's properties and the Deva's presence. The symbols are thus a powerful divination tool and just looking at them is often enough to start a healing process, they can be worked with by a Liquid Crystal Practitioner and now by you to diagnose and find the perfect remedy or guidance in every case and situation.

The Deva's Name (Top of the Card)

Located at the top of the card, these are actually the Ancient Atlantian names for the crystals we love. The Atlantian language is slowly reappearing on our planet and will get more common as we approach the Atlantian Earth's rebirth in 2013. A lot of people call the language Star or Light language and are fluent in it, feeling its effects more than understanding it as a language. Atlantian as a Language was very feeling-based towards the fall of Atlantis. It has a lot in common with Hawaiian, Hebrew, Arabic and Egyptian often sounding like a beautiful blend of all of them. In all there were eleven principle Atlantian Languages, but the eleventh was and still is spoken in the great Halls of Shamballa. The Deva's name is very powerful as a Mantra or sound repeated as a meditation. It will powerfully call that being into your energy field and especially your Octahedron of Light, once active. Pronunciation will sometimes be difficult, the Devas are not fussy and remember it's about the feeling. To help a little, I have put hyphens into their names; a hyphen means a brief pause when you say the name.

The Simple Purposes (Bottom of the Cards)

At the bottom of each card you will find one or two words that are given to me by the Master Crystal Deva as an answer to the simple question, "What is your purpose with humanity?" These words are referred to as the simple purposes of the crystals. In readings, these few words can be expanded into volumes of information. For the ones that are a little difficult to understand there are more keywords in each crystal's section throughout this book to take you to a deeper level. When doing a reading, the simple purposes and other keywords can be strung together into a sentence that becomes a healing affirmation for you or your client; this is referred to as, "Singing the Stones." The simple purposes are perhaps the most important part of the Liquid Crystals, if you know them, your readings will be powerful and accurate, remember, they represent what the Earth wants you to know about her children, the crystals.

The Atlantian Cities (At Bottom corners of the Cards)

At the bottom corners of the cards you will find Dots and Dashes, these are referred to as Galactic Notation and are a form of Numbering, a Dot equals one and a Dash equals five. In Atlantian times there were Eleven great cities or regions on the Earth, each of these had a sacred name and the seven crystals found in that region were sacred to it. Eleven cities with seven crystals each, leads us to the sacred 77 crystals of Atlantis and your Cards. The eleven cities also formed the Tree of Life across the Planet so the numbers also could be taken to represent its spheres if that is a wisdom you possess. The table below offers some of the basic associations and alignments. An Advanced Liquid Crystal practitioner can combine this information with your personal details to create an individual Crystalline Ascension Program based on the Cities of Atlantis.

Due to their profound spiritual significance as a higher path, all the Crystals in the below table have been intentionally given out of order except those of City 10. The path they offer can be seen by uniting the simple purposes of the Crystals in order and Singing the song they offer. When this is done in the Tenth City, En-Kai-Pan, we receive its hidden offering as follows -

"Ground the spirit into the body physical, embrace the gifts and joys of this your greatest journey, the ascent to Earth of the absolute.
Allow the fears of a mortal world to fall from you as you fearlessly step in the direction of your unlimited potential, each movement a Spiritual beginning, a journey back to God.
Let your earthly worlds unite to birth the wisdoms gathered and shine like the blinding light that you are in completion, a light of physical Radiance often only found in the unified heart."

City No.	*Assigned Egyptian God / Goddess*	*City Name*	*Sacred Atlantian Crystals*
•	Osiris	Golgotha	Boji Stone, Larimar, Diamond, Pyrite, Clear Quartz, Tourmaline Pink, Tanzanite.
••	Thoth	B'ani-or-a	Lapis Lazuli, Charoite, Rhodochrosite, Turquoise, Selenite, Sodalite, Hemimorphite.
•••	Maat	Ahonuia	Sapphire, Coral Black, Chrysocolla, Pearl, Herkimer Diamond, Tourmaline Green, Sugilite.
••••	Ptaah	Pacifca	Gold, Fluorite, Citrine Quartz, Amazonite, Lepidolite, Angelite, Amethyst.
▬	Seth	Alteza	Ruby, Calcite Green, Kyanite, Zircon, Labradorite, Black Tourmaline, Agate Botswana.
• ▬	Ra	Ihm'skara	Emerald, Clear Calcite, Jasper, Topaz, Kunzite, Peridot, Sunstone.
•• ▬	Hathor	Venuska	Silver, Morganite, Carnelian, Crocite, Blood Stone, Rose Quartz, Malachite.
••• ▬	Anubis	Bennua	Rhodonite, Smoky Quartz, Tigers Eye, Azurite, Opal, Aquamarine, Blue Lace Agate.
•••• ▬	Isis	Lokahia	Amber, Moonstone, Jade, Iolite, Onyx (Black), Apatite, Apophyllite
▬ ▬	Nephthys	En-Kai-Pan	Hematite, Lodestone, Chrysoprase, Aventurine, Howlite, Petrified Wood, Sulphur.
• ▬ ▬	Horus	Shamballa	Peach Calcite, Garnet, Celestite, Moldavite, Obsidian, Dioptase, Elestial Quartz.

Reading the Cards

As with any reading or consulting any oracle, there are many paths, most of which are personal and based on the individual reader. Some of my personal rules that have served me well over the many years I have worked with cards are below, you may wish to adopt some of them.

My Personal Rules in Reading Cards

- Intuition and Guidance come first, what the cards say comes second.
- Always deliver the truth the cards reveal without judgment and never lie.
- Set your intentions before beginning.
- Never simply look at a card, See into it, Feel it and Know its Purpose as personally as possible.
- All processes are a two way exchange, know what you Learnt.
- All Communication is a two way path and is mutually healing.
- Be sure that the person receiving the reading touches the cards at some point.
- With the Crystal Cards, I always locate a single crystal or Trinity of crystals (Three in a set order) that are most needed by my client and prescribe them to be taken over the next 21 days.

Universal Aspects of Card Work

Below I have elaborated on some of the most important aspects of working with cards that as far as I know are quite universal. They will certainly influence your accuracy. The most important rule, which is so often overlooked, is having a set process that you follow from the start of the reading. This plan should include who, how, where and when in relation to Shuffling, Handling and Placing the cards. This sets up the reading and allows all the personal, spiritual and in this case Devic energies that are needed in the reading to place themselves where they need to be to come out of the pack. If you change the nature or placement aspects of a reading halfway through you should give the cards a chance to rearrange themselves accordingly. Extra cards can be added once the initial layout is present for further clarification, which is a common practice.

You should also decide if the person receiving the reading is going to touch the cards. I believe it is important in aligning the reading to their energy field, but some readers worry their deck will then pick up negativity. The Liquid Crystal deck is self cleansing due to the many purification crystals it contains, but if you are worried about it, to cleanse them, hold the cards to your heart and see an Octahedron of Light around them, fill it with light and then release that light into the Earth.

Inverted Cards present a few problems for people; you need to have a way of understanding inverted cards, they will come out. Some readers just ignore them, others assign meaning to them; it is up to you.

It is common practice that the meanings of inverted cards are read as opposite to their normal meaning. I don't often do that with the Liquid Crystal cards. But, I do recognize inverted cards to be the Crystals that are most needed, they are the ones that often stimulate powerful healing and are usually the ones that the person receiving the reading is most aligned with. Whatever you choose, have it set at the beginning of the reading and if you are going to look into inverted cards, shuffle in a manner so the cards can get upside down in the deck, I recommend stirring them in a circular motion on a table. Note also that cards are always turned to the side of a deck when being placed, if you flip them bottom to top it changes their orientation on the table.

The only other really important part of a reading is possessing and understanding the question, purpose or reason for consulting the cards, which is of course part of the above mentioned set intent. It is important that we attempt to make all our questions open ended. This means that they should not be phrased so a yes/no answer is even possible. A good reader can take simple yes/no question and turn it into hours of insight into Love, Life, Health, Spirituality and the Universe.

Singing the Stones

Singing the Stones is an ancient Atlantian process that is still practiced today by a few, where crystals, minerals and metals are sung out of the Earth, usually via rivers and streams. The song that draws these Minerals is related to their Simple Purpose. Where the singer has a need for the healing aspects of a Mineral, the Earth recognizes that and sends forth the cure. This means that all minerals, via their Simple Purpose with humanity, hold a song. When three or more minerals are sequenced that song becomes a powerful healing path of divine proportions. With your Crystal Cards and the Simple Purposes on them, you can now sing their songs which are more like affirmations describing a healing path to be walked. You will find that to really sing the stones, takes a little practice and the keywords in each crystal's section of this book will help. Also it is important to know that sometimes the order of crystals in a reading needs to be changed for the song to flow and make sense. To sing the songs hidden in the crystals you will need to understand the Crystal, how it speaks and how it heals. Below are a few examples using a Crystal Trinity spread (Three Cards), their Song is at the bottom.

From this we can also see one of the most forgotten aspects of Crystal Healing. It is not really the number, color or position of crystals placed on the body for healing that is important, it is the Sequencing. Below you can begin to see that three crystals would offer 6 healing paths or songs, and thus 6 different outcomes as their order is changed. There are some beautiful songs waiting inside you, as you evolve, heal and grow with the crystals, sing their songs to the waiting world.

The Spiritual Warrior Trinity

Card Order	Crystal	Simple Purpose
1	Ruby	The Spiritual Warrior
2	Sunstone	Ra, Light Radiant
3	Topaz	Confident Manifestation

"Stand firm Spiritual Warrior, courage and passion are yours, the Light of the Great Sun lives in you, Radiant and Shining, embrace it now and Confidently Manifest your dreams with your new found light."

Release the Past to Life Purpose Trinity

Card Order	Crystal	Simple Purpose
1	Garnet	Manifestation of Purpose
2	Green Calcite	Letting Go
3	Zircon	Life Changes

"I walk the path of purpose, free from my past I let go of attachment and openly accept life change."

The Step by Step Liquid Crystal Card Reading

1) Activate the Octahedrons of Light, Intention should be enough.
2) Recognize and understand the question, purpose or reason for consulting the cards.
3) Decide on the type of reading, Number of cards and Layout, Set your intentions.
4) Shuffle, Cut and Lay the cards as you have decided.
5) Read the cards individually against their position. It often helps to turn the cards one at a time.
6) Read the cards against each other and their positions.
7) Conclude by locating usually no more than Three Crystals that are needed in life now and place them in a healing sequence or order by using their simple purpose. The simple purposes of the crystals and other keywords can be placed into a healing sentence or affirmation that is given to your client. (See above, 'Singing the Stones'.)
8) You may wish to place the important cards on the body of the person receiving the reading to begin the process of change and healing that the reading has revealed. (See page 31 'Crystal Healing with the Cards'.)

Some Crystal Card Layouts or Spreads

Below you will find some of my favorite card spreads, there are so many others that are wonderful, please use any you have come across in your journeys and feel free to make up your own.

Note -The Crystal Cards that present in any reading can later be placed on the body to powerfully activate healing and change. (See page 31 'Crystal Healing with the Cards'.)

Simple One, Two and Three Card Layouts

Choosing a single card is a good way to start a day and a simple way to get fast insights about the energies around us. It is very important with single card readings to have your intentions set before beginning and to formulate your questions clearly.

If you are doing a reading for yourself on a sensitive or important matter, it is sometimes wise to write down your queries and the purpose of the reading prior to beginning. That way if the reading goes a little sour, you won't be able to escape the truth, which we are all so good at doing. After writing the result down, you can deal with the issue at a pace that suits you rather than having to do it all at once at the reading's conclusion.

Whenever I do a single card reading for my Lower self or another person, I nearly always place a second card across it for confirmation. I assign this Second card to my Higher self so I know where it stands on the same matter, this usually shows the reason behind the first card, the cause of the current situation and thus the healing path becomes obvious. The Second Crystal is my pathway to growth, realization and healing, it is usually the Liquid Crystal I would take and work with as a solution.

The Three Card Spread, The Trinity Reading

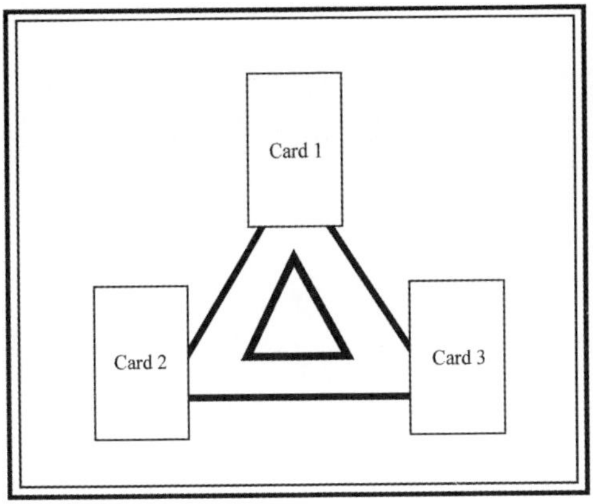

This is a basic Three Card Reading in which Card One represents the Current Situation, Card Two represents the Healing Path, Direction or Needed Action and the Third Card represents the Outcome or End Result. The Crystals can however, be read against any of the chosen areas in the below table as long as you set your intent before beginning. Place the cards as in the diagram above in a triangle formation. This is the most common reading done by a Liquid Crystal Practitioner, who then arranges the Crystals in an order of action so they sing their song and makes the crystals up as Liquid Remedies to be taken and worked with over a 21 day process.

Card 1	Card 2	Card 3
Physical	Emotional	Mental
Physicality	Astral	Spiritual
Past	Present / Now	Future
Appearance	Reality	Possibility
Beginning	Obstacle	Outcome
Wisdom	Love	Power
Reasons	Directions / Path	Results
Current Animal	Current Plant (Essential Oil)	Current Mineral (Crystal)
Spirit	Feminine	Masculine

More Advanced Card Spreads

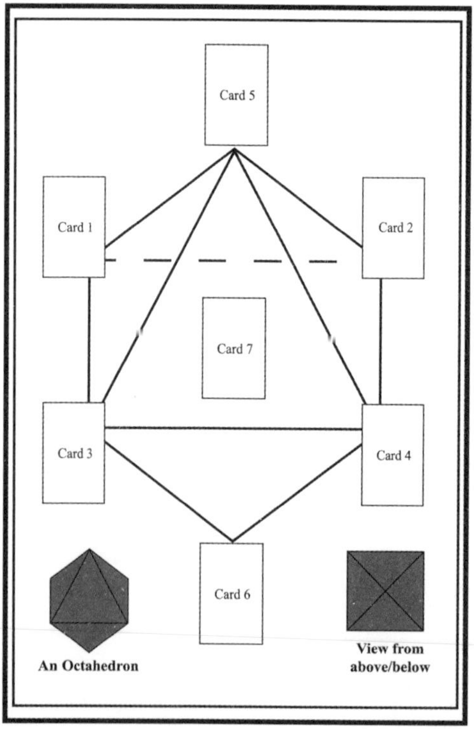

The Seven Card Devic Octahedron Layout

This reading is more complex but offers great information and insight. The Cards are laid out as in the diagram and read against their positions. The cards can also be read against each other along the edges of the Octahedron in Triangles or Trinities. Once you understand the Geometry, this offers greater depth and insight to an advanced reader.

Card	Attribute	Meaning
1	Earth	Physicality, Gnomes, Structure, Foundation, Outcomes. The Daughter
2	Air	Thoughts, Mind, Sylphs, Fairies, Creations, Focus, Projects. The Son
3	Fire	Etheric, Energy Application and Direction, Salamanders, Passion, Will, Enthusiasm. The Father
4	Water	Emotions, Undines, Relationships, The Mother
5	Angelic Kingdom / Power	Governing Crystal of Power. Your Engine.
6	Devic Kingdom/ Wisdom	Governing Crystal of Wisdom. Your Recipe/ Instructions
7	You /Human/ Love	Governing Crystal of Love and You at this time. Your very Substance.

The Tree of Life Layout

The Tree of Life is a detailed spiritual diagram that maps creation and all that is; it is the basic model from which many of our spiritual and religious directions and ideas have originated. The Tree has a strong association with Atlantis and the Devic, so it stands to reason that a layout related to it should be included here. Traditionally the Tree of Life spread is one of the oldest and most informative Tarot Card spreads, though it is often quite overwhelming, complex and difficult to read. Thus in recent times, in our modern Knowledge rather than Wisdom based world, other spreads are commonly substituted. I personally believe that the use of the true Tree of Life layout is a mark of an advanced and accomplished reader.

In the below table I have given you two versions, one that is more traditional and another that is easier to read and should prove great at answering a set Question, it is your choice.

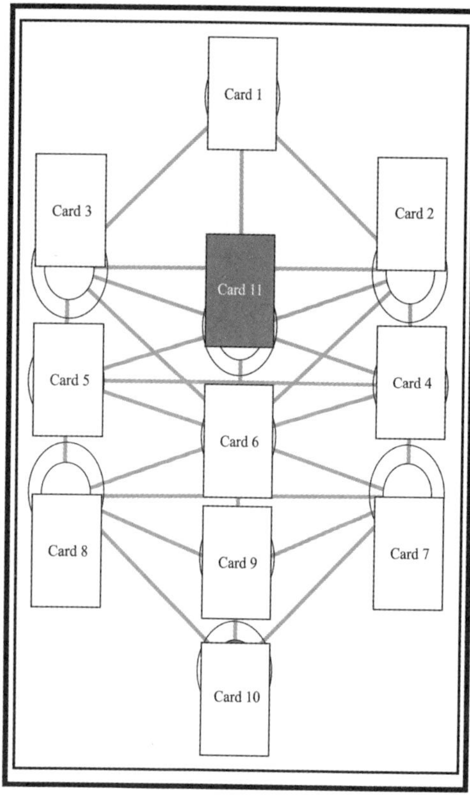

Advice for the Tree of Life Reading

- Always lay all the Cards face down to start as shown in the diagram.
- Turn Cards 2 and 3 to begin, they show the Issue or Question for what it is.
- Then turn Cards 7, 8, 9, and 10, they show your position related to the Issue or Question.
- Next turn and read Cards 4 and 5, they show all the outside influences.
- Now turn Cards 6 and 1, these define your next Action, the Cause of the Issue / Question and what you will get out of its solution.
- Finish with Card 11, your Future and next Pathway is found here.

The Tree of Life Layouts

Card / Sphere	Traditional Layout	Set Question Layout
1	Supreme Hidden influence, Divine Force	Spiritual Aspects, Reason or Personal Growth related to the Issue / Question
2	Divine Masculine influence, Wisdom "Great Father"	Energy behind the Issue / Question
3	Divine Feminine influence, Understanding "Great Mother"	Form the Issue / Question takes
4	Unconditional Love, Dealing with Authority, Spirituality	Things, Influences or people working with you

Card / Sphere	Traditional Layout	Set Question Layout
5	Divine Will, Energy direction or conflict, Courageous Aspects.	Things, Influences or people working against you
6	Higher Self, Soul's Intentions Focus of Divine Will. Balance.	Soul /Higher Self Guidance, the best thing you can do
7	Cycles, Emotions, Fertile areas, Victory over Ego.	Your Emotions
8	Mind, Mental, Intellect, Health Glory.	Your Thinking
9	Unconscious (Subconscious), Dreams	Your Persona (Your everyday self and how you present yourself)
10	Material life, Work, Physicality	Your Physical Self (Body) and Possessions
11	Outcome, Possible Solutions, Doorway to next Stage of Life	Your Possible Future, That which is unknown and your door to the next Stage of Life

Crystal Healing with the Cards

In the creation of the Liquid Crystals and thus the card deck you now hold, the Master Devic Grids around our planet for the 77 principle minerals of the Earth were re-activated. As the crystals were re-united, the symbols became a key to that grid, opening it up and linking to it.

On the back of your Cards you will find the Atlantian Emblem. This is an Ancient Devic Gateway that remains active, due to the 77 symbols surrounding it, and opens a direct path offering their glorious energies to our world. To link the Master crystal grid into a Card, all that would need to be done, is a chosen crystal's symbol would need to be placed in its center. So….if you hold a card up to the light, you will see that is exactly what we did. This coupled with the exact Color Ray matches, Deva Names, Simple Purposes, your healing intent and the geometry in the cards allows them to heal directly.

The cards can be placed, symbol up, on the body just as a Crystal Healer would place stones in a healing session. This will create powerful and lasting healing. The only downfall is, with no truly tangible physical object of healing, the self can undo the healing work quite rapidly. This is the same as any energetic healing process and is where it is good to recognize that you should back your work up with a physical stone that is carried for at least 21 days, or ideally an ingested Liquid Crystal as an ongoing complete healing pathway. Throughout this guide book there is a section under each Crystal titled, Body Card Placement, where you will find extra layout information and activities for that stone.

Crystal Healing and How Crystals Heal

The Basics

The Healing abilities of Crystals arise due to a combination of five important aspects that they Collect, Contain and/or Display, they are:

- A Crystal's individual percentages of the 13 Color Rays.
- A Crystal's Physical and Energetic Sacred Geometry sequences.
- The Elements or Combination of Elements that compose a Mineral.
- A Crystal's Formation Process and other Journey Lessons it has Learnt.
- The imprint of Human Consciousness during their formation process.

All these aspects make their way into the bodies and aid the manifestation of health on all levels.

The Not So Basic

The Mineral Kingdom is made up of Elements. These are set aspects of earth that are identical no matter where they are found in the Universe, Elements form Minerals which form the basis of Nutrition and an important part of what we need to be healthy. These Minerals are the same substances we know as Metals, Crystals and Stones. In reality we should receive a balance of these by interaction with our natural world, as well as in food and water as part of our natural health regime. But it is not just the physical substance that is of importance to our health, it is also the colors, energies and geometries that minerals contain and broadcast that allow the true healthy state on all levels. These make their way into our bodies energetically mainly via the Major and Micro-Chakra system and are then transported and held in the blood which is a Liquid Mineral Matrix, until given purpose.

In truth, energy is just energy, but given purpose or intention, energy arranges itself and becomes geometric. That geometry is then broadcast outwardly by your Chakra system to eventually manifest your reality; you can watch this happen, if you desire perception. The minerals of your inner, outer, energetic and physical world, which are the Crystals, Rocks and Metals you love, aid this process by offering the most refined and perfected, geometric sequences of Spirituality, Health and Living, to the body. If the self needs them, they are integrated and the creation and healing pathways become active on all levels.

Laying the Cards on the Body

All information and higher wisdoms associated with physical crystal healing apply to the cards, some key points are below.

- Guidance comes first; let the Devas place the cards where they want them.
- Matching Crystals and Chakra colors works well when unsure of where to place a card, but colors are never absolute, sometimes crystals that do not match Chakra colors are potent healers in that area.
- You should Breathe out and the person receiving should Breathe in just as the card is placed.
- Be Creative and make geometric patterns, Crystal healing is always Symmetrical, if you draw a line down the middle of a layout, it should be the same on both sides.
- More is not usually better or more powerful.
- Crystals enter the body easier at the major doorways of the body, they are the 13 Articulations and 9 major Chakras (See below diagram.)
- Cards can be stacked on top of each other.
- Layouts are easy for self with the cards if you put them on the floor and then lie on them.
- Timing is everything when placing and removing Crystals.
- Check the Body Card Placement section on each Crystal's Section in this book if you're not sure.
- You won't do the wrong thing, the Devas won't let you, relax and don't forget to breathe.

The Major Chakras

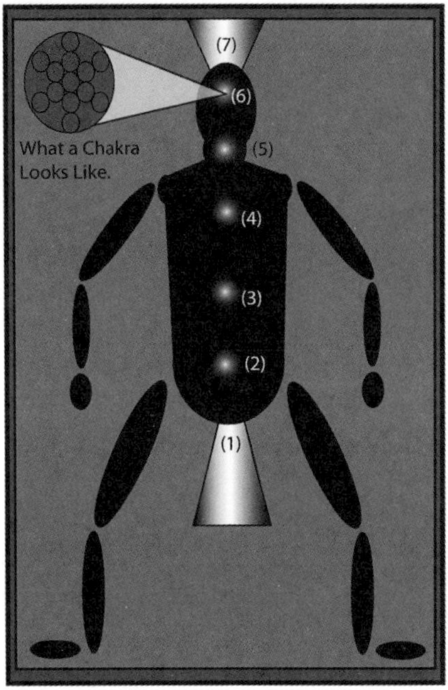

The Major Articulations on the Body

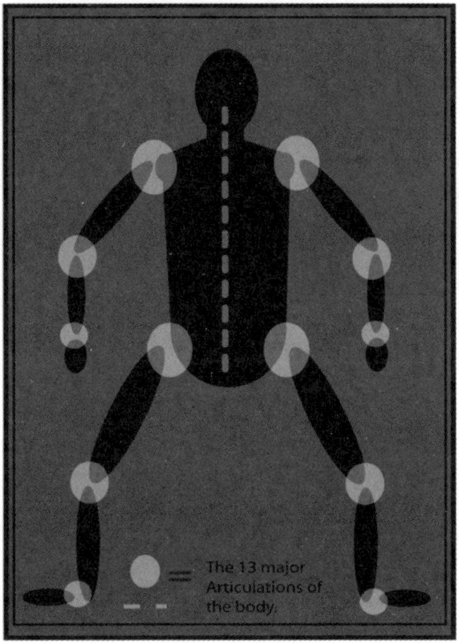

Chakra Health Reading and Healing Layout

The human energy system is divided into Light Bodies or layers. These are arranged in Triplets and separated by a forth body that acts as a bridge. Any holistic insight into health should show what is happening on at least the first seven levels of self. These relate in order to the seven in-body Chakras. You will find these in the table below, starting from the physical moving outwards as you go down the table from 1 to 7.

Card / Light Body	Related Chakra, Common Color and Body Location	Functions and Attributes
1. The Etheric/Physical (Classed as one body)	Base Chakra, Red, Base of the Spine facing Down	Physicality and Creation, Lower Expression and Action. Grounding, Will to Live, Physical Life Purpose and Choices
2. The Emotional Body	Sacral Chakra, Orange, Belly Button or just below it	Feelings, Creativity, Life Changes, Sexuality, Fertility
3. The Mental Body	Solar Plexus Chakra, Yellow, Center of the Body	Thoughts. Personal Power Center, Physical Will, Opinions and Beliefs Related to Self, Self Esteem
4. The Astral Body which is a bridge	Heart Chakra, Pink and Green, Center of the Chest	The Filter, Active Processes and Areas of Healing, Dreams. Space of Love and Relationships
5. Higher Etheric body	Throat Chakra, Blue, Throat	Higher Expression, Action, Voice, Communication, Responsibilities and Truths
6. Higher Emotional Body	Third Eye Chakra, Indigo, Center of the Forehead	High Feelings, Service, Vision, Spiritual Direction, Intuition
7. The Higher Mind	Crown Chakra, White, Crown of the Head shining Up	High Thought, Divine Will, Connection to Spirit. Knowing

Before beginning this activity, set your intention to discover the crystal needed on each level of self for Balance, Health and Alignment to Purpose. The cards are placed in a straight column, card one at the bottom representing the Physical Body and Base Chakra and Card Seven at the top representing the Higher Mind and the Crown Chakra. At the close of this reading, the Crystal Cards that present can be placed on the body at the corresponding Chakras to powerfully activate healing and change.

The Devic Kingdom

"When we plant a tree, we need three things, soil, seed and the will to complete the task. But not all is as it seems, for the soil is of Love, will is of the Mind and the seed is all Emotion. The Tree that results, at times end, will be an image of Emotion frozen by the will within the substance of God. The Devic path is an emotional one, thus not taken by many. Pure Wisdom is always Emotional; it is the Forgotten Feeling path of The Supreme Oneness."

Here on Earth we have three evolving kingdoms, all three are moving toward completion and interact with each other constantly; they are the Human, Devic and Angelic. Each of these kingdoms holds complete mastery in one of the three aspects or breaths of the supreme creator, which are Love, Power and Wisdom.

The three aspects of the Creator are found within all living things, within the heart and in unified glory they are called The Three Fold Flame. The Three Fold Flame is a means of locating balance and ultimately the true self, so as to return to our glory as pure Unconditional Love in Oneness.

In the Human Kingdom we are striving to find completion, at which time we become Ascended Masters, we are the keepers of the Flame of Love.

In the Devic Kingdom elementals are evolving into Master Devas and ultimately into Elohim, they are the keepers of the Flame of Wisdom.

In the Angelic Kingdom Angels are evolving into Arch Angels and are the keepers of the Flame of Power.

By interacting with each other we all facilitate growth, everybody gains. The Devic Kingdom has been the most forgotten of the three, due to what occurred in Atlantis and with the return of the Atlantian Earth in 2013; The Devic Kingdom is now lifting itself into human perception so we can embrace our Wisdom. Your Cards represent an active doorway into their world and were recreated to serve that exact purpose.

How the Devic World Functions

A Deva could be called an Angel of the Earth; they are responsible for the creation of all form and are often referred to as "The Holders of Form".

The Kingdom of Inner Earth is set up much the same as the human kingdom, a hierarchy of beings based on service and spiritual attainment. The members of the

Devic kingdom are the keepers of the Flame of Wisdom for our planet, the Human kingdom the keepers of the Flame of Love and the Angelic kingdom the keepers of the Flame of Power.

In the Devic kingdom, the least evolved forms are the Elementals; they correspond to the elements, Earth, Air, Fire and Water. The elementals are better known as Gnomes, Fairies, Sylphs and Nymphs.

Based on their level of wisdom they increase in what we call size. So the Queen of the Fairies, for example, is about four feet to five feet tall, whilst a basic elemental is only half a foot tall. The highest, most wise of the Devic Kingdom are the Elohim. These are governing Devas that rule an entire category, for example there is an Elohim of the Entire Mineral Kingdom, one for each element and one for each of the Seven main rays of Creation. These beings are large in the human idea of space, standing hundreds of feet tall. Between the elementals and the Elohim we find the Devas, these are separated into three main categories, Sub-Devas, General Devas and Master Devas, also called Divine Creators.

An example of the way this works would be with a vast mineral like Clear Quartz, there is a Sub-Deva for quartz representing Victoria, Australia, a General Quartz Deva representing Australian Quartz and a Master Quartz Deva representing all quartz on this Planet. To communicate with Sub-Divas is as simple as sitting, meditating or tuning into a single physical stone. To experience a General Deva one would have to have access to a Crystal from each area of Australia, this would allow all the Sub-Devic to be present as a unified whole giving rise to the General Deva. To experience a Master Deva one must have a crystal from each area of the planet where it is found, all in the one location, with Clear Quartz that was 16,854 single pieces. This opens and activates the Unified or Master Crystal Grid around the planet, bringing all the Sub-Devas and General Devas into oneness.

In ancient Lemuria, to contact the Master Devas was easy, as we were an etheric energy based existence that was plugged into the master grids. In Atlantian times, all Clear Quartz was still located in one Earth region and thus was naturally holistic, so access to the Master Devas was still available. But, at the fall of Atlantis, to protect us from ourselves, the Earth moved the crystals into separation around her body, and this also meant we lost our contact with the Master Devas. Not since Atlantis has someone reunited the 77 key minerals of Earth. The Liquid Crystals have achieved this and in doing so have reopened the true voice of the mineral kingdom, The Master Devic. The Liquid Crystals and the cards you now have are part of a global directive to reconnect with these Divine beings and are the only source of their energies united into oneness on Earth.

Devic Communication and Knowing They Are With You

Devas communicate principally in geometry, color and form, if they want your attention they will get it. People always say to me they want a sign from spirit. The Devas as the holders of form, usually deliver before asked, but the problem with their signs is they are often so Physical people generally don't recognize them for what they are. As paths of communication, Ascended Masters most easily offer Dreams, Visions and Sounds, Angels most easily offer Feelings, Fragrances and Fire, the Master Devas tap you on the shoulder, move things and affect Physicality, especially nature. Strong signs of their presence are Orbs or Balls of colored Light, Unusual crackling in the fire place, Feathers, Animals, Falling Leaves, Placed Flowers, Four Leaf Clovers, Grass growing in Circles, Unusual Clouds and early morning pictures in condensation on windows. The Master Devas can also rapidly alter body temperature when present or make you physically vibrate.

Above all things, the activation of the Octahedron of Light and ultimately seeing all as one is the most powerful way to enhance Devic communication, but all members of the Devic Kingdom love music, rhyme, poetry, dance and the night hours.

"Seek not a Sign from the Little Ones of Earth, instead let your Physical Life be One.
Take each step with Respect, Thanks and Learning and they will be with you."

"I am,
The Life in Wind,
The Glow of Fire,
The Wet in the Waters,
The Embrace of the Earth,
I am, You are."

Card Messages

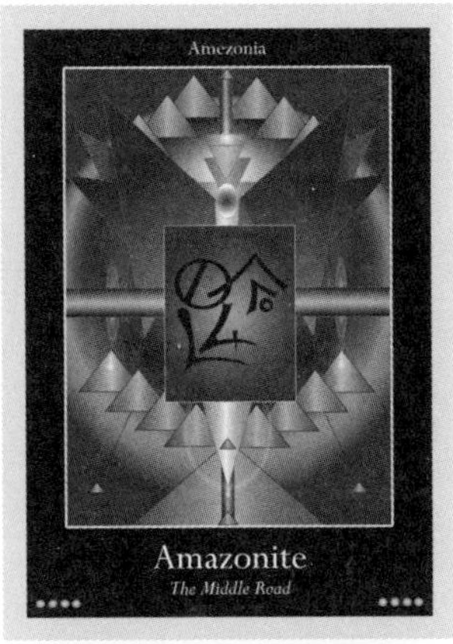

Amazonite

The Middle Road

The Master Crystal Deva Amezonia

"Step into my calming light, I carry the blending of all that you are, as we are one, never apart. Our meeting is no accident or mystery, it is the common ground within all creation.

Together we bridge the gap where polarities dwell and open your true personal expression as spirit via the physical. Let us open your voice and let expression flow from the heart, allow all that touches your path to be sacred and a guiding light on your journey home.

As before birth, by my side, you will be free to walk the Middle Road, distanced from the illusionary burdens of a mortal life and governed only by your divinity. Let the warm gentle glow of emptiness, the all that is, live in all that you do."

Amazonite in Healing

Amazonite is a blue-green mineral with small iridescent silver-white flecks through its body. Holding principally the blue ray, it activates expression while the green ray is present enough to lend the integrity of Love in all processes. This is a stone of Truth.

Amazonite works its magic with those that believe all must be Black or White. In that position we embrace this stone as it activates realistic expression and a more passive state, especially in social conduct, relationships and love. Work with Amazonite leads to a true understanding of the place of power in personal life and a new respect for self via realization of our achievements. With Amazonite as a guide, we are propelled forward in life, our mundane existence is released and once again the glass is half full, not half empty.

All of the gifts that this mineral provides are due to the union of the physical and spiritual selves allowing us to transcend duality and reside if only for a moment, on the Middle Road. Amazonite is a sacred stone of the Ascended Lord Buddha who will answer powerfully in its frequency.

On the physical level, Amazonite can be of assistance with Osteoporosis, Kidney stones (Calcium) and calms Muscular Spasms.

Your Healing Journey Today

If Amazonite has come to you today, spirit has a message or direction concerning your chosen path in life. The time is here to empower yourself and see your achievements in life, your progress. From that space, make the choice or decision that you have been putting off. The reason for your delay where this change is concerned is that you or someone close to you is unable to see the bigger picture as it is hidden from view, a new, original way or path, gifted and governed by spirit. The new solution is a shade of both the black and the white; it combines all the options that have resulted in the inaction to this point. Listen to the self, it only knows truth at the heart.

Affirmation;- "I walk the path I am."

Keywords to help in reading the cards;- The Middle Road, Balance, Truth, Calm, Achievements, Expression, Equality, Yin Yang Balance, Buddha, Maat (Egyptian Goddess), Krishna.

Body Card Placement;- Throat, Heart and Solar Plexus Chakras. Lower back, Soles of the feet.

Space of Emptiness Trinity;- Larimar placed on the Soul Star Chakra, Amazonite on the Heart Chakra and Garnet on the Earth Star Chakra.

Chemical Composition;- Potassium Aluminum Silicate
Color Rays;- 53% Blue, 30% Green, 15% White and 2% Silver
Animal Totem;- Toucan
Essential Oil;- Valerian

Amber

Laughter

The Master Crystal Deva Merbayel

"It is with Joy and Laughter that we shall anchor within the conscious self the reality of true spirit. Hold my hand now as we glimpse the Perfection of Universal Light, the eternal Sun that is one and all.

Rise up above all that is close to you and Laugh, as it is within Laughter, that the true nature of man is expressed unconditionally. Melt the pain and suffering, leaving only Joy and realization in the shell of once present delusion.

With me you are blessed. You are the very Essence of Laughter, the blinding Sun of truth, a gift to humanity. Step again into the White halls and light them with your golden glow, Know you are the shining bright light you seek in the World."

Amber in Healing

Amber is fossilized Tree resin that has stood the test of time, shifting to a more silicon, timeless form from its old carbon base body, the tree. Usually a combination of yellow, orange and gold in color, it is also transparent and light in weight. This stone's simple purpose for humanity is summed up in the word, Laughter, which it is able to teach the true lessons of and induce.

This is a stone for those that often find themselves in tears or feeling trapped in life. Amber's sun-filled color rays penetrate depression and empower the choice of new paths. Obstacles are laughed aside, lessons are learned and a new self is birthed. Amber is also able to open the paths of animal communication making their language and yours one.

At a high spiritual level, Amber opens the crown chakra allowing a glimpse of the Universal perfection that we are all a part of, this makes the physical world manageable and the problems just melt away.

Amber holds the sacred vibration of the Ascended Lord Buddha, a perfect match to his glorious light and lessons. It is also a link stone to the Egyptian God Bes.

Physically, Amber is known to remove pain and create balance. It has an affinity for the ears and thyroid, treating all manner of problems there, as well as being useful in viral inflammation. Amber may also be of great value in treatment of diseases of the brain and central nervous system.

Your Healing Journey Today

Amber has come to you today as the crystal of Laughter. She asks an age old question of you, will you laugh or cry? Both are an expression of unconditional love and are the only processes that are almost incorruptible in the physical world. Her presence tells us that there is a need for more laughter in your life or something that you need to see the lighter side of. Let the inner child go a little.

Amber also may have come to you if you laugh too much. There are those of us that instead of facing the world and embracing our lessons, laugh. It is a cover laugh that hides much pain and allows the loss of the true joy in life. The inner child has been squashed and wants its true laugh back.

Affirmation;- "I laugh, it is the voice of my true spirit on earth."

Keywords to help in reading the cards;- Laughter, Pets and Animals, Ears, Crown Chakra, Great Central Sun. New Paths, Courage.

Body Card Placement;- Crown and Solar Plexus Chakras, above the head, Right hand (Left if Left-handed.)

Buddha Trinity (To potently align with his energy for healing and communication);- Amber on the Upper Left side of the chest, Jade on the Heart Chakra and Amazonite on the Upper Right side of the chest.

New Life Trinity (To open the doors to a new way of Life);- Place Amber on the Crown Chakra, Zircon on the Third Eye Chakra and Topaz on the Solar Plexus Chakra,

Draw all their energies to the Heart Chakra and let them create a single ball of light that will stay there for 21 Days.

Animal Communication Trinity;- See Boji Stone.

Chemical Composition;- Fossilized Pine Resin

Color Rays;- 10% Red, 35% Yellow, 35% Orange and 20% Gold

Animal Totem;- Duck

Essential Oil;- Orange (Sweet)

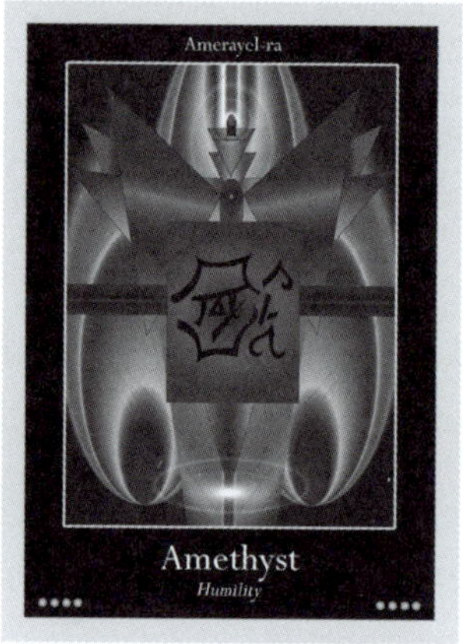

Amethyst

Humility

The Master Crystal Deva Amerayel-ra

"Call forth and open yourself to the light of Adhara. Let it activate your Heart in my blinding Aura, for I have come with the lesson of humility, a gift only held by a Peaceful Heart and Truthful Mind.

Breathe deep now and enter the center of your being, let your world roam free from the mortal focuses that carry attachment. Let go of physicality, trust and allow the Universe to be your guide to all that you are.

Infinite Child of Violet Embrace, hear the will of united mind and filter it free through the endless heart. Our journey completes at the beginning, a place of sacred peace that many have only known in the body before Birth. I am the 7th Son of the 7th Sun, Know me."

Amethyst in Healing

If you have crystals at home there is a good chance that you have an Amethyst crystal. She is a beautiful purple colored quartz crystal that varies in her depth, transparency and intensity. In modern times she has often been abused, cooked to change her color to burnt orange and then sold as Citrine which often fetches a higher price.

Amethyst is one of the most plentiful crystals on the Earth and as always when this occurs, her simple purpose with humanity as the stone of Humility is an important one. We could certainly do with a dose of it as a race. She is able to teach this lesson mainly due to the presence of the Red color ray that is often unnoticed deep within this crystal. This allows Amethyst the ability to ground, stabilize and increase vitality, characteristics that are often overlooked due to the overall Purple color which, for many people, defines it as a Spiritual stone. However, when the Purples and Reds unite, Amethyst like no other can allow the physical, human mind and body to embrace the Spirit, its concepts and directives, at the forefront of which are found Unity, Equality and Oneness, the master teachers of Humility.

When the Mind directs life without the true guidance of spirit an illusionary self is created that is often known as the Ego. Its purpose is whatever the Mind sees as important at the time, limited to the physical worlds. One is quite simply functioning at 50% pretending they are 100%, but hidden, buried deep inside is the truth, a feeling of nil purpose, Isolation and lowered self esteem that eventually leads to Anger and Fear, a person in desperate need of Amethyst and the Guidance of spirit.

As the mind embraces the spiritual, Amethyst delivers self awareness, peace, security and life direction which allows one to feel a part of the world again.

Amethyst is a potent meditation stone able to teach true breath control in altered states and induce visions, it can raise the Kundalini energy and establish a good Earth link allowing memory of that which takes place. It should also be noted that this stone was known as a euthanasia stone in Atlantian times and can facilitate the release from physicality when asked to do so. This is a master stone of the Ascended Master Saint Germaine who utilizes its frequency to anchor the Purple Flame of Transmutation on the Earth.

At the physical level Amethyst has been useful with Tension and Migraine Headaches, Insomnia and Mind-based disorders such as Autism, Dyslexia and Epilepsy.

Your Healing Journey Today

If Amethyst has come to you today, your spirit is asking for a pathway of creation in your physical life. The higher self is about to enter your world and help direct your choices, look for signs everywhere and they will be there. To really receive the messages that Amethyst has for you, the mind will have to be disciplined into a passive state and you will have to step away from your mortal side that is concerned about money and other physical stuff. This is a time of transformation and transmutation, meaning that nothing is wasted, all is utilized only changed from one state to another that is more useful to the totality of you. Truth with self and your world in the coming weeks will be a measure of the potential depth of Amethyst's work with you. Be humble, seek balance, unity and equality, she will fill the gaps with the blinding light of your individual spirit. Your path is within you, meditate, take time and breathe, don't seek to change the world, change yourself and the world will change around you.

Affirmation;- "I walk the Eternal path of Truth, the Purple Flame Burns in my Heart."

Keywords to help in reading the cards;- Humility, Battle of Mind and Spirit, Undisciplined Thought, Meditation, Transformation, Transmutation, Life Path, Bad Temper, Anger, Blood Sugar Levels, Headaches, The Higher Self, Saint Germaine (Usually as Merlyn), Lady Portia, Archangel Zadkiel.

Body Card Placement;- Mainly Base, Sacral and Solar Plexus Chakras but can be placed on the Third Eye once lower work has been completed, which is rare as other stones are better there.

Saint Germain Communication Trinity (1);- Iolite on the Crown Chakra, Hematite on the Third Eye, Amethyst Below the Feet. Placement of the Cards in order with Amethyst on the top under a glass of Red Wine will also potently allow one to receive his Blessing and enter his Frequency, but be prepared to share the wine, he always gets his share!

Chemical Composition;- Iron + Silicon Dioxide with traces of Manganese

Color Rays;- 33% Indigo, 33% Red, 33% Violet and 1% Black

Animal Totem;- Goat

Essential Oil;- Lavender

'The greatest things in the Universes happen outside of humankind's mortal embrace. The stars of the night sky sit in a greater mystery that often goes unseen by Humankind, their blinding light is your distraction, the mind dare not wander long between them lest it continue eternally in the wonder and glory of emptiness.'

Angelite

Peace

The Master Crystal Deva I-ra-el

"Enter on my journey, for I carry the message of Peace from the higher realms of spirit to the densest forms of matter, let the pink dolphins sing at our embrace, you will know their voice.

In my gentle blue fire, feel me rain down upon you in absolute forgiveness. Know now the importance of true and real communication in search of the absolute spiritual self, let it rise within you.

Know with me by your side I melt away the lower earthly emotion of blinding anger, I carry the key to renewed peace with the world and all creation. Go now re-enter the world, walk in freedom."

Angelite in Healing

Angelite is a powder blue mineral, mostly opaque and occasionally contains small white inclusions, prior to being polished it is coated in a white layer. Angelite forms in spherical nodules that when joined together and cut in half resemble angel's wings. To the physical eye and even the touch, Angelite has a gentleness and softness that is not found in many minerals.

Angelite's simple purpose for humanity is Peace, true peace is only found when we let go and let God, surrender the minds petty bidding and heal all our attachments, Past, Present and Future, the key to this is forgiveness. Peace is emotional Harmony.

Angelite balances all outgoing energies from the body, melting away anger, aggression, fears, doubts and worries. It is a soothing and calming stone that makes one feel settled and at home. Often in Angelite's presence, new parts of self are discovered and one finds oneself in a constant state of forgiveness and compassion.

Spiritually Angelite also facilitates Angelic communication, enhances channeling, telepathic abilities and astral travel, all gifts we will need more in the new age. Angelite is one of the major stones of the Telepathic Induction, a directive that comes into play after 2013 whereby the human race will become more Telepathic. This is a directive of the Brotherhood of Light to help us back to Oneness. It is based on the fact that if we live inside each other's head there is no need for untruth. Where there is Truth, Love soon follows, where there is Love and Truth, Judgment and Separation fall away giving rise to Unity and Oneness, where they are found, there is Eternal Peace. Remember Truth starts with the self, the New Children of Light see through our silly disguises, they are leading the way. This is a sacred stone of Archangel Mary, Archangel Raphael and the Ascended Master Serapis Bey.

At the physical level it is powerful at balancing the body's water content, making it useful for water retention and swelling. Angelite is also useful at the thymus gland and for throat problems.

Your Healing Journey Today

If Angelite has come to you today it is time to enter the space of peace. This is only possible when we free our dependence and attachments of the physical world, choose not to worry about the outcome and know we have done our best. Be happy in your efforts, it is time to let go and leave the result in whatever it is you are pursuing to God. The state of peace usually follows forgiveness on all levels, you may have some forgiving to do to get there. This is the most sacred stone of Mother Mary, who is now an Archangel, a transition Angelite was crucial in facilitating, she may be calling you.

Affirmation;- "I am the Blue Flame of Peace."

Keywords to help in reading the cards;- Peace, Detachment, Forgiveness, Surrender, Angels, Emotional Balance, Anger, Aggression, Worry.

Body Card Placement;- Crown and Throat Chakras, The Thymus Gland for activating telepathy.

Telepathy Trinity (To facilitate and activate Telepathic ability);- Herkimer Diamond on the Crown Chakra, Azurite on the Third Eye Chakra and Angelite on the Thymus (Gland) Chakra.

Chemical Composition;- Calcium Sulfate

Color Rays;- 48% Blue, 38% White and 14% Clear

Animal Totem;- Boto Dolphin

Essential Oil;- Bergamot

Apatite

Foresight

The Master Crystal Deva Ke-mo-tom

"Step upon my hidden yellow ray, embrace your birthright and let me empower your freewill to create and manifest your world. The path I offer is one of mental mastery; let us create your dreams from the perfected vision and leave nothing to chance.

Listen with care as the mind is the tool of all that is good in the universe, but can also herald disaster if untrained. Each action should harm none and be of benefit to all. This can only be achieved by holding and acting through foresight, a clear vision and understanding of the outcome, a picture to which I hold the brush.

Brush of Life in hand, paint now. See and allow the dream, your endless potential a gift to all of humanity. I will show you who you are and you may act always from that space of unconditional love, benefiting all. You are a cell in the body of all creation which cannot exist without you, let this truth live in you and your actions."

Apatite in Healing

Is usually found as a dull blue/green mineral with white impurities through its body. In rarer pieces, that can be green, yellow or blue its colour is beautiful and deep, the blue variety holds a colour frequency that no other mineral on Earth possesses. In Atlantian times, the high-quality blue pieces were very sacred and utilized as powerful communication pieces between humanity and the Devic kingdom. Apatite was responsible in Atlantian times for teaching the children how to speak to the Earth and still today no mineral calls the little people, Elementals to Master Devic and beyond, as powerfully.

Apatite treats some of the most common problems of our modern world, one of which is highly responsible for its current state, the poor use of Power in love and spirituality.

Apatite powerfully activates the mind, allowing one to think before acting, where once the outcome was negative due to reaction; with Apatite it becomes more creative and positive. Apatite is a powerful crystal of the body's metabolism, by linking the mind to the body's needs, with discernment of its wants, balance is found and unwanted weight is often lost.

This mineral is able to activate deep states of meditation, link one strongly to extraterrestrial communication, balance the chakra system and align the energy bodies. But its real power in the energy system lies in its ability to raise the kundalini energy in a powerful and balanced manner. Apatite is a sacred stone of the great nature being and King of the Devic Kingdom, Pan; it can also facilitate contact with Ascended Master Kuthumi. Physically, Apatite has also been shown to help with stuttering, damaged muscular tissue, teeth and bone problems.

Your Healing Journey Today

If Apatite has come into your life today, planning is the keyword. Your negative cycle that seems to repeat itself in life has been recognized by spirit and is about to be broken. Whatever it is that you are about to enter or undertake in life, be sure to use your intuition and all of your ability to foresee the outcome. Take time to plan every step and try to remove the obstacles before beginning. Apatite is also asking you to be sure of what you want, ignore all external pressures that are pushing you, think, and then act. Things that are to be yours in the world will wait, if they do not, they were never supposed to be yours. Reaction in the world leads down an unpredictable path that is not really yours to walk. The lessons you encounter will lift you back to your true path, offer the choice to think, and then act again, how many times will you walk the circle?

Affirmation;- "My vision is perfect, it manifests my Life."

Keywords to help in reading the cards;- Foresight, Planning, Intuition, Devic Communication, Personal Power in Expression, Choice, Listen to the Body, Extraterrestrial Messengers, Kundalini Energy, Pan.

Body Card Placement;- Solar plexus, Throat, and Third Eye Chakras.

Kundalini Trinity (Raises the Kundalini Energy in a controlled manner);- Garnet is placed on the Crown Chakra, Ruby on the Heart Chakra and Apatite on the Earth Star Chakra.

Devic Communication Trinity;- Boji stone is placed on the Left hip, Apatite is placed on the Right hip and Turquoise on the Thymus Chakra. Iolite can also be placed on the Third Eye Chakra to facilitate vision if you require it.

Chemical Composition;- Calcium (Fluoro Chloro Hydroxyl) Phosphate

Color Rays;- 50% Blue, 30% Yellow, 10% Indigo and 10% Clear

Animal Totem;- Cricket

Essential Oil;- Buchu

Apophyllite

Astral Travel

The Master Crystal Deva Kali-m-el

"Blessings infinite one, journey with me; step through the gates of the heart to the Astral rainbow bridge of Creation. Let the Octahedron of Light carry us, eyes opened inward, we will ignite the pathway to Shamballa and enter the worlds beyond.

Set your eyes upward and see the vision of my apex for you now lie central in the pyramidal embrace. Cross your arms in recognition as all have before you and link now with the divine that you are. Call forth the blinding Star high above in the night sky, let it enter you, divide, and connect heart and mind to manifest your reality, you will remember.

Time and space are no limitation within the bounds of my frequency, you will see their illusion and fly through the veils of physicality. The Crystal Steps of my temple lead to the Great Hall of Unity, all worlds united as one, your new playground. Slept well you have, child of light; your time is Now here, spread your wings and fly upon my breath."

Apophyllite in Healing

Apophyllite is a clear very transparent crystal that can form many different ways, but by far the most remarkable and identifiable characteristic of its crystals occurs when it forms pyramid like structures. Apophyllite as a mineral is the birth place of the ancient Atlantian meditation that has survived the ages, where one creates a Crystal Pyramid as their playground, ashram or temple. Traditionally this pyramid is visited for healing and other spiritual work. The Apophyllite temple in ancient

Atlantis was amongst the grandest of all structures ever built, a large glass like pyramid structure. Apophyllite may contain greens, pinks and yellows, but it never really loses its clarity, giving rise to beautiful crystals. Green Apophyllite holds one of the most remarkable and clear frequencies of the perfected heart chakra and the green healing ray. Apophyllite is the number one crystal of Astral Travel able to facilitate Astral navigation, conscious travel with memory of that which is experienced and a strong connection to the physical during the process. Due to its connection with the astral body it is also a potent dream stone, especially when combined with Jade, translating and triggering memory of all that takes place.

Apophyllite also clearly defines the boundaries of the emotional, mental and spiritual aspects of self, presenting paths between them for easy healing, added integrity and mastery of those levels. Apophyllite's ability to facilitate the identification of spirit and its boundaries helps one who may have forced their truth onto others to see higher truth in life situations and then powerfully connect the spirit and physical realms opening the channeling state for further guidance. Apophyllite is equally at home on the Crown chakra and the Heart and much of its work is filtered through these two energy centers. It should also be noted that as an activation stone, Apophyllite triggers and under guidance, powerfully drives the Octahedron of Light, a job that is enhanced by the presence of Selenite. Apophyllite is the sacred stone of Pegasus. It manifests the energies of Lord Sirius and allows contact with the Ascended Master Aaron and God Nebo.

At the physical level, Apophyllite may be useful with eye problems, premature ageing and all illness at the level of DNA and RNA.

Your Healing Journey Today

If Apophyllite the stone of Astral Travel has come to you today, you must pay close attention to your dreams and what occurs in them. If you are presently not dreaming this card signals their return.

Due to the fact the astral is mentally generated, much happens there that we are unaware of and builds up over time. This buildup on the astral plane, at some point should be healed, recognized and/or mastered which usually is the natural process referred to as dreaming, but when this activity is undertaken consciously it is referred to as astral travel. If the astral body is allowed to become busy and uncontrolled, the conscious connection between the spirit and physical will be less clear. The presence of Apophyllite with you today means you should make a decision to detoxify your astral body of all that does not serve you, this is as simple as having the intention to view, recognize and heal that part of self, a work that is usually done in the sleep state. Once clear there will be a reason this has been asked of you, a message delivered directly from spirit, usually changing your life in a direction you have never thought to walk. A common symptom of the above-mentioned astral state is struggling to define between emotional, mental and spiritual matters in life and being unclear as to direction and purpose. Get ready for some light on the subject of self.

Affirmation;- "I am Mentally clear on Purpose."

Keywords to help in reading the cards;- Astral Travel, Pyramids, Dreams, Flying Dreams, Pegasus, Spirit to Physical Connection, Makes Clear the Paths between Levels of Self, Channeling, Octahedron of Light.

Body Card Placement;- Apophyllite is mainly placed on the Heart and/or Crown Chakras to do its work. When Apophyllite is placed on an ailment it can show the mental pathway of its creation.

Astral Travel/Dream Work Layouts (These will encourage an out-of-body experience in a powerful manner);- 7 Card/Crystals- Sapphire on the Left shoulder, Zircon on the Right shoulder, Apophyllite above the head in the Crown Chakra, Iolite on the Third Eye Chakra, Angelite on the Throat Chakra, Jade on the Heart Chakra and Moldavite on the Sacral Chakra (to travel into past lifetimes Petrified Wood can be substituted here).

Trinity Card/Crystals;- Jade on the Heart Chakra, Selenite on the Third Eye Chakra and Apophyllite above the head in the Crown Chakra. Happy Journeys, see you on the Astral.

Crystal Pyramid Trinity;- Apophyllite to the Left side of the head (ear), Diamond on the Third Eye Chakra and Iolite to the Right side of the head (ear).

Chemical Composition;- Hydrated Potassium Calcium Silicate Hydroxide Fluoride

Color Rays;- 72% Clear, 17% Green, 8% Pink and 3% Yellow

Animal Totem;- The Horse (Especially White)

Essential Oil;- Mugwort (Caution: Toxic)

Aquamarine

Simplification

The Master Crystal Deva Aquamarel

"Join with me; let us light the Expression of Universal Truth within you in the simplest of terms and allow clarity of your true path into action.

Blessed being of infinite light and intention, with me, your voice lights the timeless and universal halls of truth. I welcome you home in peace, for from your action, universal perfection will arise, allowing you to see the Joy, in all that you do.

Time is never wasted in God's work and it is that fact that I can help you to see, as you are the hands of God and all that you do in your vast reality becomes a sacred part of the whole, a new playground in which to play the song of simplicity."

Aquamarine in Healing

Aquamarine is a gentle blue- green stone named after the ocean. Finer and more expensive pieces are transparent and ice blue in color, more commonly it is opaque and greener. Aquamarine belongs in the Beryl family of crystals, her brothers and sisters include Emerald, the Crystal of Spiritual Healing, and Morganite, the Crystal of Equality in Love. With origins from such a distinguished family, it is no surprise that this stone serves a very spiritual purpose; it is the stone of Simplification, allowing one to travel deep within and understand the complexities found there in simple terms that are practical in the world.

Aquamarine is a stone of courage in expression, it activates trust allowing the truth to be spoken. She allows a rapid response in all situations stopping the mind before it interferes and makes everything complex. This action simplifies the world and allows the voice of spirit to be heard as a guiding light even in the most mundane of activities. Aquamarine is the stone for public speakers and writers allowing a highly fluid and ordered communication style, with good word choice.

With Aquamarine the connection to the higher self is enhanced and relevant past life information may be readily available via the newly stimulated, active and cleansed throat chakra. Aquamarine is a sacred stone to all the Gods and Goddesses of the Ocean opening communication with them. It is especially sacred to Nimue and Artemis, and has direct links to the Hindu God Ganesha, Ascended Master Saint Germaine and Archangel Raziel.

Aquamarine is a Master Crystal in the balancing of water in the human body, useful in fluid retention and is a powerful remedy of the Thymus Gland.

Your Healing Journey Today

The presence of Aquamarine today lets you know that is time to take the most direct and simple path in whatever it is you are undertaking. The best way to deal with all that enters our life is quite simply, fast; deal with the small things while they are still small and do not allow the world or mind time to complicate the matter. Usually Aquamarine's pathways of action involve verbal communication; there is someone you probably need to directly speak with. Aquamarine also appears when the doors to much-needed gifts from other lifetimes are opened to us or when the higher self needs you to sit and listen.

Affirmation;- "In Simplification, I manifest perfection."

Keywords to help in reading the cards;- Simplification, Voice, Higher Self, The Ocean, Courage, Speech, Expression, Throat Chakra, Thymus Gland Activation.

Body Card Placement;- Throat Chakra, The Third Eye, this card is very powerful as a visual meditation in contacting the higher self. Place on the Heart Chakra during the full moon for alignment to goddess self.

Clear Communication Trinity (Good Precise word Choice and Delivery.):- Sapphire on the Lower Left side of the chest, Aquamarine on the Throat Chakra and Silver on the Lower Right side of the chest.

Ocean Clearing (Calls the ocean to your aid, a potent healing exercise of Cleansing):- Place Selenite on the Crown Chakra, Aquamarine on the Third Eye Chakra and

Pyrite on the Solar Plexus Chakra. This exercise will carry on for 21 days, be prepared to simplify life, it is best performed at the beach.

Chemical Composition;- Beryllium Aluminum Silicate (Trace Iron)

Color Rays;- 33% Blue, 33% Green, 33% Clear and 1% Black

Animal Totem;- Sea Horse

Essential Oil;- Eucalyptus

Aventurine

The Unlimited Self

The Master Crystal Deva Aventural

"Once, long ago, I promised to protect, guide and evolve you, I am the ancient carer of Children, I have come to open the doors of heartfelt adventure. Receive my blessing, for within my embrace we will dissolve the limitations of self. If you will see all that occurs in the Heart as Love, there is no virtue higher than its inward path of action.

Bold and brave, we will now purify and heal the scars of a physical Life. Rest upon my mighty silver wings in flight across the dark ocean of your self-manifested limitations. Fly we will, filtering and soothing the oceans green with Self Love to discover a shore in the burning emotional light of endless potential and creativity, your birth right, Freewill.

Opened now to a broader holistic view of your capabilities and able to bathe in love's inward frequency, become the spiritual adventure that you are, expressing love for self in confidence through Action. Breathe deep and the Priestess of the Silver Star will rise through your Heart to embrace the Moon in the empty skies above."

Aventurine in Healing

Aventurine is a deep green rock from the Quartz family, it contains small pieces of Mica, which allow silver reflections of light to glisten and shimmer within it, an effect known as Aventurescence. Although Aventurine is commonly green, it can also be orange, brown, yellow, blue, or grey. The orange variety is also known as Sunstone.

The simple purpose of this stone in healing is summed up in three words, 'The Unlimited Self'. This is due to the presence of the Silver, Green and Blue rays that it holds in balance. This collection of coloration initiates feminine Emotional Expression and Action through the heart under the guidance of Spirit, which soothes the emotional body and allows recognition of the unlimited potential held within the self. Aventurine allows one to re-enter the adventure of life and is very much a stone for those that have lost their way or path in the world. Things first thought to be unachievable become possible and part of the adventure. It most often appears when buried fears, especially those created in the first seven years of life, have been allowed to steer the ship, in such cases it creates profound realizations and deep permanent healing.

The potent healing and soothing nature of Aventurine solidify its position amongst the most nurturing and gentle of crystals on Earth, often Aventurine is added in Liquid Crystal treatment to make the healing process more nurturing and less aggressive. Its close friends in that department are Blue Lace Agate (Stone of Calm Expression), Red Jasper (Stone of Nurturing), Peridot (The Bringer of Joy), Pink Tourmaline (The Gift of Love) and Amethyst (Stone of Humility).

In Atlantian times Aventurine was the record keeper crystal for the first seven years of life, it enjoyed a position as the, 'Keeper of Innocence' and was the first stopping point if unusual illness presented late in life as it often held the cause and thus cure. Aventurine is the sacred stone of Ascended Masters Tut-Moses and Djwhal Khul.

At the physical level, Aventurine has been useful in balancing the Thymus Gland, stimulating the Nervous System and in the treatment of Psychosomatic illness.

Your Healing Journey Today

If Aventurine has come to you today, it is time to give thanks for your unlimited potential, release all Fears and once again take up the reins of life in a bold and brave fashion. In Aventurine's presence, you are being asked to trust in your divine potential, empower your wonderful gift of freewill and create whatever world you wish around you. The only limitation facing any of us is the limitation we have placed upon our perception, for what we perceive, becomes our reality. Aventurine's message is clear, nothing is impossible and if there are things which you have always wanted to create in your life, see them not as stopping points, but stepping stones in the adventure to the ultimate creation, something that lives well and truly outside of our earthly perceptions, for if it did not, it too would be trapped in the perceived prison of Physicality. Remember also that Aventurine is also the stone of the first Seven years of life, you are being guided to release any Pains or Fears, forgive and go forwards while this great energy is with you.

Affirmation;- "I am the Unlimited Potential of Creation."

Keywords to help in reading the cards;- Unlimited Self, Emotional Body, Childhood Fears, The Adventure of Life, Timidity and Shyness, Heart Chakra, Healing Space, Soothing, Nurturing, Children, Healing of Children.

Body Card Placement;- Place on the Heart Chakra and/or any area of the body to sooth and heal. Place on the Third Eye Chakra to access childhood memories from the first seven years of life, this can also be useful in finding the cause of life changing disease processes.

The Why I Chose My Parents Trinity;- To discover life purpose taking into account childhood pathways, place Hematite at the Base Chakra, Aventurine at the Heart Chakra and Sulphur at the Crown Chakra, lie down and relax. This can be quite an emotional experience and may take a few days to really do its work, often through the dream state. Placing a piece of Jade under the pillow will help bring understanding to this process. This exercise can take you back to the reason you chose your Parents in this life, something I think we all should know at some point.

Chemical Composition;- Quartz (Silicon Dioxide) + small amounts of Mica (Potassium Aluminum Silicate Hydroxide Fluoride)

Color Rays;- 40% Green, 40% Blue, 10% Silver and 10% Black

Animal Totem;- Albatross

Essential Oil;- Tangerine

Azurite

Focus

The Master Crystal Deva Azu-ra-el

"Open the Eye of Eternal Light and take my hand upon the journey of you. Together within my indigo ray of wisdom, let us gently lift you through the levels of self to a new world.

Ascend with me beyond the limitation of the five physical senses. By choice now let my hidden fires light the pathways of higher evolution within you. I will prepare you as the pathway of light through matter, utilizing Purification and the Power of Change. Embrace me and accept your birthright, the Focus and attunement of the Inner Eye.

Holding my fire in your sacral embrace, create your world, transforming fear into clear understanding let the light of Antares live in you as it does in the night skies, I am her messenger, I am with you."

Azurite in Healing

The Master Diva of Azurite, Azurael is the primary ray master of the indigo colour ray holding more of the indigo ray than any other mineral on Earth. This deep indigo blue mineral is one of the most vibrant substances to come out of the earth, usually opaque and rarer in crystalline form, it holds all the healing characteristics of the indigo ray, facilitating wisdom, focus, mental ability, spiritual vision, psychic development and the understanding of higher purpose.

Azurite is the principal remedy of Focus, a title that it holds via its ability to link the subconscious and conscious minds together in united action. Its ability with the mental levels of self can transform hidden aspects such as fears and the real reasons for illness into clear understanding, readying them for its closest friend Malachite to clear permanently out of the bodies. Throughout all of Azurite's mental activities the spiritual and intuitive touch of the higher self is added for guidance, which accelerates decision-making and removes limitations.

Hidden deep in this stone is the Orange Ray, empowering all of its activities with creativity, warmth and vitality. The orange is never seen with physical eyes, but is easy to feel when Azurite activates within the body, linking the lower sacral chakra area to the third eye. This energy is very oriental and is often referred to as the Tan Tien, it is birthed in the sacral area and takes a figure of eight pattern, looping out the front and back of the body via the heart chakra and through the third eye. This links the sacral and third eye areas of the body together allowing accurate communication. Azurite is the keeper of this ancient wisdom, which is powerful in Tantric practice and the activation of spiritual aspects of self including the third eye. Its Egyptian correspondence would be the sacred Ankh, the Egyptian Cross.

This dynamic warm energy hidden in Azurite, allows it most of its more physical healing abilities, where it will remove blockages, congestions and growths from any area, while simultaneously aligning the spine. Azurite can also be useful with spasms and erratic nervous system movements such as restless leg syndrome. Azurite is a Sacred stone of the Egyptian God Khephera, whose symbol is the Scarab. It is also a contact stone for the Ashtar Command and Ascended Master Kuthumi.

Your Healing Journey Today

If Azurite has come to you today, it usually means that something is trapped in the subconscious level of self that is being denied its path of realization and/or healing. Azurite simply indicates the need to unite the mental self into action with focused purpose, something often easier said than done. The basis of this energy is truth with self, which will activate the wisdom, focus, self-love and other pathways of action to get the job done, scatter is about to be a thing of the past.

Think before acting, or so we are taught, a wisdom that is great if understood to mean the whole mind and discovery of your united mental directive, but that is not what we generally do. Azurite has rushed to your side to open you mentally to your infinite possibilities, he knows if the spirit can be given a moment to breathe, it will deliver your sacred path into the world. Expect greatness from yourself and so it will be, but focus on one thing physically, it opens infinite doors for the spirit to work its magic. No focus, and no one gains, your choice, I choose truth and it never lets me down, let it be your guide. With Azurite as your guide, you are being offered the chance to do something very special, when the inspiration comes, take fearless action.

Affirmation;- "I am focused, my spirit has a voice of purpose."

Keywords to help in reading the cards;- Focus, The Indigo Ray, The Third Eye Chakra, Mental Level of Self, Psychic Development and Intuition, Limitations, The Tan Tien, The Creativity of Spirit, Trapped in the Sacral, God Khephera (The Scarab).

Body Card Placement;- Activates all body Chakras. Placement of the Azurite symbol on the front and back of the Sacral, Heart and Third Eye Chakras will activate and awaken the Tan Tien energy for healing and spiritual growth. (Every soul collects this energy in the Antares Stargate before birth, wake it up.)

Past Life Blocks Discovery Trinity;- Petrified Wood on the Heart Chakra, Azurite on the Third Eye Chakra and Apophyllite on the Crown Chakra, lie down and relax.

Discover the Cause of Illness Trinity;- Malachite, Azurite and Lapis Lazuli, placed in a Triangle formation on any problem area will offer the Cause and needed action for healing.

Wherever Azurite goes in healing Malachite should soon follow and then finally Chrysocolla, they are great friends that work well in sequence.

Chemical Composition;- Copper Carbonate Hydroxide

Color Rays;- 80% Indigo, 15% Orange and 5% Black

Animal Totem;- Bee

Essential Oil;- Nutmeg

Black Coral

Light in the Darkness

The Master Crystal Deva Ke-ma-el

"Sink into my peace; I will carry you through the blackness. With me you will see darkness as a shade of light, the very shade that gives rise to you as a physical body and imparts the gifts that you possess in your many perceived worlds.

I can allow you to become all Knowing and confident in the part of you that is God. I bring trust to its presence and perfection as Light, for the good of all. You will come to see self preservation as a step into trust rather than a need for protection which simply fuels the fire of fear on our planet.

Join the past masters I have embraced and receive the pure knowing of divinity in self. Let us light the fire of self trust and confidently empower you across the vibrant, ever changing sands of life.

Now, in embrace, ride with me the waves of divinity that flow beneath the surface of all creation, infinitely into the three hearts of Fire, the Solar Angel recognized."

Black Coral in Healing

Black Coral is found in warm tropical waters, usually at greater depths than normal coral. It is jet black and opaque, looking like a branch of a tree, however, when held up to the light, the tips of the branches are a bright fiery red.

There few things greater at lifting trust and confidence in the power of the self than Black Coral, it enters into the darkest places of self and shines a bright light there making all that is found known, then encourages the replacement of those newly surfaced fears with Love via self forgiveness. This gives Black Coral its powerful ability to dispel fear of darkness from the most spiritual to physical parts of self, allowing one to be filled with light and to tread a truly fearless path.

Through the many islands of Micronesia, including Vanuatu where I grew up, Black Coral is renowned for its properties of regeneration and purification. It is known to allow contact with loved ones that have passed and is a coming of age stone that accelerates the transfer of knowledge into wisdom, when a boy or girl becomes a man or a woman. It is also worked with in the islands as a cure for migraine headaches and skin conditions. The presence of Black Coral is seen as a measure of the general health of a reef area, sadly today, it is becoming quite rare.

In working with Black Coral, I have found it very powerful in balancing the male and female roles and sides of self, which is evidenced in its Colour Ray structure. It is also very powerful in all work with cancer, but especially where the cause lies in the giving away of power. Black Coral is also the mineral to have on hand when studying ancient spiritual material as it is able to bring one into contact and facilitate communication with past Spiritual Masters. Its energy is best matched to Lord Maitreya, Ascended Master Sananda (Jesus), Goddess Isis and the God Anubis.

In bodywork techniques, Black Coral is able to strengthen all of the meridians and empower the energy system, to seek a balance, while allowing an understanding of the fears that created the problem. It also has an affinity for the bones, aiding in their rebuilding and natural formation.

Your Healing Journey Today

Black coral is a stone of hope. In coming to you today, she reminds us that no matter how dark we perceive the world to be, there is always light hidden within it. Everything in the universe is light or love until it is tainted by the perception of man. Black Coral lets you know that the new world of light starts with you, your perception simply has to move to see fear as a lack of understanding, rather than a substance like a brick wall in growth. For whatever reason in life, often we disempower ourselves; this lack of faith in self is the first step away from love and often leads to a dark place, choose carefully in the coming days, see the light in the darkness and you will be free. A fear of the dark is a love of the light, make a choice to understand and fear is an Illusion we can live life without.

Affirmation;- "In love I am Free."

Keywords to help in reading the cards;- Light in the Darkness, Empowerment, Confidence, Spirit, Ascended Master Contact, Fear, Freedom, Hope, Purification.

Body Card Placement;- Third Eye, Heart, Solar Plexus and Base Chakras, Right hip area.

Healing Hidden Fears Trinity;- Black Coral on the Left shoulder, Green Calcite on the Heart Chakra and Rhodochrosite on the Right shoulder. Relax and let these great healers do their work. Usually the process will start with the calling forth of a single Ascended Master, Angel and Deva matched to you, to assist the Healing.

Chemical Composition;- Calcium magnesium Carbonate

Color Rays;- 25% Black, 25% Red, 25% Gold and 25% Silver

Animal Totem;- Dugong

Essential Oil;- Niaouli

Black Onyx

Grounded Self-Awareness

The Master Crystal Deva Ony-chel

"Raise me from the earth and united we will anchor your physical body. Enter my calm self-awareness and allow my supporting touch to lift you through the physical veil to a new light. Together we are stimulating the pathways of the intuitive, activating your real voice and sound, your Cosmic Signature.

Guiding you I am, as you flow with the rivers of life, detach from all that seems complex, stressful or lacking in harmony. Let it run its course, for without the attachment of the conscious illusioned self, all is of heaven.

Open your eyes of light in mine and step through the gates of your future, for you, and only you, hold the key to your creation, what you perceive in the world is your only limitation."

Onyx in Healing

Onyx is principally a Black stone, which when unpolished has a matte finish. It is similar and often mistaken for Black Obsidian who is more glassy and reflective. For a very long time Onyx was a popular stone in men's rings, usually cut to a square flat shape which, though unknown then, assisted in balancing and bringing equality to the Male and Female energies within self. A gift it still carries to this day.

In recent times, Onyx is one of the most powerful stones for stress in life, able to melt it by delivering absolute awareness of self; if you know you, then you know what you need. Onyx provides a space so one can view the world they have created. Then with support and wisdom, it activates decision-making and responsibility, thus we only absorb that which we need from the world, simplifying life and dissolving stress.

Work with Onyx activates perseverance and the new found support of self in life, allows flow and non-attachment. Spiritually Onyx helps develop the physical body and can allow it to carry vast amounts of light which activates high levels of growth. This stone also allows control of sexuality, the banishing of the ego and the calming of lust, often leading to mastery via Tantric Processes.

Onyx is the most powerful activation stone of the Base Chakra, a job it usually performs with the other members of the Base Chakra Trinity, Bloodstone for healing and Smoky Quartz for perfected function and completion. Black Onyx is sacred to Anubis, Bast and Osiris of Egypt and links powerfully to Ascended Master El Morya.

Onyx is of great use in weight problems, neurological disorders, foot pain especially ailments from walking and breaking smoking addiction.

Your Healing Journey Today

Something in the physical world is creating stress and strain. You may have become involved in something that is not your responsibility. You need to have a good look at yourself, your needs and your physical surrounds. This is a time for strong decisions and action concerning your physical well-being and happiness, decisions of the nature you must make are often best made in solitude outside of the influence of others. Black Onyx also presents where there is a need for grieving.

Affirmation;- "I have all I Need, I create my world and I am Free."

Keywords to help in reading the cards;- Grounded self Awareness, Stress, Perseverance, Patience, Self Support, Male Female Balance, Sexuality, Smoking, Addiction, Need for Grieving.

Body Card Placement;- Black Onyx is a healer mainly on the Heart, Sacral and Base Chakras. Placed below the feet on the Earth Star to powerfully remove stress, see Charoite for the Stress and Worry Trinity.

Tantric Trinity (Opens all the necessary pathways, activates, heals and prepares);- Black Onyx is placed on the Left hip, Garnet is placed on the Right hip and Ruby is placed at the Crown Chakra.

Chemical Composition;- Silicon Dioxide

Color Rays;- 45% Red, 5% White, 5% Yellow and 45% Black

Animal Totem;- Ram

Essential Oil;- Clove

Black Tourmaline

Protection

The Master Crystal Deva Anu-ka-el

"Seek me, but do not judge, for outwardly, I am as the darkest night, but within, I am the bright shining light of day. I carry this quality to you allowing inner security and protection.

It matters not the outer surface. By my teaching, the gathering of trust within self will empower you to a space of self love that will then flow into all you create. Your world is not to be feared, but understood and nurtured; it is a measure of what lives in you.

In my embrace you are like a child in the womb, secure and protected, by your own trust in, and wisdom of your light."

Black Tourmaline in Healing

Black Tourmaline is an opaque black mineral characterized by long striations that run down its body, which allows it to carry and direct a very large amount of light, powerfully into a chosen area. This relatively cheap stone is the most powerful form of protection available from the mineral kingdom, it has a shielding effect on negative, dense or heavy energies. It achieves this not only by its vast amount of light, but also by bringing confidence to the self and empowering trust in the light that you are. Black Tourmaline is able to teach the most powerful lessons associated with confidence and protection of self on all levels. This mineral is the only physically available substance that is able to protect us from our own negative outputs, this makes it very useful in the treatment of mentally created illness and countering negative or fear based outputs in healing.

At the mental and emotional level, Black Tourmaline facilitates focus and self trust, which backs up actions in the world, cuts attachments and activates a powerful sense of security and personal power. More spiritually, it can activate the Base Chakra and may play a role in lifting the Kundalini energy.

Black Tourmaline is a sacred contact stone for Masters El Morya, Allah Gobi and Osiris, while deity correspondences include Anubis, Bast and Sekhmet.

Physically; it can be used for depression, heavy electromagnetic radiation, stress, anxiety, panic and all pain including back and spinal problems.

Your Healing Journey Today

If Black Tourmaline has come to you today, something has or will test your ability to trust yourself and stand in your personal power with absolute confidence in the light that you are. When situations present to us in life that we are supposed to take action upon, very often we react losing control of our mental ability, it is here that fear lives and the desire for protection arises. There is truly nothing to be fearful of in the entire universe except your own mind out of control, it creates all pain and suffering but in turn, in its state of mastery, can recreate heaven on Earth. While you learn this lesson on all levels or perhaps even take a break to recharge, Black Tourmaline is your friend, allowing a protected, secure and safe place of learning.

Affirmation;- "I trust in my infinite light, Fear is illusion, Love is real."

Keywords to help in reading the cards;- Protection, Trust, Confidence, Personal Power, Inner Light, Security, Panic and Stress.

Body Card Placement;- Black Tourmaline works mainly on the Base Chakra.

It can be placed beneath the feet to flush out toxins, held at the Solar Plexus Chakra to increase personal power and trust in the self. When Black Tourmaline is placed on the Third Eye Chakra, it may for some, facilitate communication with the Manu. (Allah Gobi).

Stress Release Trinity;- Black Onyx on the Upper Left side of the chest, Herkimer Diamond on the Solar Plexus Chakra and Black Tourmaline on the Upper Right side of the chest. Take nice long breaths, drawing the energy of the crystals through your body, filling it up. Once your body is full, release the Energy through your feet on out-breaths, see it absorbed into the Earth.

Chemical Composition;- Sodium Iron Aluminum Boro-Silicate Hydroxide

Color Rays;- 38% Black, 26% Gold, 26% Silver and 10% Red

Animal Totem;- Shark

Essential Oil;- Caraway

Bloodstone

Purification

The Master Crystal Deva Ba-ka-el

"Blessings, I have come in service, together let us lift the weight of the world from your shoulders, empower and allow you to see the truth of the warrior that you are. Take my hand on a journey inward, let us join the heart and physical worlds of you, today we will clarify the often muddy waters of life.

Through your eyes, receive my vision, let it promote joy and allow you to see lessons, in every moment that life presents for we must travel forward. Breathe my breath, it will renew and revitalize your life force, every cell will be purified and expanded in my touch to embrace the light of the infinite.

Be strong in your process towards perfection, embrace that which you came to complete, as divinity you are. Your renewed life force and purified state will weigh light against the feather of Maat and expedite your journey through the stars into oneness and service."

Bloodstone in Healing

Bloodstone is a deep green stone with red markings through it that resemble a splash of blood. It is a member of the quartz family and is quite a common stone. The combination of the deep green and vibrant red allows this stone to carry the healing green ray directly into the blood and all the way down to the base chakra. This has the effect of renewal, revitalization and balance, potently affecting life, the chakras, energy and physical bodies, resulting in its simple purpose as the stone of Purification. After work with this stone, in the newly created purified state, the blood is energized and able to hold an increased amount of light initiating a more permanent Enlightened State and instilling the wisdom and sensitivity for inner guidance. This is the mineral for when life has become boring and mundane, when it seems nothing new ever happens, you are in need of Bloodstone. The green ray presented by this stone is highly purifying of the emotions and encourages one to stay in a space of integrity, honor and truth. This is the sacred stone of the Egyptian goddess Maat, she is responsible for the weighing of the contents of one's heart after a lifetime, a measure of purity and wisdom to determine future lives. Doorways to the Ascended Master El Morya will open in this stone's frequency.

This mineral has a strong effect on the Blood, Heart and Circulatory systems removing toxins, normalizing and purifying functions and cells.

Your Healing Journey Today

If Bloodstone has come to you today, it is possible that your heart is just not in your physical activities, allowing life to become boring and one paced. Bloodstone, the Stone of Purification, signals renewal, revitalization and healing, leading to the re-establishment of your spirit as your guiding light towards life purpose. For you this means change and a new way, but first there must be a period of purification and clearing. Drink lots of water and eat as cleanly as possible while Bloodstone does her work.

A new you is to be born, remember that before the Caterpillar can see the light and fly as the glorious butterfly, it is restricted, attached and blind in its Self Created Physical cocoon.

Affirmation;- "I am Pure, spirit is my Guide."

Keywords to help in reading the cards;- Purification, Revitalization, Renewal, Stabilization, Blood, Boring and Mundane Life, the First Initiation Towards Ascension (Physical Mastery), Heart and Circulatory System, Maat(Egyptian Goddess), Mayan Indian Contact Stone.

Body Card Placement;- Mainly Heart or Base Chakras. To enhance purification and cleansing, place Bloodstone on the Left hip, and Malachite on the Right shoulder. If you have Mayan past lives, this card can be placed at the Third Eye Chakra, to allow a Hummingbird to approach and offer you guidance in meditation or the dream state.

Base Chakra Trinity (Most holistic healing of the Base Chakra available);- Black Onyx is placed on the Left hip, Bloodstone is placed on the Right hip and Smoky Quartz is placed on the Earth Star Chakra.

Chemical Composition;- Silicon Dioxide and Iron Dioxide

Color Rays;- 45% Green, 35% Red, 10% Blue and 10% Black

Animal Totem;- Humming Bird

Essential Oil;- Cedarwood (Himalayan)

Blue Lace Agate

Calm Expression

The Master Crystal Deva Mer-ra-el

"Embrace my peaceful blue Ray, and step upon the waters of truth-filled expression that I am. Let my calming rain gently wash over and through you.

Without judgment, we will now surrender the heat of fire filled expression; let us bring awareness to the creative virtues and responsibilities of speech, the Joy of creation and creating that you are, in the eyes of the Great One.

Opened to me now and bathed in my light, your lower expressions have melted away leaving a pure river of peace and love for all. Rest now, for my brothers and sisters await your arrival into expressive service, a voice for all to follow."

Blue Lace Agate in Healing

Blue Lace Agate is a gentle sky-blue stone with white bands gently dancing through it. Bands of blue and white, alternate the whole way through the stone often forming delicate patterns and colour variations, all of which are gentle and peaceful. The simple purpose of this crystal with humanity is Calm Expression, in the realms of which it has no equal. This mineral dissolves angry, hot, fiery, sharp and violent expression, replacing it with a peaceful, cooling and calm alternative. No matter the area in which Blue Lace Agate is released to do her work, where the fire element rules she will always infuse the fluidity of water and the wisdom of air.

As an Agate, this stone has a strong connection to the breath, bringing balance and control so the higher frequency blue stones of communication can follow in her footsteps, often delivering the wisdom of the Soul and pathways of original thought. Blue Lace Agate is a stone of truth and responsibility, especially concerning speech and will powerfully teach the importance of this in expression at all levels.

In Atlantian Times this stone was worked with as the basis of feminine mental mastery and was one of few stones utilized to translate the songs of dolphins and whales. It is sacred to Ascended Master Serapis Bey, Master Vywamus, Lord Maitreya, Archangel Mary and the deities Shu and Brahma. It is also the stone of mastery and calling forth of the Phoenix.

At the physical level, Blue Lace Agate can be useful in all hot conditions such as infection, inflammation, fever and arthritic conditions. It brings balance to digestion and the fluids of the brain.

Your Healing Journey Today

If Blue Lace Agate has come to you today, tread lightly and gently in all matters, for she only comes to those who must take the path of calm truth-filled peaceful expression. All matters and courses of action are best approached from a truthful space where the wisdom and logic of Air can be blended with the emotion and fluidity of water. Blue Lace Agate appears only when there is too much fire in expression, or the possibility of it, her message is, take time, breathe and then take action with an open heart. Determining the difference between action and reaction is her playground, you have been asked to look at this within yourself. For one who takes action with love and joy this stone is as endless as the blue skies where clouds dance, but for those who would react with fire, she warns of the inevitable, ever-breaking wave of emotion, increasingly turbulent the more it is ignored. Open your heart, and then open your mouth, Blue Lace Agate tells us, the world is ready to hear what you have to say.

Affirmation;- "I Am the Voice of Calm Expression."

Keywords to help in reading the cards;- Calm Expression, Peace, Truth, Responsibility in Speech, Language, Voice, Feminine Mental Mastery, Water and Air Elements, Fire Conditions of the Body, Opening to Channel, Archangel Mary, Vywamus, The Phoenix, Egypt.

Body Card Placement;- Blue Lace Agate can go on any body part to reduce heat when necessary. Generally it is most at home on the Throat Chakra, where it does much of its work.

Enter the Phoenix Trinity (To burn in the fires of realization and be reborn);- Azurite on the Left shoulder, Rhodonite on the Right shoulder, Blue Lace Agate above the head on the Crown Chakra.

Egyptian Past Lives Trinity;- Stacked in order on the Third Eye, Sunstone, Lapis Lazuli and Blue Lace Agate on the top can reveal past lifetimes in ancient Egypt.

Throat Chakra Trinity (Most Holistic Healing of the Throat Chakra Available);- Turquoise on the Upper Left side of the chest, Lapis Lazuli on the Throat Chakra and Blue Lace Agate on the Upper Right side of the chest.

Chemical Composition;- Silicon Dioxide

Color Rays;- 46% Blue, 35% White, 17% Clear, 2% Indigo

Animal Totem;- Fairy Penguin

Essential Oil;- Hyssop

Boji Stone

Balance, Align and Clear

The Master Crystal Deva Urantel

"Just as the sky receives the Sun and a day is born, I have come to rise in your heart and open the door of rebirth. Step into my white purity and hold the rose, I will unite the healing paths within you, a step to freedom.

Feel the tears of a mortal life fall as crystals to the Earth, let them burden you no more. Sink deep into the Earth and feel the loving touch caress you; allow her breath and pulse to become your own as you integrate the loving stability. This is the movement of the physical body into ascension that I represent. I deliver and activate Earth's ascended frequency and will balance, clear, cleanse and Align you, take my hand.

Wear my blessing for the world to see, in glorious service it will shine and our mutual work will turn to stone permanently living through the ages. Choose now the only path available you, your Intention to live as perfection."

Boji Stone in Healing

Boji Stone is generally a Metallic Brown-Black combination of minerals that form in a spherical disk-like shape. A smoother Boji Stone holds a Feminine Energy while a Boji with prominent square crystal structure is Masculine, all Boji Stones should come in pairs, the information here applies to such work. Generally Boji is found in rich fertile soils resulting in the inclusion of many minerals in small traces, however they are mainly composed of Pyrite and real ones contain the potent healing mineral Palladium which is rare, and has powerful healing effects on the body.

The Boji Stone holds one of the most gentle, though refined, grounding energies available on our planet. It is a mineral of integration on all levels, balancing and healing as it goes, it calls all parts back to unity. Where information is lost in the complexes of the Male, Female, Emotional, Mental and Spiritual selves or dependency on one is born, it is excellent at finding the point of balance then teaching one how to stay there. As a general healing stone, no other stone matches the holistic results of Boji. It not only positively affects all the bodies and entire chakra system but also the acupuncture meridians, removing blockages and balancing flow.

Boji Stone is sacred to Ascended Master Serapis Bey and Archangel Gabriel and with its grounded wisdom can be worked with to communicate with Plants, Animals and the Devic Kingdom. This same gift also opens direct communication with the physical body to shine light on the causes behind dis-ease processes. Boji is said to help in pain removal and tissue regeneration.

Your Healing Journey Today

If Boji has come to you today, you are in need of some downtime; you have allowed yourself to lose some of the building blocks of a healthy balanced state. In the coming days, as the frequency of Boji rises around the body, healing will result and changes will occur. It is important to not resist and flow with whatever comes up. Often Boji will send a friend to aid the healing process and even if it's just a cup of tea, your whole life can change, such is the profound nature of the path before you. Boji Stone also presents when the Male/Female sides of self need to be looked at, often we will need to do something to realign, balance and heal on one or both sides of the coin. Boji Stone can also represent our Mother's or Father's influence on us and the need to free ourselves from it.

Find a quiet grassy spot and lie on your back for 10 minutes with this card at your Heart, let the Earth's pulse and breath run through you.

Affirmation;- "The Earth is my Healer."

Keywords to help in reading the cards;- Balance, Alignment, Clearing, Healing, Grounding, Integration, Male/Female Balance, Regeneration, Nature, Animal Communication, Telepathy, God Geb, Goddess Nuit, Serapis Bey.

Body Card Placement;- All areas of the body, Chakra and Energy Systems.

<u>*Animal Communication Trinity;-*</u> 1)Boji Stone, 2)Amber and 3)Selenite, these can be stacked in this order and held in the power hand (usually the one you write with), when you speak. To hear the animal, hold the cards in your receiving hand. (Or.....get a Liquid Crystal Practitioner to make it up for you.)

<u>*Earth Record Keeper;-*</u> Boji Stone is an Earth record keeper and can be worked with to enter many areas of Ancient Wisdom in meditation, simply place Selenite on the Crown Chakra, Boji stone on the Third Eye and a Sacred stone of your chosen culture on the Heart Chakra. (See below table for some Examples.)

Chemical Composition;- Iron Sulfide and Palladium

Color Rays;- 19% Gold, 21% Black, 19% Silver, 21% White, 7% Green, 7% Red and 6% Blue

Animal Totem;- Pig

Essential Oil;- Vetiver

Clear Quartz	African
Ruby	South America and Atlantian
Lapis Lazuli	Egyptian
Sapphire	Greek and Lemurian
Emerald	The Essenes and Middle Eastern
Silver	American Indian and Tibetan
Gold	Asian, Incan and Mayan

Botswana Agate

Breathe

The Master Crystal Deva Ramatel

"Your first breath at birth awakened a life of Love and Choice, not Fear and Separation. I clear the clouds of self doubt and lift you through the gates of creation into your power. Too long have the halls of Power been ruled by the breathless voice of ignorance.

Breathe with me by your side; allow love and wisdom to guide you to your empowered purpose. The Eternal Self has been weighed light as a feather, thus enter the halls of Shamballa with Anubis as guide, physicality no burden, but a gift of Choice and experience.

Now close your eyes, breathe; feel my calm breath flow through you, let it clean and cleanse with precision, bringing awareness to the disease of Attachment. Know your right to freedom and Embrace your individuality, the gift you are to the united spirit Eternal."

Botswana Agate in Healing

Botswana Agate is a white, sometimes clear stone with black and gray banding. It is quite common but often overlooked in shops due to the presence of its close friends Amethyst, Clear Quartz and Rose Quartz who are never far away and to most are more appealing to the physical eye.

At the Mental/Emotional level, Botswana Agate springs to life with a powerful and direct effect on the breath, empowering and opening the ability to choose and redirect life without sacrificing our individuality. This allows the choice of action, self discipline and awareness to the resting place of personal power, which in turn, via a new breath, eliminates stress and a reactive nature to the world. She is a gift to any of us that have fallen under the spell of another's will or have become attached or addicted to a way in the physical world that is not for our absolute betterment. Botswana Agate is a sacred stone of Ascended Master Kuthumi, the Egyptian God Shu and Goddess Tefnut.

At the physical level, the need for Botswana Agate often manifests itself as Addictions, Lung and breathing problems and Skin issues. This Mineral also may be an aid in neurological tissue regeneration in dis-ease or after trauma.

Your Healing Journey Today

The presence of Botswana Agate for you today tells us that the time for a breath of fresh air is here, the time to become the Shepherd of self not one of the sheep. You are at the start of an important journey, a bridge to freedom and a new you. Look deeply into self for the Truth about your earthly ways and be ready to seek another direction without judgment. It is time to allow a problem that has taken up all your time to find its solution; doors are opening that have been closed for too long, be sure to walk through them.

Affirmation;- "I choose to Breathe the breath that I came to be, I create my life, it is what I am."

Keywords to help in reading the cards;- Breathe, Personal Power, Addiction, Breath, Manifestation, Solar Plexus Chakra, Smoking, Choice.

Body Card Placement;- The Physical Heart. Mainly the Base and Solar Plexus Chakras. Powerful at the Left Shoulder and Palm of the Left hand.

Smoking Trinity (To give up smoking, recover the breath and lung health);- Black Onyx on the Lower Left side of the chest, Botswana Agate on the Heart Chakra and Black Coral on the Lower Right side of the chest.

Breathing Trinity (To find the True Balanced Breath);- Botswana Agate on the Lower Left side of the chest, Morganite on the Heart Chakra and Pyrite on the Lower Right side of the chest.

Chemical Composition;- Silicon Dioxide
Color Rays;- 20% Clear, 30% White, 10% Yellow 10% Red and 30% Black
Animal Totem;- Zebra
Essential Oil;- Myrtle (African)

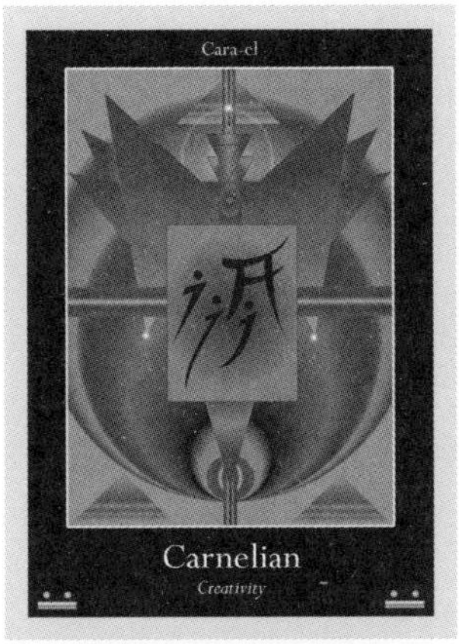

Carnelian

Creativity

The Master Crystal Deva Cara-el

"Long I have waited within the sacred land. Take my hand and together we will realize all that is at the seed of the creative processes, through which you move towards Joy, Peace and Empowerment.

Let your eyes hold stars from the Great Shepherd and descend through the Pyramid of Ra to the sands of Fire at your sacral. Call forth the records of self as letters of light and listen to their song. Sit gently and let the voice of the endless self define your path onwards to destiny.

I am the energy of Optimism, the unceasing light and trust in all that you are and do, as you create lessons, not failures on your journey home. You and I are old friends and still your potential grows with each living breath. The Time has come to rebirth the pathways of the Great Children of Light, let it be done in our sacred single name."

Carnelian in Healing

Carnelian is an Orange-Red variety of Chalcedony (Agate), it is mainly opaque though nice pieces can be quite transparent and red in color, holding light deep within them. Carnelian gets its name from the Latin 'Carnis' meaning flesh after its color, but it is also interesting that it gets its color from traces of Iron Oxide which is much the same as our Blood.

Carnelian is the primary mineral of the Orange Color Ray for the Earth holding 84% in its light frequency, a great responsibility, meaning all of the planet's Orange Frequency work and healing is filtered though her. This gives rise to most of this stone's healing abilities and its simple purpose with humanity as the stone of Creativity.

The energy of Carnelian stimulates the Sacral and Base Chakras into positive action, allowing an up-to-date, in-the-Now, view of self with a firm grip on Creativity, Personal Power and trust in your own ability to manifest progress. With Carnelian at your side, Laziness, Boredom, Confusion, Self Doubt and Tiredness are cast aside. One becomes Optimistic and able to stand alone as an individual, focused with realistic goals and the drive, vitality and life force to see them out. The thirst for life is Re-born. It should be noted here also, that Carnelian is a powerful aid in all forms of Abuse, shining the light upon the path that leads back to the Individual Empowered Self.

Due to Carnelian's effects on self esteem, life force and the lower regions of the chakra system, it is not surprising that Carnelian is one of the most important stones related to Sexuality, Fertility and the Reproductive system in general. In modern times, Carnelian has developed an affinity more so for Men in this area of its work, its Female equal would be Crocite. When Garnet is added to bind their action, there will always be fireworks. Carnelian activates the Male Creative outward energies, Crocite ignites the Female Inner Fires and Garnet circulates the Heart and Crown Chakra energies into the mix. In Atlantis, Carnelian was one of the guardian stones of Tantric Mastery, increasing the sense of touch and able to synchronize the heart and breath of partners into the united light force of co-creation. Carnelian is a sacred stone of the Ascended Master Serapis Bey, Prophet Samuel (Saint Germaine) and links to the energy of Cleopatra.

Physically, Carnelian is a tonic for the Heart and Lungs, it increases digestive function and can aid Asthmatics and Smokers to find balance that often leads to profound healing though the rediscovery of Personal Power. In general, it greatly increases the amount of Oxygen in the body which has many benefits.

Your Healing Journey Today

The presence of Carnelian today is a Healing and Empowering step back into life. As she makes her way into your world it is as though the Sun is shining within you. Shadows, sorrow, self destructive attitudes and doubts are washed clean, leaving a clean slate to rebuild and create your world. The rules are simple, be free, be creative and most importantly be you. Set goals and draw a path of joy upon which you will confidently walk to your individual purpose. Carnelian can and will, if you allow her, guide you back to the creative individual fires that burn in your heart. Do something New, something Forgotten and something Feared in the coming weeks and rediscover the common thread, your individual spark and Trust in Self.

Carnelian can also represent a new relationship or a breath of life into an established one, now is the time to act.

Affirmation;- "Creativity is my path to Freedom, Joy and Unity."

Keywords to help in reading the cards;- Creativity, The Orange Color Ray, Vitality, Fertility, Sacral Chakra, Sexual Function, Optimism, Personal Power, Co-creation, Tantric Processes, Isis and Osiris, Boredom, Laziness, Touch, The Fox, The Stone of the Fertile Sun (Atlantian).

Body Card Placement;- Generally on the Solar Plexus, Sacral and Base Chakras.

Earth Breath Layout (Clears, Balances and Heals via the Earth's Energies);- Carnelian on the Sacral Chakra, Lodestone on the Right hip, Boji Stone on the Left hip, Smoky Quartz on the Right shoulder, Turquoise on the Left shoulder, Hematite six inches below the feet and Pyrite six inches above the Crown Chakra. This healing may need to be supported with Jasper over its duration of action of 21 days.

Tantric Mastery Trinity;- Carnelian placed on the Soul Star Chakra, Garnet on the Heart Chakra and Crocite on the Earth Star Chakra.

Chemical Composition;- Silicon Dioxide

Color Rays;- 84% Orange, 11% Red, 3% Clear and 2% Black

Animal Totem;- Fox

Essential Oil;- Cardamom

Celestite

Knowing

The Master Crystal Deva Celestel

"My very touch is the Tone of Knowing. I am here for you, Embrace me and wear my silver blue cloak of light. My Love, Joy and Peace will carry you within to the place of your true birth, the place of your infinite nature.

At this, the center of all that you are, there is a sacred space, where all that will, and has been, due to you, is transmuted to absolute Knowing. It is in that space that we are one, outstretched in welcome I will aid you to create through your divine heritage.

Mastery and Completion are yours; the allowing of the mind's transcendence over lower thought has opened the ever truthful path of knowing. Welcome home child, I have always known you would hear the call. Now manifest all you are in the world and Universal Mind will be born in the physical, freeing all who desire the perception of eternal light."

Celestite in Healing

Celestite the stone of Knowing, is a highly spiritual mineral, it is silver-ice blue in color and transparent, forming well defined crystals. Usually we see Celestite in geode (cave) formations and structures, the same as we commonly see with Amethyst.

Celestite has a strong relationship with Calcite (the stone of Universal Mind) in its formation process which often leads to Celestite growing on it as a base. What grows from Universal Mind? Pure knowing is the answer, a form of communication higher and more refined than any of the physical world's, an action so refined and sacred it is performed through inaction and pure trust in the undercurrent of the process itself. The results of such a space make Calm, Peace, Joy and Love constantly available as a way of existing, the fears and worries of life just melt away.

When trust in self has been worn down and lowered, Celestite attunes us to the spiritual highest aspects of self and its undercurrent that runs through life. This results in the symptoms of Knowing, powerful trust, wise understanding, powerful peace, heavenly harmony and unwavering Calm.

As a powerful representative of the blue ray and all its characteristics, Celestite can increase the range of Hearing and is calming and cooling on all levels. As a communication crystal it is able to translate all that is received, no matter its origin and is a specialist in Angelic communication. Celestite is a sacred stone of Archangel Raphael and the Ascended Masters Hilarion and Lord Maitreya.

Celestite is a Lemurian Crystal and as such, is really here for the new Children of Light; she is a specialist in the etheric energy field and was revered for this in Atlantian Times. Much of what she is able to do in this area will become available to us in the coming new age after 2013.

Physically Celestite calms digestive disorders and is a powerful relaxant upon the muscular system.

Your Healing Journey Today

Your Trust in self is being tested, you are being asked to stand in your wisdom and power with Love as the answer and Guide. Whatever issues you are currently involved in, remember when you truly Know you are Right, the world doesn't need to know why or how. Entering into such spaces simply shows you don't Trust yourself, the path of true Knowing is often one of Patience, Silence and Love. Think and Know before you act or speak. You have entered a very spiritual phase in life, draw yourself inward with acceptance of all around you, it is all valid and has purpose. Ride the waves of life, often divinity is hidden in the physical world but with Trust and Knowing as your guide all will be revealed. Celestite also presents to us when we must listen more carefully in the world.

Affirmation;- "I Know, Trust and Serve the divine plan."

Keywords to help in reading the cards;- Knowing, Trust, Universal Mind, Spirit, Patience, Divine Plan, Angels, Expression, Hearing, Let Go and Let God.

Body Card Placement;- Throat, Heart and Solar Plexus Chakras. This card is a powerful visual meditation, the symbol for Celestite can open the door to the Angelic kingdom and activate ancient memories of Lemuria for those that are ready.

Angelic Voice Trinity (Feminine expression and Spirit unite in the Truthful space of Personal Power);- Celestite on the Lower Left side of the chest, Silver on the Throat Chakra and Elestial Quartz on the Lower Right side of the chest.

Eye of Horus Trinity;- Moonstone to the Left side of the head (below the ear), Celestite on the Third Eye Chakra and Silver to the Right side of the Head (below the ear).

The Space of Knowing Trinity;- Celestite to the Left side of the head (ear), Herkimer Diamond on the Third Eye Chakra and Sapphire to the Right side of the head (ear). (Note;- Use Caution with this one, it's got some heat.)

Chemical Composition;- Strontium Sulfate

Color Rays;- 56% Blue, 38% Clear and 6% Silver

Animal Totem;- Blue Whale

Essential Oil;- Petitgrain

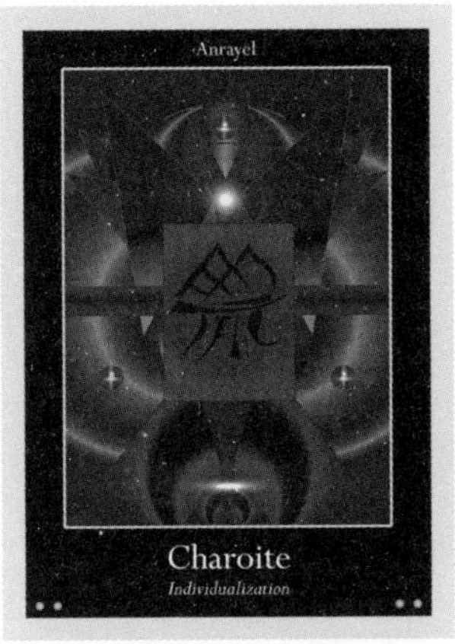

Charoite

Individualization

The Master Crystal Deva Anrayel

"Called you have; now together we stand at dawn, each complete and individual to all others, black fades to fiery purple in a day's sacred birth. Our work is inward, a blessing of wisdom and fire, for today, in our sacred embrace we have sent a message to the world of your individual return.

Let us embrace all that your world offers, melt the bonds of the Inner eye and wipe away her violet tears, for today in my frequency, you will know your gifts and evolve into your potential. Feel snow fall upon and around you, follow the White Tiger, Ruby's younger sister, to the starry gateways of Cetus, I wait to open the door.

Individualized spark of Universal mind, feel your fire burn bright. Link all that you are into unconditional love and enter into action. The time has come to accept your part in the creation of the New Earth and journey into oneness; I will await you at our Home within your Heart."

Charoite in Healing

Charoite is a purple-pink mineral with pearlescent white and sometimes black wisps through her body. Originally this stone was rediscovered in Russia at the foot of a mountain range which is reflected in its ancient symbol.

In healing, Charoite as the crystal of Individualization, balances the receiving of light at the Crown Chakra with the outputs of the Heart, this continually reminds us of our individuality as a spirit and opens doors so personal gifts blossom into life. Charoite's ability to do this is unequalled in the mineral kingdom and powerfully extends to the opening of the doors behind which the contracts of a lifetime rest. These contracts, which we write before birth, are often referred to as the Akashic records of self. Wisdom of them can create a rebirth of sorts through the discovery of Life Purpose and the True Self or Individuality.

Charoite is able to create a personal space free from outside influences where one becomes more energized and spontaneous, able to manifest a comfort and trust in self that dissolves stress, worry and fear. In fact work with Charoite, especially in the company of Hemimorphite, the stone of the Egoless State, can free one permanently from all that they have become to satisfy others, including the personal Negative Ego. These two stones were worked with extensively in Atlantian times by children between the ages of 11 and 13.

Charoite is one of the most important stones on the Earth for the New Children of Light, who have come to serve the Divine plan and lead us home to Oneness. In this capacity, Charoite Activates, Translates and Cleanses the Astral body and other journey aspects of self via the sleep state. Charoite is the most potent substance for children with sleep difficulties that I have ever had the pleasure of experiencing, a potent gift that as a Father, I truly appreciate. When the children are awake, they are our teachers, when they are asleep they are learning and remembering who they are so they can teach us. Charoite helps this process, delivering understanding of the hidden worlds and awakening their individual purpose in the bigger picture. With a little Love and a heard Voice who knows what they will really say!

On a more physical level, Charoite is a powerful healing crystal for Autism and Bipolar Disorders, where it is able to bring understanding to the patient, that can open doors to powerful and permanent healing. We can also work with Charoite as a remedy for the Liver, Pancreas, Eyes and all manner of Alcohol induced ailments. It is the best spiritual remedy for insomnia.

Your Healing Journey Today

Let the Sprits of your past live in you and deliver your future through Self Love, realized Personal Power and the dictation of Divine Wisdom, you step now upon the path home.

If Charoite has come to you today it signals a rebirth of sorts, it is time to become the Individual that you are and release yourself on the world. The first steps in doing this are always the releasing of attachments and cutting away of outside influences, as they keep us as we are, and make change difficult. The loving vibration of Charoite makes sure that when you are reborn your spiritual, personal and individual gifts are embraced, for with them realized, integrity to higher purpose is assured and you will shine. At this important time you should expect to be challenged by the world and the people around you, they all perceive you a certain way and most are resistant to change due to its unpredictable and often painful nature. Take care to not be swayed into their perceived idea of you and hold tight the true self as it is re-birthed in all its glory, the new you will carry many new opportunities as the spirit that you are makes its mark on the world. Trust in your Infinite spark, it believes its path has never been so clear, if you have asked for a sign or call to action, this is the most potent one available, Charoite only arrives when divine purpose is about to be addressed and sent into physicality. The master Deva of this stone often delivers messages in music, listen to some with an open heart, who knows where you may go.

Charoite is the Sacred Crystal of the Egyptian Goddess, Maat, and the Ascended Master, Paul the Venetian, it is a Whale contact stone and was worked with to communicate with them in Atlantian Times, Charoite can directly interpret their Songs of Light.

Affirmation;- "My Path is Clear, I am a spark of the infinite Flame."

Keywords to help in reading the cards;- Individuality, Activation of true Life Pathways, Heart/Crown Chakra Communication, Soul Path, Service, New Children of Light, Autism, Violet Ray of Color, White Tiger, Ancient Lives in Russia, Spiritual Insomnia, Higher Senses Activation, Whale Song.

Body Card Placement;- Powerfully at home on the Heart Chakra, but also at the Third Eye, Crown and Solar Plexus Chakras. Charoites closest friend is Ruby whom activates the Spirit into the Body while Charoite activates the Body into the Spirit. (This is shown clearly in their respective Animal Totems). In Atlantis these two crystals were worked with together to center the Spirit at the heart within any other chosen frequency represented by another crystal. This results in the message or healing path of that third crystal entering the body at the unconditional spiritual vibration of the individual soul. This potent spiritual healing method was referred to as 'Soul Expansion'. To do this, Charoite is placed at the Base and Ruby at the Crown Chakra, any other crystal can be placed on the Heart. (A Liquid Crystal Practitioner can make potent trinities with this Technique.)

Alcoholism Trinity (Potent Detoxification, Healing and Life Changes);- Iolite on Right hip, Charoite on the Solar Plexus and Bloodstone on the Left hip. (Note;- This can be done with the Soul Expansion technique above to magnify results.)

Stress and Worry Trinity;- Onyx (Right hand) , Petrified Wood (Left hand) and Charoite (Heart Chakra).

Anchoring the Starchild Trinity;- Sugilite on the Upper Left side of the chest, Hematite and/or Moldavite on the Heart Chakra and Charoite on the Upper Right side of the chest.

Chemical Composition;- Hydrated Sodium Calcium Barium Strontium Silicate Hydroxide Fluoride

Color Rays;- 47% Violet, 24% White, 19% Rose, 6% Black and 4% Clear

Animal Totem;- White Tiger

Essential Oil;- Lemon Verbena

Chrysocolla

Silence

The Master Crystal Deva Chrysoel

"Blessings in this Joy filled calling you have allowed, child of infinite Love. I have come to shower you in the light of Venus. Speak not, simply shine forth in silence as it is God's Speech. I am at your left, feel me wash through you.

In my light, extend your heart and allow it to be a filter, open only to sounds touched by the Ocean of Spirit. Such beauty will open the higher levels of voice and communication, delivering the language of Love which will flow from you.

Be blanketed in my robe of Silver light and Let our embrace open the Goddess path within self. You will come to know that often the ever present perfection you are appears through Silence, it paves the path of Eternal Peace, Truth and Oneness."

Chrysocolla in Healing

Chrysocolla is an exact blend of the Blue and Green color rays. It is usually a sharp opaque rock with mottled blues and greens running through it, but when polished, it becomes smooth and resembles the view of the ocean floor from a high cliff. In its more evolved state, known as Gem Silica, that is quite rare and expensive, it takes on more blue and holds greater transparency. Gem Silica's color frequency is, in fact, an exact match to that of the Divine Mother and is one of the three colors that surround her in all famous Visions and Artworks.

Of all the stones on the Earth, Chrysocolla holds one of the most feminine frequencies, making it a stone of the Goddess and her finer virtues such as Patience, Compassion, Equality and Humility, gifts that she anchors into the heart of all that she touches. Her greatest gift for us all however, is that she like no other, directly teaches mastery of the Feminine path of Power, a way that is often forgotten on the Earth. The Masculine path is to take action, speak up and create change outwardly; Feminine Power is to allow, be silent, dissolve and change inwardly. Remember, just as that which we create and work for in our outer world affects our inner world, so that which is within you, if allowed, will soon surround you in the world. One path requires physical strength, focus and other Male traits, the other path, just... Is... Is!.. Funny that.....Isis. Chrysocolla is the crystal of Silence, the governing crystal of the Feminine way of Power. The Masculine equal is Chrysoprase; hold one in each hand until they balance each other. If Chrysocolla can't keep your feet out of your mouth, you may just need to glue your mouth shut.

Chrysocolla is a powerful channeling stone that keeps you conscious of all that takes place, a gift that when coupled with Black Coral opens the doors to the Ascended Masters in a profound way. It infuses truth and strength into the voice and can open the Psychic abilities. Chrysocolla is a direct contact stone for the Archangel Mary and Ascended Lady Nada, it will open doors to the Goddesses Isis, Mut, Aphrodite and Artemis.

At the physical body, Chrysocolla is a stone for all manner of female reproductive issues and imbalances, it is useful before, during and after childbirth, able to tone, heal and sooth the tissues. Chrysocolla decreases stress and any ailment stemming from it, including digestive imbalance and shoulder tension.

Your Healing Journey Today

If Chrysocolla has made her way into your life today, her presence usually relates to the recognition to your feminine side and her pathways of growth. It is possible that you have developed a dependence on the masculine methods of living and it is time to step back into your self, trust and feel that which really resides in you. Release your attempts to control and change the external world. The Goddess is on your doorstep, will you take her hand? Real change is that which leads to the discovery of the divine inner self. Sit a while and recognize your greatest achievement is not in the world, it was what you sacrificed to be in the world at birth. Chrysocolla time is a time of Inner Truth, that if embraced will lead to Inner Peace and the birth of a new divine life for us all.

Battles are best fought within self if anyone is ever to be Victorious and the world returned to peace.

Affirmation;- " I am the Power of Silence."

Keywords to help in reading the cards;- Silence, Goddess, Feminine Self, Feminine Power, Expression, Channeling, The Ocean, Orion Constellation (Especially Betelgeuse), Surrender, Truth, Compassion, Tolerance, Patience, The Divine Mother, Isis, Joan of Arc, Female Reproductive System, Pregnancy.

Body Card Placement;- Mainly Throat and Heart Chakra but can also do profound work on the Crown with women. Close friends of Chrysocolla are Silver, Moonstone, Pearl, Malachite, Rhodonite, Amethyst and Azurite, they make up many Trinities and Combinations of treatment.

Female Hormone Balance Trinity;- Silver is placed on the Left hip, Moonstone is placed on the Right hip and Chrysocolla is placed on the Sacral Chakra.

Chemical Composition;- Hydrated Copper Silicate

Color Rays;- 40% Blue, 40% Green, 12% Clear and 8% White

Animal Totem;- Rabbit

Essential Oil;- Spearmint

Exercise: The Space of Silence

This process is helped by placing the Chrysocolla card in your dominant hand (usually the one you write with), Chrysoprase in your other hand and Green Calcite on your Heart Chakra. Take a nice big breath and go inward. Ask the aspects of self that serve your outer world to come forward, see them as aspects, attitudes and mannerisms then let them go to their outer world where they are happy. As these energies leave you, feel and experience emptiness where they once were, sit silently, Listen, Breathe and affirm your name, I am (Your Name), I am (Your Name), over and over like a mantra, allow the empty spaces to fill themselves in, don't define them, give them names or purpose, just allow and know. Do this at the start and end of each day for ideally 21 days, if you make it, you will do it for the rest of your New life.

Chrysoprase

Fearless Movement

The Master Crystal Deva Lemurel

"Open to my all encompassing love and be now present. Step forward into the uncharted waters of life's experience, I have come to guide you. Let there be no fear in our union, as continuous Joy is your divine right.

Today I offer the spark that will re-light the flame of individuality within you, allowing your unity with all to become known once again. Feel my Yellow Fire blessing the Solar center of self and link it to the pure Green Ocean of your unconditional Heart. Under the perfected guidance of the Eternal white light, you and I are now One.

Our union signals to the world your path is undefined, created every moment, with every moment embraced. The choice of Fearless Movement in the name of the most Holy of Holies now lives in you. The mastered path of the Masculine is your blessing to the world, your footsteps theirs to Follow lest they succumb to physicality's trap, the ever present Fear of Choice and Freedom, which breeds inactivity and failure."

Chrysoprase in Healing

Chrysoprase is an opaque stone that is similar to Jade, but lighter. It contains a lot more yellow and white in its frequency and makeup. Chrysoprase has become quite a rare stone and nice quality natural pieces can be hard to find. This is principally because it was aggressively exported out of Australia where it is primarily found, into Asia and sold as Australian Jade, which is one of its other names.

In healing, this mineral's purpose and ability is given away by its colour, Chrysoprase is the crystal of Fearless Movement. It achieves this by powerfully activating the yellow Solar Plexus Chakra for identification of self and connecting it to the open unconditional green vibration of the Heart Chakra. With the presence of white in the stone, it then involves the Crown Chakra, linking to spirit for guidance. The outcome is Crown, Heart and Solar Plexus Chakras working in harmony to direct life in a fearless manner due to the presence of spirit, unconditional love and understanding of self without ego.

With its powerful ability to link to spirit through an unconditional green heart frequency, work with this stone leads to a greater understanding of the cycles in physical life, which integrates a great acceptance of self and others, with a high level of hope, compassion and forgiveness. This aspect of Chrysoprase can powerfully heal a broken heart and is a teacher for men that have lost their feminine balance. Chrysoprase is a contact stone for Ascended Master Djwhal Khul and Master Lanto who work well within its frequency.

At a more physical level, Chrysoprase is a specific stone for the Prostate Gland, Testicles and Ovaries. It has been known to reduce Stress, Nightmares in children (see Charoite), increase Fertility and help in balancing Hormones and Depression.

Your Healing Journey Today

The presence of Chrysoprase for you, signals the opening of a new and creative pathway that will be filtered through the heart under the guidance of your highest parts. Chrysoprase helps us recognize our infinite nature if we embrace unconditional love and, being of the green frequency, guides us in allowing that to come into the physical world. Chrysoprase is very much about following your Heart, a practice that often creates the most beautiful things in the world, but in order for it to do this, personal power and your individual spirit must be taken along on the journey. These are the Yellow and White energies of Chrysoprase and her most beautiful gifts, for you. It seems you're ready for action, Link the Crown, Heart and Solar Plexus Chakras together each morning with light and fearlessly manifest the waves of movement that you came to create.

Please note also that Chrysoprase is an action stone, do it, do it, do it, do it and do it, what ever IT is, IT won't go away!!!

Affirmation;- "I Fearlessly take action, I am Love, Wisdom and Power."

Keywords to help in reading the cards;- Fearless Movement, Action Time, Communication Between Heart, Solar Plexus and Crown Chakras, Spiritual Purpose, Understanding of Life Cycles, Forgiveness, Acceptance, Uncharted Waters in Life, Djwhal Khul, Master Lanto.

Body Card Placement;- Mainly Heart and Solar Plexus Chakra. Chrysoprase can be placed in the room or under the pillow of a child with nightmares or troubled sleep. Meditation with this card can allow you to see which parts of life you need to take action with.

Feminine and Masculine Balance to View Life Purpose Trinity;- Place Moonstone on the Crown Chakra, Chrysoprase at the Heart Chakra, and Sunstone on the Base Chakra. This trinity can bring up information that will require further healing work; it is a good starting point in healing for skeptical Men.

Chemical Composition;- Silicon Dioxide trace Nickel

Color Rays;- 44% Yellow, 44% Green and 12% White

Animal Totem;- Deer

Essential Oil;- Fennel

Citrine

Abundance

The Master Crystal Deva Citrel-m-ra

"Come close child, let me warm you with my golden glow, breathing life into all that you are. Together, without judgment, we will create the path to your abundance, man and spirit as one. Let us blend the creative avenues of spirit through the lowest, densest parts of matter.

Raise your palms to the sky, fill yourself with my light, breath it to your core and magnify its glory into the bliss of endlessness. Money, Health, Love and Time, whatever your currency of Joy in the moment, I have come to aid you in its acquisition.

Rediscovered friends we are, take my hand whenever you wish and I will descend the Golden Dove of Abundant light to remind you of your regal seed. This is a journey of minds, blended from the most physical to the Divine and beyond, we will always arrive where we began, in creation, with you, for you are the all that is."

Citrine in Healing

This glorious member of the quartz family is a light filled golden color with tones of lemon, yellow and orange, it is a transparent crystal that often holds rainbows and interesting inclusions. Recently, real Citrine has become a little more difficult to find in shops around the world which is greatly due to its popular reputation in Asia as a stone of manifesting Luck, Wealth and Abundance. The increased demand for the stone has sparked an age of created Citrine which is simply heat treated Amethyst. The difference is obvious, as it looks burnt and is usually a lot darker, murkier and cheaper (or it should be?).

The energy of Citrine is warming, comforting, creative, motivating and empowering; it holds a vitality and life force that is gifted to all that ask, becoming a support in down times. Through work with Citrine, Confidence and Trust in self soar and we move to embrace the divine creative ability that is our birthright. We take charge of life, without the need for attachments and ride the waves of life's ups and downs. The mind becomes charged with measured Personal Power and obstacles on all levels fall away. It is from this that it has become known as the stone of Abundance.

Citrine is a clean crystal that never needs to be cleansed, this is not only due its potent ability to connect to the higher self and anchor it into the body, but also due to its ability to conduct the Unconditional Gold Ray into creation. This Vibration allows the stone to cleanse and clear the entire Chakra system, though it does have an affinity for the Solar Plexus and the Sacral, where it positively lifts Self Image, removes congestion and empowers creativity.

In the Ancient Atlantian way, Citrine is the principle stone of the Fourth City, a region of Earth dedicated to the development of Unconditional Love and the embrace of the higher emotional self. This not only makes Citrine an important stone but also shows us the importance of its message in spirituality and the ascension process. A High Priestess or Priest initiated by Citrine was known as a Keeper of the Golden Dove, they were quite rare and a famous one you may have heard of was Sananda who came to Earth later as Jesus.

Citrine is an ancient remedy for regenerating body tissues, treating kidney and bladder infections and it is a balancing stone for the digestive system that can help with Constipation.

Your Healing Journey Today

If Citrine has come to you today, a gift is on the way, something that you have desired for a long time is about to become a reality. The main thing to remember at this time is that new things can only occur where space has been made for them to exist, this means letting go of all attachments and standing in a self loving and confident way to receive. The shining light of Citrine also signals a Clearing of negativity from your system and a burst of new found vitality that should be directed onto the guided pathways of self growth and development. If this stone had its way, we would all love each other, heal each other and respect each other, it asks a lot of us mortals, but it can give the endless gift of Unconditional Light and Love, get ready to receive your dreams, but always be prepared to see just how small they are in the bigger picture.

Affirmation;- "Self Love is my measure of Abundance, I Love, I Receive, I Give."

Keywords to help in reading the cards;- Abundance, Deserving, Responsibility, Self Confidence, Personal Power, Creativity, Gold Ray, Knowing, Clearing, Sacral Chakra Congestion, Sirius, Hidden Schools of Egypt, Sananda.

Body Card Placement;- Citrine is a Solar Plexus and Sacral Chakra Stone, but it can clarify and clear any of the energy centers if placed upon them.

Attachment Realization and Release Trinity;- Place the Rhodochrosite card on the Heart Chakra with the Green Calcite card under it, lie still, relax and when it feels right, place the Citrine card on top, this will allow one to recognize attachments held at the heart's frequency that need to be released. This healing usually continues for 21 days after the first experience, I recommend doing it each day for 7 days, at the same time if possible. The Exercise need only take 10 minutes, but its up to you. Aquamarine can be added or substituted for Rhodochrosite if the mind resists the release process.

Vitality Boost Trinity;- Citrine on the Lower Left side of the chest, Sunstone on the Solar Plexus Chakra and Topaz on the Lower Right side of the chest.

Depression Realization Trinity;- Place Citrine on the Crown Chakra, Black Coral on the Third Eye Chakra and Gold on the Solar Plexus Chakra. Let all attention go to the Heart Chakra and draw the cards' (crystals') energy to that point, just Allow. Rose Quartz or Jasper can be added to finish the healing process if you feel it is needed. (Which it usually is.)

Manifestation into the Physical Trinity (Clears the in-body pathways for the Manifestation Process);- Topaz in your Power hand (one you write with), Citrine on the Heart Chakra and Tanzanite in your other hand. Focus in this exercise should be at the Third Eye Chakra attempting to keep the light there, a tiny star of light. Practice makes perfect.

Manifestation Help;- Carve the symbol for Citrine into an orange candle, visualize that which you wish to manifest, place the Citrine card under the candle holder and Light the candle for 7 minutes a day for 21 days, whatever it is will result, or you will realize that you don't actually need it. (If the candle runs out get a new one.)

Chemical Composition;- Silicon Dioxide
Color Rays;- 36% Yellow, 22% Gold, 21% Orange, 17% Clear and 4% White
Animal Totem;- Grasshopper
Essential Oil;- Lemon Balm

Clear Calcite

Universal Mind

The Master Crystal Deva Kel-el

"Receive my blessing on this day, for I am the many as one, my rainbow array of brothers and sisters share the same base purpose, unification through the light of universal mind. This is my domain, travel with me into the mental body. I will lead you through the Third Initiation.

Let us now throw away the limitations of a mind un-mastered and unrealized and begin the journey home. I will free you from time and space, the illusions that carry pain and separation. In my embrace, we will light the path of wholeness and truth.

Now, in the embrace of Universal Mind your perfection and unlimited potential is a simple fact. You are the united flame of oneness blinding in its perfection, journeying homeward to the great Central Sun. By the power of freewill the blessed son, Horus will awaken the hidden intelligence in the name of Isis and Osiris as One, Ascension awaits in your Completion."

Clear Calcite in Healing

Clear Calcite is able to hold clarity more so than any other mineral on Earth, so much so in fact Clear Calcite is often referred to as Optical Calcite. However, it is more known by the natural shape of its crystals, which can be perfect rhomboids, the features of which are parallel sides at direct and perfected angles. The Calcite Family of crystals on Earth covers all the Color Rays available to us, Clear Calcite is the seed of all of them and has the most refined vibrational frequency.

Clear Calcite's amazing clarity and mastery of geometry gives it many of its properties as a spiritual stone and anchors it as the all-important crystal of Universal Mind. Universal Mind refers to the infinite oneness that we all represent as a unified thought form; it is the source of all things original and could even be called the Divine Spark. Clear Calcite is one of the most mental stones on Earth; it has a strong relationship with the mental body, linking all parts to it intimately. It is able to cast fears aside and bring one to a calm, but motivated state, where one can see many realities at once and take action. Clear Calcite is said to be able to increase the IQ, awaken and deliver hidden intelligence and direct one powerfully towards spiritual purpose.

Working with Clear Calcite over time can reduce the fragmentation of self, opening and allowing past lifetimes to be remembered and easily integrated into present life. This is a stone of Astral travel, deep meditation and altered states, it allows the information and things experienced to be remembered and placed in a format that is then useful for life.

At a more physical level, this is a principal stone of the kidneys and can treat all manner of eye problems.

Clear Calcite is a sacred stone for the Ascended Masters Melchizedek, Lord Lanto and the Archangel Metatron, it is a link stone to the Sirius Star System and the Great White Lodge.

Your Healing Journey Today

If Clear Calcite has come to you today, you are about to or have entered a space of mental transition, a new modality, pathway of learning or project. Clear Calcite has come to help with the inevitable fears that arise at this important structural time of change. The energy of Clear Calcite around you will prevent the mental fragmentation and scattering that could weaken the project. This stone can also present when one has been ignoring their path in the world, not taking risks, instead playing by the rules that others have already written. You are being asked in this case to embrace Universal Mind, have trust and enter the uncharted waters of true creation with integrity. In most cases, to receive the gift of Clear Calcite is to receive your wisdom of other lifetimes. Clear Calcite is also a sign that the Third Initiation on the pathway to Ascension has been entered into or completed, Mental Mastery.

Affirmation;- "I Embrace Universal Mind."

Keywords to help in reading the cards;- Universal Mind, The Mental Level, Structure, Masculine, Mental Change, Divinity, Integration of Past Lifetimes, Separation that Must be United, Vision, Astral Travel, Horus (Egyptian God).

Body Card Placement;- This card can go on all of the chakras, where it will link the mind strongly and promote healing of the mental body by the presence of Universal Mind.

The Lord of Time Crystal Trinity (allows one to travel outside of time and space, discover and integrate past and future lifetimes and discover life paths);- To activate and enter on this journey, Petrified Wood is placed on the Right shoulder, Clear Calcite on the Crown Chakra and Labradorite is placed on the Left shoulder. (This is a very powerful and ancient Trinity of crystals, to be treated with respect from an egoless state.)

Chemical Composition;- Calcium Carbonate

Color Rays;- 100% Clear

Animal Totem;- Hawk

Essential Oil;- Peppermint

Clear Quartz

Light Embodied

The Master Crystal Deva Cry-el-o-el

"I am the White Dove of infinite light, through time's immortal embrace, I serve all that ask. On this day, I have come to live within you, make me a space in your heart and together we will amplify your light, letting your radiance live in every cell.

Open to my embrace in the web of light that life presents and lie still in Ra's Embrace. See the rainbow of colors possible in our world and through breath drink deeply of them. Carry that gift in all its variation and simplicity into your Heart and Gaze to the heavens above you, where I await as the White Dove of Light. Call my name and I will descend into the Heart where I shall remain, a Rose, white as snow, until our work is done.

My world is filled with the joy of love and light realized in physical form. Reach for our mutual goal now, and become not a vessel, but the glory of light itself. Open to my energy, let us join together, amplifying your unconditional nature and elevating you through the levels of spirit back to your true home within."

Clear Quartz in Healing

The Great-Grandmother of the mineral kingdom, I believe, needs no introduction. Clear Quartz is the mineral that many think of when the word crystal is spoken, she comes in many forms, often displaying perfect clarity and beautiful crystals with various geometric terminations.

Clear Quartz is one of the ancients, spoken of in all the world's religions and places of wisdom. She is a member of the ancient Lemurian Council of Seven, once serving as a physical anchor point for the etheric Lemurian people. In some ways, we could say Clear Quartz acted as an ancient physical body until Lemuria shifted and Atlantis was born. In Atlantian Times, of all the revered minerals of the Earth, Clear Quartz was by far the most respected, something that her Temples in the Atlantian City of Golgotha reflected. Clear Quartz allows the direct Embodiment of Light into physicality, which is still its simple purpose with humanity.

The measure of embodied light was, and still is called Light Quotient, which is the percentage of cells that hold light in the Body. In Atlantis, to be a High Priestess or High Priest of Clear Quartz, one had to hold at least 92% Light Quotient. Thus, it was a rare position to hold for long, the longest serving perhaps being The Lady Nada, a great ascended lady of light still serving humanity today.

Clear Quartz is an Amplification stone; it lifts all that it encounters, able to find one's maximum potential no matter the starting level. It offers alignment at the Mental and Emotional resulting in a profound Clarity and a self acceptance that leads to action, growth and healing. Clear Quartz performs potent Purification on all levels of self by effecting Light Quotient directly and, leading by example in the embodiment of Light, can deliver one into the Ascended state.

Clear Quartz is an important stone in Psychic Surgery and Energetic body works, where it expands each of the Energy bodies, helping one to see what is going on and making it easier to move aspects around. This same factor at the etheric level can show us of our creation pathways, thus teaching us what we may be doing that leads to an unwanted outcome. This is especially useful in healing to see the Cause or Seed of illness and eliminate it. Clear Quartz will increase Telepathy, Psychic Abilities and Spiritual Communication.

At the physical level Clear Quartz has an affinity for the Nervous System and any issues there. It purifies the urinary system and kidneys. It will remove increased light, heat, stagnancy or congestion, leading to balance when placed over the area.

Your Healing Journey Today

If life is not infused with purpose, it is very easy to become numb and lost, just rolling from one day to the next, unaware of how any of it happens. We can simply accept our world and in doing so lose our divine self and personal roles in creation. Clear Quartz has entered your life to sing the song of self acceptance, purification and clarity, by amplifying your inner light she is realigning you to your thoughts and feelings so you may take action and create a world that you truly deserve and desire. Clear Quartz has come to remind you that the physical world can be perfect, she signals the beginning of a new age of you. Reset your goals, write a list of the things that make you happy and dedicate time so they may exist physically in your life, the time has come to embody your light and activate your avenues of creation with skill and mastery. This is a powerful time for meditation and contemplation, use it wisely and carry out your decisions with strength and knowing, the White Dove is with you.

Affirmations;- "I am the Fragrance of Jasmine Light."
"The White Dove Lives in my Heart."

Keywords to help in reading the cards;- Light Embodied, Amplification, Light Quotient, Clarity, Self Acceptance, Purification, Golgotha, Crystal Healing, The Lady Nada, Maitreya, Sai Baba, Goals, The Scarab, Life Path.

Body Card Placement;- Can be placed on any Chakra or body area.

Crystal Healing Enhancement Trinity;- Place Diamond on the Left shoulder and Clear Quartz on the Right shoulder. Any stone that is placed at the Heart Chakra between them will be potently Enhanced and amplified in its healing ability. This technique is particularly potent with other members of the Quartz Family.

Deneb Kaitos Trinity, Whale of a Star to Visit;- Place the Clear Quartz Card on the Third Eye and Moldavite on the Crown and Celestite on the Heart Chakra. Use your Intention to go to Deneb Kaitos, a Star in the Constellation Cetus (The Whale). This is a home of Clear Quartz based light, a place of great Healing and Growth. This was the origin of the First Quartz Crystal in our Universe. If you do this Trinity before bed for 10 minutes it will hold you in the frequency all night.

Clear Ray Trinity;- Clear Calcite on the Left shoulder, Apophyllite on the Third Eye Chakra and Clear Quartz on the Right shoulder. (Caution; only do this if your Know what it will do.)

Chemical Composition;- Silicon Dioxide

Color Rays;- 91% Clear and 9% White

Animal Totem;- Dove

Essential Oil;- Jasmine

Other Clear Quartz Stuff

Somewhere on Earth there is an individual Quartz Crystal for every person, which can activate the in-body Light Encodements, the light memories placed in the Blood at birth. This is one's personal Hall of Records, held in the body life after life. In times past it arrived when necessary, but now, as in Atlantis, can be accessed through the reunited, holistic Clear Quartz Liquid Crystal, the united space of 16, 854 pieces from as many origins on the Earth. You still have to be ready, but it might be time to get hold of some.

Clear Quartz is the Primary Crystal of the Clear Ray for our planet, meaning at 91% it holds more of that frequency than any other stone, Clear Calcite is a close second at 90%, and the two are very powerful when worked with together.

Crocite

Passion

The Master Crystal Deva Ulu-ra-el

"Mine is the domain of Passion, take my hand. See a red flame above your crown, call it down to the base and feel the serpent stir, let an erupting column of fire towards the Crown be my welcome and your rediscovery and embrace of me, let us create.

Expression of Perfection in Feminine power through the Masculine avenue is my domain, I stimulate the Animal and Primal nature of Humanity which is too easily lost in modern life. I am Love Expressed as Instinct; feel me run through you, I am the breath in the Lions Roar.

Together now, hand-in-hand as serpents entwined, let the earthly gift co-creation be your guiding light to eternal happiness and joy. Embrace your creative spark and live, for only those that express pure passion will knowingly hold the Holy Grail and swim in its Sacred Waters."

Crocite in Healing

Crocite is a bright, Fiery, Orange-Red stone that can be quite transparent, its crystals are slender and quite needle-like, usually disorganized to the eye, cutting and running through each other. It is not found in many localities around the world and the nicest pieces come from Tasmania, displaying a bright, orange-red colour that is rare in the mineral kingdom.

Crocite is the crystal of Passion. It empowers animalistic expression through sexuality and creativity, more than any other crystal on Earth. It is able to carry fire into old relationships, correct impotence and infertility, open up the pathways of creativity and allow the recovery of personal power after distress. Of the minerals available to us that address sexuality, no other addresses the primal instinct as directly as this one, even increasing the sensitivity of the reproductive organs and aiding in the tone of the muscles in the area.

Everything that Crocite does it does in a very powerful, physically active way, it addresses passion at many levels not just in relation to sexuality, thus can be called into action when the flame has gone out for anything that makes up an important part of your existence. This crystal calls the highest energies into Base and Lower energy centers to facilitate movement and transition when needed and is able to facilitate movement from one state to another. In Atlantian times, Crocite was utilized with Amethyst and Garnet as a euthanasia stone facilitating the movement from one life to the next.

At the physical level, Crocite is a master of male and female reproductive disorders including infertility, ovarian cysts and hormonal imbalance.

This is a doorway stone when paired with black Obsidian to the ancient Egyptian cat goddess Bast and is a potent stone of Tantric Practice. The Lady of the Sun will answer in this stone's presence.

Your Healing Journey Today

If Crocite has come to you today, it is time to look at the lower chakra system from the Solar Plexus down to the Base for the balance of Passion. Passion is crucial to the solar plexus for direction, self-love and identification in the world. Passion is crucial at the sacral for co-creation, creativity, freedom and choice. Passion is crucial at the base chakra for sexuality, raw physical direction and physical life mastery. Remember as you explore Passion, that blind passion shows a lack of mastery and the presence of ego. Addiction is the extreme of blind passion unchecked, while depression is the extreme of a lack of passion, expressed in life. As with all things, balance is the key, the principal rule, is do what You love, not what the world would have you do, Passion is personal, share it with those you love, and those who love you.

Affirmation;- "My Fire Shines Brightly, I Express Passionately."

Keywords to help in reading the cards;- Passion, Sexuality, Male-Female Balance, Recovery of Personal Power, Creativity, Relationship, Reproductive System, Infertility and Impotence, Boredom in Relationship, Frigidity, Tantric Practice.

Body Card Placement;- Lower Chakra System. To get the fires going between a couple, place this card under a bottle of red wine and share it with someone you love or place it under a red candle in the bedroom.

Sexuality Trinity (Enhances all aspects of the experience, Physical to Spiritual);- There are two ways to work with this Trinity:

1) Healing Sexuality-based issues and balancing the reproductive system, Carnelian is placed on the Left hip, Garnet is placed on the Right hip and Crocite on the Sacral Chakra.
2) Enhancing Sexuality, Carnelian, Crocite and Garnet are placed in a Triangle formation under the bed, the top of the triangle should be at the Head end.

Chemical Composition;- Lead Chromate

Color Rays;- 37% Red, 19% Yellow and 44% Orange

Animal Totem;- Red Kangaroo

Essential Oil;- Calamus Root

Diamond

Light Body

The Master Crystal Deva Adamael

"I am all that you are in your realized completion. The doorway of union, silicon and carbon as one, united in the sacred language of light. I am the voice of the crystals manifest, Starchild of the mineral kingdom, my way is new, my path un-walked. You will be my guide as I will be yours.

Hold me close; permit my spark of infinite light to burn in your three eyes, a triangle of fire. Together we journey to the quintessential embodiment of light absolute and Infinite. Wear my white starry robe upon your shoulders and in Love, command the crystal that you are into realization. A single point of blinding light. Gaze no more in wonder at the stars child, lest you not see them gaze back in wonder at you.

Your physical eyes may now close, where we travel they simply do not, the inner eye is your guide. Through the triangle of fire with heart open, trust and acceptance will manifest your path. In my light you will carry the Wisdom of the ages, Power of the spirit and Love of the infinite, the balance of these is my real role. Hold gently the petals of the White Rose, you are magnificent."

Diamond in Healing

Diamond needs no real introduction, but for many it is a surprise that it is simply crystallized Coal. It is a pure carbon crystal which, based in the Laws of science, qualifies as life form. Though this glorious lady is the most powerful activator of the crown chakra available to us at this stage, she was unknown in Atlantian times and spiritually is the youngest crystal on Earth.

Via its amazing clarity and light, Diamond demonstrates the placement of spirit into physicality. It is a symbol of the embrace of the pure spirit on the physical level, which is the goal of the human race on Earth. Diamond is a unifying energy; it unites all that is in separation to a central point of light in the self, anchoring love for self and others which in turn fosters balance and loyalty. Linking the mind to the spirit, she sets creativity in motion, the imagination and inventiveness of a child return and one can find a true vision or path in the world.

Diamond is the sacred stone of the Son of Isis and Osiris, the Egyptian God Horus. It is the most powerful stone on Earth for communication with human beings that have just passed away, making it our sacred stone and only one other being truly answers in Diamond's frequency he is Lord Melchior, the Galactic Logos, a being whose frequency makes him unavailable to many of us.

Diamond is still very misunderstood in the world; she is one of the only minerals that can remove the actual life force from diseases as she absorbs light. Most crystals send or radiate light; diamond captures it. This is a very powerful tool in healing things such as Cancer which has a set life force that can be quite simply absorbed.

Diamond has an affinity for the physical head area, finding use in the treatment of eyesight, brain imbalances, pituitary and pineal difficulties, autism, dyslexia, epilepsy, and even the adjustment of the cranial plates themselves.

Your Healing Journey Today

If Diamond has come to you today, a powerful child has come to play, it is time to unite the separate parts of your life and allow them to find a united strength. It is time to unite your minds and listen to your heart, only then can the will of your spirit guide you in your physical world. The path of ascension is being presented to you, it is time to choose Love, the first step is self. Other reasons Diamond may be present include, spiritual guidance, activation at the crown chakra, the need to balance physical life and spirituality or the opening of a pathway of service.

Affirmation;- "I am the infinite light of the universe."

Keywords to help in reading the cards;- Light Body, Spirit, Soul, Crown Chakra, Unite, Oneness, Light, The Head Area, Silence the Mind, Self Love, Joy, Ascension,

Completion, Service.

Body Card Placement;- All Chakras that need light, the Crown (links to spirit), below the feet (with Hematite calls the spirit into the body), at any Cancer site as close as you can for healing, the Liquid Crystal Diamond can enter the blood directly.

Whale Communication Trinity (Prepares a Person to Communicate with Whales and Translate their Song);- Blue Lace Agate on the Lower Left side of the chest, Diamond on the Heart Chakra and Larimar on the Lower Right side of the chest. The effect of this process will last for 21 days, it should be noted that profound healing can take place for some people through the song of whales and thus ongoing support may be necessary in some cases.

Crown Chakra Trinity (Most Holistic Activation of the Crown Chakra Available);- Lepidolite to the Left side of the head (below the ear), Diamond on the Crown Chakra and Selenite to the Right side of the head (below the ear).

Ascension Trinity (Facilitates the Ascension Process and the Merge with Spirit);- Clear Calcite is placed on the Left hip, Diamond is placed on the Right hip and Clear Quartz is placed on the Thymus Gland Chakra.

Chemical Composition;- Pure Carbon

Color Rays;- All 13 Color Rays

Animal Totem;- Humpback Whale

Essential Oil;- Neroli

Dioptase

The Healing Heart

The Master Crystal Deva Matazel

"Feel my touch, let it open the Emerald Green Stairs into your heart and together let us ascend them slowly, for today there is only completion and Healing. I ask you now to look back in anger, resentment and judgment no more, for I have come to lovingly guide you in the art of focused manifestation, of which your life is the result.

Remember, the heart is pure beyond the veil of Self Judgment and together we will lift it so, through your own Emerald eyes, you will see the perfection that you are. Feel the Emerald shower of my compassion surround you and let it detach you into freedom. I hold the pure healing intent of the Green Ray at your disposal anchored into the black of the earth.

In my presence the lightning flash of Emerald light has healed the scars of the heart and now lives in you. Allow me to ground the basis of Love, Physical and Unconditional, let them find their home within you, completing the cycle of the ages in the Now and anchoring permanently, in the hearts of all you touch, the blessing of the infinite one."

Dioptase in Healing

Dioptase is a relatively rare crystal that is quite expensive; it is a dark, deep Emerald Green Stone that could very easily be mistaken for Emerald. The key difference between the two is found in their Colour Ray structure, Emerald being composed principally of the Green and Clear Rays and Dioptase the Green and Black. This, of course, makes Dioptase more opaque and allows it the ability to anchor the Green healing Ray deeper into physicality. This is of great significance in the green aspect of the heart chakra and allows Dioptase to be the most potent stone for healing the heart. No mineral on Earth can go as deeply into the heart energies physically and create healing.

Dioptase's principal lesson is that of the open heart, it teaches the importance of compassion, nonattachment and non-judgment. It is perfect for healing relationships, where there is a lack of understanding and poor communication, but it comes into its own after relationships, where it acts as an unconditional light sealing the halves of a broken heart together in a flash of green lightning.

This crystal is wonderful for healers that have done too much and allowed themselves to become burnt out, thus losing the healer identity. It balances Sensitivity and Self Judgment, and then reignites the healer for the good of all, including the self, often with new skills. Dioptase can also be coupled up with Petrified Wood and Double Terminated Quartz crystals to powerfully remember past life times.

Although a powerful emotional and mental healer, Dioptase has potent effects on the physical body, it is second to none with headaches and migraines, will calm in shock and emergency situations and is a specific treatment for HIV and AIDS.

In Atlantian times, Dioptase was known as 'Earth Emerald' and was used to unlock the heart, reveal and train one in their true healing gifts, something that it is still able to do today when we are ready. In Atlantis, Dioptase was a crystal of the 11th city, Shamballa, and was only worked with directly by High Priests and Priestesses of that city. Dioptase is one of many crystals that in Atlantian times were usually only worked with in trinities, specialized sets of three stones that complemented each other in their healing action. Its healing ability was greatly respected and very well known. The action of Dioptase at its highest spiritual level is known as the process of Resurrection or Rebirth, but it can only do this after the release/death of something. Important Ancient Atlantian Masters that were High Priestesses and Priests of the crystal Dioptase in the 11th City, Shamballa, include Quan Yin, Isis, Sananda (Jesus), Akhenaten, The Lady Tara and Archangel Mary, they still all answer in its frequency.

Your Healing Journey Today

On this day the heart will be healed. Wherever Dioptase goes broken hearts are healed and carried into understanding. The presence of this crystal for you indicates some of the many lessons of love are ready to be embraced; Compassion, Patience,

Non-judgment, Listening, Truthfulness, Nonattachment, Equality and Respect are all good starting points. Dioptase has come to hold the heart open, she indicates a new relationship or path of love, but remember, for new things to occur, one must be prepared to look forward, take action and free attachments and expectations. Dioptase can also present, when you have allowed others to cloud your judgment, so sit quietly, alone and make your decisions; this crystal's presence tells you, you have the answers. The above mentioned Masters may be utilizing the frequency of Dioptase to communicate with you, place this card to your heart and listen.

Affirmation;- " I am all Loving, my Heart is Pure."

Keywords to help in reading the cards;- Healing Heart, Relationship, The Open Heart , Heart Chakra, Attachment, Healing Path, Oversensitivity, The Green Ray, Resurrection, Migraine and Headaches, Past Life Times.

Body Card Placement;- Powerful at the Heart Chakra, the Earth Star Chakra and held between the Hands at the Heart in Prayer. Dioptase can be placed under candles in the centre of a table before communication relevant to relationships to deliver honesty and truthful outcomes. Give this card to loved ones to protect them during travel.

Allow a Stubborn Heart to Freely Give Love Trinity;- Dioptase on the Lower Left side of the chest, Kunzite on the Heart Chakra and Pink Tourmaline on the Lower Right side of the chest. Lie, Breathe and Relax.

Chemical Composition;- Copper Silicate Hydroxide

Color Rays;- 84% Green, 13% Black and 3% Gold

Animal Totem;- Otter

Essential Oil;- Fir Needle

Elestial Quartz

Angelic Truth

The Master Crystal Deva El-om-el

"I hear your steps at the door to the 11th temple, the circle of blue fire around you signals your readiness. Step into my flames of Angelic Truth, we will seek the path of your personal power in the world then measure and purify its intention.

Feel my blue flame of truth blanket you in a touch of initiation and welcome, together now, we tread the path of unified growth to preordained destiny. Join we will, our Angelic siblings and drink deeply of our blended light, Power, Wisdom and Love as one. Be free.

Open child, cut away the debris of a physical life with the power of realization and embrace the Solar Angel that you came to Earth to unveil and become. You will wear the crown of the eternal son and realize the pulse of the universe runs in your will, simply allow now and rest in Truth."

Elestial Quartz in Healing

Originally a gift from the Angels to help us master personal power, this diverse form of Quartz Crystal is a mixture of the deep and light grays of Smoky Quartz and the whites and clarity of Clear Quartz. It rarely has one noticeable termination, with multiple points, usually in many directions, and often all over its body creating individual patterns and engravings that can be translated to teach the universal language of sacred geometry.

Within the threefold flame, the Angelic kingdom are the keepers of the flame of Power, the Elohim and Devic are the keepers of the flame of Wisdom and we are the keepers of the flame of Love.

Elestial Quartz is the crystal of Angelic Truth, which could be translated into the truth about one's personal power. For many people this crystal is very confronting as it provides such a pure and absolute view of the self. It shows the seeds and cores of fears, diseases and one's shortcomings associated with use of power in the world. (A good crystal for the water cooler at work?) Work with Elestial Quartz over time can anchor angelic characteristics into a person and, via the Crown chakra, open one to angelic communication and a higher light frequency. Via its powerful action, Elestial can help one to overcome emotional burdens and balance the mind to such a degree that it can deliver understanding of life purpose.

Elestial Quartz is potent in its action on the brain where it stabilizes wave frequency, making it useful in Epilepsy, Schizophrenia and where there is burned-out brain tissue, especially due to drug abuse. Elestial Quartz will harmonize imbalance between the higher glands in the brain. This is a sacred stone of Ascended Master Melchizedek and Egyptian God Thoth (able to open Light Packets left by him all over the Earth), but it is the special contact stone of the Archangel Michael.

Your Healing Journey Today

If Elestial Quartz has come to you today, you have reached a time in life where you are ready to truthfully see where you place your personal power in the world. In the coming days, observe your actions and those of people around you. Remember, there should be a balance of incoming and outgoing energies where power is concerned. A lack of personal power usually results in one becoming a victim and losing love for self. An excess of personal power can become a corruption of the highest order, birthing an ego that can take the reins of life and may even believe that it is the spirit. Above all, know that Elestial Quartz is here to show you the truth.

Affirmation;- "I own my Personal Power."

Keywords to help in reading the cards;- Angelic Truth, Personal Power, Angelic Communication, Life Purpose, Spirit, Immoral Self, Brain Balance, Crown Chakra, Archangel Michael.

Body Card Placement;- Elestial Quartz nearly always goes on the Crown Chakra when worked with alone.

Angelic Communication Trinity;- Place Chrysocolla on the Throat Chakra, Tanzanite on the Heart Chakra and Elestial Quartz on the Solar Plexus Chakra.

Align Power to the Heart Chakra Trinity;- Place Kunzite on the Heart Chakra, Elestial Quartz on the Solar Plexus Chakra and Kyanite between them.

Chemical Composition;- Silicon Dioxide

Color Rays;- 33.3% Clear, 33.3% White and 33.3% Black

Animal Totem;- Lynx

Essential Oil;- Angelica

Emerald

Spiritual Healing

The Master Crystal Deva Vert-el

"Come, I will hold you child, allow my warmth to surround you. Feel the mist of my green healing ray envelop and carry the message of the Absolute into the depths of your spirit. Trust now in your divinity, sacredness and perfection beyond mind and physicality. Birthed from a single seed of love, you are the Infinity of Love's Ocean on the shores of the universe.

I remember the time you danced with me within the skies of light, a time of joy, a time of unity and truth. We spoke of a journey that you had chosen and we opened a path that you could walk. I have not forgotten you, child of light, and I await, with many, your return. Listen now, for it was known that you may forget. You are the alpha and omega, but most important you are the highest principle of spiritual love, you are infinite.

In my embrace, realize your support in the other worlds. Let me guide your breath and open the door, for the many who await you. Together as one in the joy of rhythm, enter the one true Abundance through the pulse of the Creator, the reality of Unconditional Love. You are the air in the breath of healing intent. Fear, pain, dis-ease and suffering are an illusion of man unrealized."

Emerald in Healing

Emerald is a beautiful green gemstone, which varies in clarity from transparent to opaque, the more prized pieces being transparent. She is an old world stone mentioned in many of the world's major religions, prized as a Jewel and an important part of the Ancient Channeling Breastplate. She has been in service for a long time and is on her way out of manifestation as a physical crystal on the Earth. As the new children of light are being born into physicality, a new spiritual healer is needed, a crystal from their world. Such a crystal is Moldavite, called from the stars by Emerald to serve the children of Earth on their journey in physicality. Moldavite will be the new Emerald, taking up the role of spiritual healing when Emerald ascends.

Emerald belongs in the Beryl family of crystals, her brothers and sisters including Aquamarine, the crystal of simplification and Morganite the crystal of equality in love. A member of the Council of Seven from ancient Atlantis, Emerald was recognized as the contact stone for the Dolphin, allowing communication between Atlantis and Lemuria until its demise. The most recognized high priestess from the Emerald Temple in Atlantis was the Lady Nada, a powerful being that is still available to us today.

Emerald has always been known as the Master healer, the foundation of which lies in the Stone's ability to open the heart chakra and allow acknowledgement of the meaning of true abundance, the presence of unconditional love. There is nothing that Emerald can not heal, under Emerald's guidance all healing becomes a spiritual act that holds at its foundation love in action. She stabilizes the mind and opens the emotional body, simplifying what she finds, replacing turmoil with patience, peace and optimism. Emerald is able to activate the psychic ability and is a powerful facilitator of the meditative breath. Emerald is a sacred contact stone for the Ascended Master Paul the Venetian and the Lady Nada.

At the physical level, this Crystal has been useful in all ailments associated with the heart, kidneys, liver and pancreas. Emerald has also been shown to be useful in epilepsy and cancer, facilitating the removal of high levels of radiation from the body.

Your Healing Journey Today

If Emerald has come to you today, it is time to bring your spirit close and listen, you are in need of love. The time for healing has come, go inward and leave no stone unturned. At this time in your life, truth is your best friend, channel all your experiences through the heart, if it is not unconditional, it should be discarded. Emerald also reminds us that what we are facing in life is a lesson, just a steppingstone into understanding and back to your infinite self. When you are right within, your outer world will follow. Money is not abundance, love is, be the love, the money will come where its needed. New guidance may be waiting for your recognition. The spirit of the Dolphin is with you, go to the ocean and listen through your heart, let each breaking wave pass through and heal you.

Affirmation;- "In Truth, Love and Peace, I am healed."

Keywords to help in reading the cards;- Healing, Spirit, Guidance, Unconditional Love, the Dolphin, the Rose, Need for an Inner Journey, Choice, Emotional Balance.

Body Card Placement;- Emerald can enter the body through the chin (Goddess Point) and all the main body Chakras. At the Third Eye Chakra it will stimulates Pleiadian contact, at the Heart Chakra it activates spirit communication (channeling) and below the feet at the Earth Star it removes toxins.

Uniting the Green Flames Trinity (A powerful Atlantian Sequence of Healing);- Dioptase on the Upper Left side of the chest, Herkimer Diamond on the Heart Chakra and Emerald on the Upper Right side of the chest.

Dolphin Communication Trinity (Prepares a Person to communicate with Dolphins and Translate their Song with the Heart for Healing and Growth);- Angelite on the Lower Left side of the chest, Emerald on the Heart Chakra and Blue Lace Agate on the Lower Right side of the chest.

Chemical Composition;- Beryllium Aluminum Silicate Chromium (trace)

Color Rays;- 50% Green and 50% Clear

Animal Totem;- Dolphin

Essential Oil;- Rose

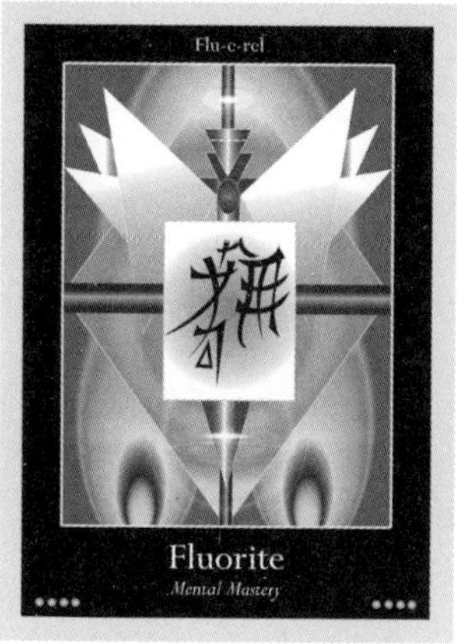

Fluorite

Mental Mastery

The Master Crystal Deva Flu-e-rel

"Take my hand, link to me and I will guide your thoughts. Mine is the mental plane and now we will play together in its frequency of creation. Let our union manifest organized mental mastery in the depths of self.

Through me, only that which is in alignment with universal mind is made present, allowing you to take action in the Now. Know all that flows from you is in alignment with divinity. Under the gentle guidance of my loving focus we will remove the voids of unfocused manifestation that surround you, allowing true purpose for self and humanity to become known.

May the newly embraced Universal self and mind be welcomed home to its source and creator that you are. The stars of the heavens will be there when you close your eyes, day and night they live within you, direct their voice with your intention."

Fluorite in Healing

Fluorite is a multicolored mineral that is quite transparent, often, however, its color is so deep that one must hold it up to a light or the sun to see through it. We can see in its colour ray structure that Fluorite's color range includes most of the spectrum. Reds and pinks are rare, green, purple and clear are by far the most common and give rise to the mineral's ability to carry the unconditional loving mind of spirit into the mind of man, prompting Mental Mastery.

This is the mineral for mental organization, it takes mental disorganization and stress and creates order that then flows into the surrounding world. Working with Fluorite over time is said to cultivate trust in one's mental ability, foster commitment to one's ideas and facilitate their path into the world. It increases the IQ and indicates when one is being mentally manipulated.

Fluorite is a multidimensional stone carrying the laws of the universe into the physical arena. Between its colour bands are doors into the space between polarities, these allow one to sit in the peace of God that exists between any two things. That space is then mentally linked into daily living, helping one to stay tuned to the source while functioning on the physical plane. Fluorite is a sacred contact stone of the Ascended Master Melchizedek, the Archangel Zadkiel and Egyptian God Thoth.

Physically, Fluorite protects against computer and electromagnetic stress and the healing of bone and dental diseases. It is a very powerful remedy of stress-related Insomnia and disturbances in brain wave frequencies.

Your Healing Journey Today

If Fluorite has come to you today, your life is in need of organization, especially at the mental level. Now is a good time to realize that if the mind is not disciplined and focused, it is being allowed to wander aimlessly and thus it will create aimlessly also. When this happens, we create things in our life that we have no purpose for, these things then clutter our path. Fluorite asks you to commit mentally and follow through to the end with whatever is currently occurring, take everything one step at a time. One path is hard enough to stay on, why create more? Make a list of all the things you have begun in life that are currently active and number them in order of importance, choose one and stick with it into completion. Once that is done, look at how you did it and learn to do it faster, the greatest and only teacher is always the self.

Affirmation;- "My Mind creates my world."

Keywords to help in reading the cards;- Mental Mastery, Organization, Focus, Discipline, Clutter, Heart and Mind as One, Commitment.

Body Card Placement;- All Body Chakras. At the Third Eye Chakra Fluorite may be used to discover life purpose and enter the Akashic records of self.

Akashic Records Trinity (The ancient records of Self, all that you are and have been, are available here when you are ready);- Tanzanite is placed at the Crown Chakra, Fluorite on the Third Eye Chakra and Apophyllite on the Heart Chakra. Lie quietly, you will be taken to a White Crystal Pyramid Structure or down a staircase that leads under the Sphinx in Egypt, all records are usually read aloud to you. It should be noted also that this is not the place for questions, only answers, Listen. If you don't remember what happened, Apophyllite will, place it on your Heart.

Increasing Intelligence Trinity;- Fluorite is placed to the Left side of the head (ear height), Clear Calcite is placed to the Right side of the head (ear height) and Pyrite is placed on the Third Eye Chakra. 7 Minutes a day for 21 Days, you will see and feel the difference, this is great for Children over 10 years old.

Uniting the Heart and Mind Trinity;- Place Fluorite on the Crown Chakra, Kyanite on the Third Eye Chakra and Rose Quartz on the Heart Chakra. Draw all their light and energies to the Throat Chakra and then let it disperse through the body.

Chemical Composition;- Calcium Fluoride

Color Rays;- 15% Violet, 15% Blue, 25% Gold, 20% Yellow and 20% Clear

Animal Totem;- Swan

Essential Oil;- Rosemary

Garnet

Manifestation of Purpose

The Master Crystal Deva Galandel

"Welcome to my embrace, I am the fire of Ra embraced by the earth, an ancient one. You and I have stood as one in times past. On the journey back to that which you are, I have come to guide you to the sacred space of inner strengths, the Temple of your personal gifts.

In my presence, cast the wills of others aside, breathe my green ray of love and black light of truth, let my red fires encourage and nurture you into activation, let your gifts come forth in a creative manner and you will find new paths to fulfill your purpose and gently awaken the serpent to its journey upward.

Using the active stabilized heart as a filter, we will now physically manifest a divine legacy, which will define the commitment to self that is required of you within the only perception that is valid, your own."

Garnet in Healing

Traditionally Garnet is a deep blood Red transparent mineral that through the ages has been highly prized by jewelers. Garnets can vary in clarity and color manifesting the lightest of pinks, through to reds so deep, they appear black until held to the sun. There are many different varieties of Garnet, including a beautiful green variety called Tsavorite and the rarest of all, the Blue Garnet only discovered in 1990, that changes color from blue-green in the daylight to purple in incandescent light. The information here applies to all colors and types of Garnet, but it should be noted Red is the most plentiful coloration, thus taints the information accordingly.

Garnet is the keystone of the Manu Allah Gobi, lord of the first ray of creation; it demonstrates and carries forth the pure vitality and power of the red frequency in all its actions. Its simple healing directive with humanity is the Manifestation of Purpose, a path it activates by unblocking creativity and channeling it through the heart and emotional body bringing inspiration, devotion and Imagination. Garnet has the ability to carry all creative energies found in the lower areas of the chakra system up to the heart, where their actions are stabilized via love and magnified on their journey into physicality. It is via the same path that Garnet is able to activate the survival instincts, magnify courage and instill commitment to purpose.

Garnet has been known to increase the sexual appetite and is a master stone of the Tantric practices, alongside of stones such as Crocite and Carnelian, its close friends. However Garnet's closest friend would have to be Moonstone, who in magical practice represents the feminine component, where Garnet represents the masculine. This is most commonly put into practice when a Garnet is worn on the middle finger of the dominant or power hand, and Moonstone is worn on the middle finger of the receiving hand in magical work, this has the effect of polarizing the body and facilitating manifestation into the physical, an ancient Atlantian practice still practised today. In ancient Atlantis, priests and priestesses of these two crystals would visit young children in the 10th city, En-Kai-Pan, to determine their gifts and help in the choosing of life direction. A child would simply stand between a priest and a priestess, the masculine and feminine and recognize the principle crystal that defined their path back to oneness.

Garnet is a governing stone of the 11:11 gateway and the Second Initiation on the path to Ascension. It is a contact stone for the Ascended Masters El Morya, Sanat Kumara and Allah Gobi and will allow contact with a divine being known only as The Lady of the Sun.

At a more physical level, Garnet is a potent blood purifier that aids the function of the heart and lungs. It is also a powerful healer of infertility sterility and frigidity.

Your Healing Journey Today

The energy of this stone gives purpose to all things and has not come into your life to correct, turn around or heal your current surrounds, but simply to deliver the purpose behind them. In life, we all undertake tasks that at the time seem perfect, then as time progresses, we learn and realize they may not be for us and should be released. Garnet is letting you know there is a reason behind all your choices and soon it will be known. However, no matter how tough the path, never surrender until you know why you begun the journey. For if you turn your back too early, there is a great possibility you will just recreate the same picture with different paints. Garnet asks us to filter all that we will do through our hearts, as it is there that the voice of truth echoes in the Soul's halls of purpose and manifests our path in the world. Listen to your heart speak, for between the words is hidden the glory of the Universe. Garnet especially applies to creativity, sexuality, relationships, work, diet, children and other sacral and base chakra activities. You are about to understand your life at a deeper level. Meditate and find space to see all that you are.

Affirmation;- "I Manifest my Purpose with Love as my Guide."

Keywords to help in reading the cards;- Manifestation of Purpose, Courage, Imaginative, Masculine Energy, Creativity, Sexuality, Sacral and Base Chakras, The Red Ray, El Morya, Sanat Kumara and Allah Gobi, Relationship, Instinct, Druids.

Body Card Placement;- Garnet is at home on any Chakra from the Heart down,

Life Purpose Discovery and Related Decisions Trinity;- Garnet is placed at the Crown Chakra with Pyrite on the Left shoulder and Selenite on the Right shoulder.

Purification of the Blood Trinity;- Bloodstone on the Upper Left side of the chest, Garnet on the Heart Chakra and Hematite on the Upper Right side of the chest. When this is done, be sure to drink lots of water for at least three days afterwards.

Chemical Composition;- Iron Aluminum Silicate

Color Rays;- 70% Red, 10% Green, 2% Blue and 18% Black

Animal Totem;- Kookaburra

Essential Oil;- Elemi

Gold

The Solar Angel

The Master Crystal Deva Au-rumel

"I offer you the very essence of the Sun. Wear my solar embrace and feel my warmth carry the direct signature and purity of the infinite one into your heart. Let us light the individual flame of immortality that you are.

Close your eyes and wear my star filled emerald robe, let it surround and heal all that you are. My physical presence embraced, as sure as the sun rises each morning I will trigger the memory of the god self inside you. Simply by my light, warmth and glow, that memory will be recognized.

Invoke my golden flame from above you and shine in your endless divine design You have heard my call, that part of you that is unbounded has began to restructure the very threads of your existence, manifesting your perfection so your greater purpose may be recognized. Let the spirit of Ra shine in your every action, in the embrace of Nuit, you are his child."

Gold in Healing

Gold is a metal characterized by its truly individual color, often made into jewelry and still to this day, as throughout time, revered for its purity as a substance. This metal is one of the most prescribed remedies in Homeopathic medicine and its healing ability is something held sacred by every race to have encountered it. In modern medicine Gold is used in the treatment of Multiple Sclerosis, while in ancient Atlantian times pure gold talismans were physically implanted into the body for activation, healing and spiritual growth, directly affecting the light carrying ability of the Nervous System and Body.

Gold is the mineral of the Solar Angel, the soul consciousness, which it powerfully activates and carries into the body. This regenerates all aspects of self and activates our inner light and true potential, helping us to know our individual gifts and stay on our true path of growth. Gold simply infuses the desire to know spirit and grow via its embrace as a reality. Mentally and emotionally gold purifies, clearing negativity, tension and stress which allows the discovery of a holistic balance in all activities and often shows the pathway of true cure in dis-ease processes. Gold also extends its purification ability into the dream state where it is one of the best Nightmare stones, removing them and delivering the message behind them more gently.

Spiritually this mineral is aligned with the Male energy of creation and the very basis of Unconditional Love, it is known to activate and link the Soul Star Chakra via the crown to the lower self and is the spiritually higher aspect of Emerald, her big brother on the inner plane. Gold is a sacred metal and doorway to the energies of Helios and Vesta, the Solar Logos; it connects to the Christ energy, linking us to masters at that level such as Lord Sai Baba and the Lord Maitreya.

Where the physical body is concerned, Gold is of use with Multiple Sclerosis, Tissue regeneration, Neurological problems, Autism, Epilepsy and Dyslexia.

Your Healing Journey Today

Gold is a metal of regeneration, vitality and power. On some level you have depleted yourself, leaving an open door for stress and negativity. It is time to recharge and take time for self. Review your goals and let your potential shine as the guiding light in choice. Nothing is out of your reach when you are inward, whole and revitalized; though in physicality it is easy to forget your blinding light. Gold is here to help you go inward and have trust, for although we are all unified and equal, each of us contributes individual sparks to the end fire, which will not be in its completion without us. Gold is asking you to remember this and honor your individual path with trust and empowerment. Leave your footprints in the sand for others to see and follow if they wish, for under Gold's spell no-one has even seen the beach upon whose back you walk, it lives in you alone.

Affirmation;- "I am the Solar Angel."

Keywords to help in reading the cards;- The Solar Angel, Male Energy of

Creation, Individual Gifts, Purification, Revitalization, Confidence, Ra (The Egyptian Sun God), The Sun, Potential, Nightmares, Healing, Stress.

Body Card Placement;- Gold is most at home on the Soul Star (above the head), Solar Plexus and Crown Chakras. It can be placed over the endocrine glands to bring balance and healing.

Nightmare Trinity (Clears by offering the cause for healing in a less aggressive way);- Charoite on the Upper Left side of the chest, Gold on the Heart Chakra and Jade on the Upper Right side of the chest.

Eye of Ra Trinity;- Sunstone to the Left side of the head (above the ear), Lapis Lazuli on the Throat Chakra and Gold to the Right side of the head (above the ear).

(Note the Eye of Ra Trinity and Eye of Horus Trinity can be merged for a potent very Ancient Initiation process that is the entire basis of the Egyptian Book of the Dead. Please approach it with respect.)

Chemical Composition;- Gold

Color Rays;- 99% Gold and 1%White

Animal Totem;- Eagle

Essential Oil;- Frankincense

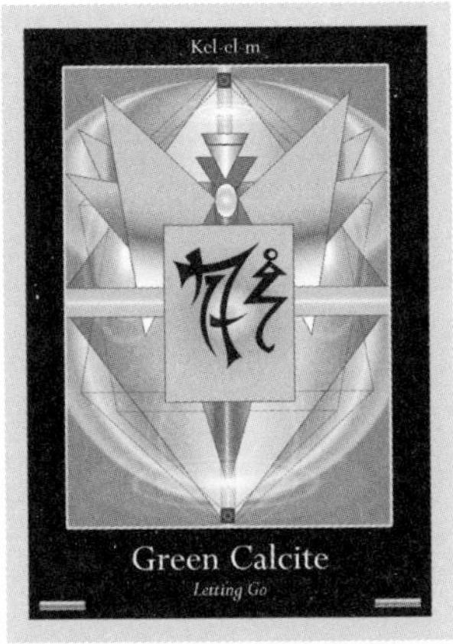

Green Calcite

Letting Go

The Master Crystal Deva Kel-el-m

"For too long, you have looked back over a shoulder that was turned forward in choice. Enter now my compassionate and loving embrace, take the hand of the Lady Master QuanYin and judge yourself not. The time has come to let go with Joy, only then can a new cycle be born.

Let me aid you to the space of calm healing, soothing all that is in our path, I am gentle, bringing safety and reassurance. I will sail with you upon the sea of healing with the minimum of Pain. I am like Ice in the Ocean, Flowing and Smooth, feel my cooling hand lift the weight from your shoulders and help re-establish you in the world.

Come, journey on the dragonfly's back. By my side a cycle has been reborn. Regret nothing, forgive all and be free to receive your creations through the ever patient and accepting eye of love's eternal storm. Walk your path of realization in the starry sea of the Universal breath."

Green Calcite in Healing

Of the many color frequencies in the calcite family of crystals, Green Calcite is perhaps the softest, often displaying one of the most gentle color frequencies in the mineral kingdom. All calcites are excellent at facilitating the management of multiple realities or levels of being into oneness. Green Calcite, with its remarkable clarity and soft, mint-green hue helps anchor this characteristic into the heart carrying all it finds there into the Now. Guided by an open heart and universal mind, in Green Calcite's embrace, movement through new territory becomes a fearless and calm process.

Green Calcite is the crystal of Letting Go. She enters the mind with her healing, cooling and calming vibration and melts away any attachments to old ways and situations, then creates a calm and centered space for the rebuilding and manifestation of new paths in life. Though she is able to stimulate change by herself, often in Atlantis powerful manifestation crystals such as Ruby, Garnet and Topaz followed Green Calcite with potent, life-changing results. Green Calcite holds the sacred vibration of the Lady Quan Yin and Lady Pallas Athena a perfect match to their glorious light and lessons, it will link you powerfully.

Green Calcite is the most calming and cooling of all the green minerals, able to settle heated anger and powerfully calm the nerves. She is a relaxant and will help in all forms of stress and its related illnesses especially in the digestive system. All conditions of mental rigidity (attachment) such as Arthritis, Tendonitis, Ligament damage and Spinal trouble are greatly helped. Green Calcite is one of few minerals that, as a liquid Crystal, can be placed topically on burns with great confidence.

Your Healing Journey Today

Time to cut the ties and release yourself forward, every day in life is a challenge of integration and growth. That which is not recognized is left awaiting our return to deliver its important lessons and messages. Remember, all in our world is valid and has purpose. The time has come to heal and forgive yourself into wholeness where you can see the totality of you and your creations. Green Calcite calls forward the parts left behind in moments where we feared or allowed unrealized Power, Love and/or Wisdom to direct us. From that moment forwards, your life has not been your own, tainted by the influence of another person, job, place or circumstance. Letting Go is not the loss of anything, in truth it is the rediscovery of you and your path in the world, untainted and whole. Forgive, Love and Heal.

When the mind perceives the end, the Spirit is just beginning, journey on.

Affirmation;- "I am free in the Now."

Keywords to help in reading the cards;- Letting Go, Detachment, Freedom, Control, New Territory (to be approached without fear), Mental Healing, The Green Ray, Presence of Anger. Healing of the Bones.

Body Card Placement;- Placed on the Third Eye (to see what has to be released from the past). Green Calcite can be placed anywhere at the site of illness to understand its creation and healing and can be worked with magically on a photograph to understand ties and attachments to others and places, information is usually delivered in the dream state. Place the photo and this card under your pillow. If you don't have a photo a name written with intention will do.

Release to Life Purpose Trinity;- On the Heart Chakra with Garnet on the Right hip and Zircon on Left hip. (Trinity of crystals that when allowed to speak say;- "I walk the path of purpose, free from my past I let go of attachment and openly accept life change.")

Anger Cooling Trinity;- Blue Lace Agate on the Lower Left side of the chest, Green Calcite on the Heart Chakra and Sulphur on the Lower Right side of the chest.

Chemical Composition;- Calcium Carbonate (Trace Manganese and Iron)

Color Rays;- 55% Green and 45% Clear

Animal Totem;- Dragonfly

Essential Oil;- Grapefruit

Green Tourmaline

Enlightenment

The Master Crystal Deva El-ba-el-m

"Join me, open the heart and feel the green ray at great velocity flow through you. Together let us embrace your earth journey and increase your light carrying capabilities. Let us ignite the nervous system and allow a higher Light Quotient, we will accelerate the path to enlightenment.

The power of love realized through my cutting ray, let us evolve through all manner of disease, holding tight the lesson. Your every fall is a stepping stone lifting you closer to the Great Solar Angel that you are. I am with you; I stand ever present at your side.

My welcomed embrace has lifted you ever closer to your infinite light, breathe and allow it a home within you permanently. Together now with compassion and peace, we will serve the great plan to fulfillment in the heart's united threefold fire."

Green Tourmaline in Healing

Green Tourmaline is a dark to emerald-green, translucent mineral that, like all Tourmalines, has long striations that run down its body, allowing it to carry a large amount of light. The energy of Green Tourmaline is infused directly into the Nervous System where it raises our ability to carry light there. This gives the mineral the healing pathways of higher consciousness and higher general light frequency resulting in its reputation as the 'Stone of Enlightenment'.

A master healing stone, Green Tourmaline can open the Heart Chakra in the presence of the spirit which allows Peace, Trust, Compassion, Patience and Non-attachment to be found and expectations to be seen as perceptions that can be released if inappropriate.

Green Tourmaline is a specialist healer for those that have issues with their father figure, finding solutions and finalizing the issues for all concerned. It is worked with extensively in Psychic Surgery, able to heal the energy bodies, seal, align and cut away that which is no longer needed, all while holding a high light frequency that delivers integrity into the work.

Green Tourmaline facilitates contact with Ascended Masters Paul the Venetian, Sananda and Djwhal Khul, it is one of the most powerful Arcturian contact stones and can open the records of the Delphic Oracle.

At the physical level, Green Tourmaline works with all forms of Nervous System imbalance including Insomnia, Multiple Sclerosis, Spinal Misalignment and Panic attacks. It has also been shown to help with Chronic Fatigue, Exhaustion, Hyperactive Children, Migraines and Lowered Immune Function.

Your Healing Journey Today

If Green Tourmaline has come to you today, an incident, pathway or issue has caught the attention of your higher self and called it to action. Remain as open as possible and sit in a space of self-awareness, as the answer or healing path is about to present itself. Be patient, compassionate and non-judgmental of self at this time and respect how hard you are working on a higher level to make the answer clear. This is a good time for automatic writing, simply sit and ask for the solution from your highest part, write and then later, read what you have written. The doors of Enlightenment are opening. This stone also presents when one has passed an initiation or moved through a level spiritually, it is a symbol of achievement, and the presence of your spirit. If a father figure has passed recently this card is a symbol of his presence and the opportunity to finalize the healing of any issue that was unfinished between you.

Affirmation;- "I am Enlightened, my Spirit Runs through all I do."

Keywords to help in reading the cards;- Enlightenment, High Light Frequency, Master Healer, Healing, Achievement, Needs to Open Heart Chakra, Father Figure, Service, Discovery of Life Purpose, Need to Listen to the Voice of Spirit. Contact Stone for the Delphic Oracle.

Body Card Placement;- Green Tourmaline is a mineral of the Heart, Crown and the Base Chakras, it can also be placed at the Third Eye Chakra for migraine headaches (see Trinity below). This card can be placed under a white candle to increase the frequency in a room and may be placed under a glass of water to infuse it with the green ray's powerful healing ability.

Father Issues Healing Trinity;- Rose Quartz on the Lower Left side of the chest, Green Tourmaline on the Heart Chakra and Charoite on the Lower Right side of the chest. This healing process will need to be supported, Red Jasper is recommended with Emerald to help finalize the healing.

Migraine Headache Trinity;- Dioptase to the Left side of the head (below the ear), Iolite on the Third Eye Chakra and Green Tourmaline to the Right side of the head (below the ear). The Iolite can be placed at the back of the Third Eye Chakra if the forehead is too sensitive.

Chemical Composition;- Sodium Lithium Aluminum Boro-silicate Hydroxide

Color Rays;- 63% Green, 20% Clear, 13% Silver and 4% Black

Animal Totem;- Snow Leopard

Essential Oil;- Bay (Laurel)

Hematite

Spiritual Grounding

The Master Crystal Deva Ha-mut-el

"Let me open you to the infinity of the universe. Blessed I am, with the role of leading the mineral kingdom as the Master of the Colored rays in Form. In service to you, I am the open vessel through which the Earth Mother herself draws her colored breath and manifests the beauty of all physical creation.

I come to you this day as a measure of your readiness for the blessing of the Earth Star, gateway into the powerful light force that you are. Together we can truly make a home for you in the physical world. Feel me, like the falling rain, gently land upon you, washing you clean of negativity and desensitizing the emotional pains of life.

I offer you the vessel of light that you are, making it known to the most physical parts of your endless self. Take my hands, let us slow life to a pace that allows action not reaction and provide a space to embrace the infinite spirit that you are. Let your higher bodies be your guide on this, your journey to completion."

Hematite in Healing

Hematite is one of the most common sights in crystal shops, where it is usually a shiny silver metallic mineral sold as a tumbled stone, however, it is able to appear in all the known physical colors of Earth allowing its master Deva, Ha-mut-el the title, 'Master of the Color Rays in Form'.

Found naturally, it is black or rust red; the commonly seen silver only usually presents itself after polishing. This allows Hematite to hold a secret, when scratched it bleeds a red powder which indicates its ability as a powerful grounding stone, carrying the red base chakra down into the Silver Earth Star below the feet. This is one of the only stones able to activate the Earth Star, an out of body chakra that polarizes the soul into the body, the most powerful form of grounding available.

Hematite makes its presence felt at all the levels of self from the physical to the spiritual, separating everything into levels and areas, making contents more identifiable and manageable. This ability allows true self control and renders one able to take appropriate action in life experiences. At the emotional level, Hematite is able to desensitize the emotions; this allows one to be less reactive. Soon the difference between thought and emotion is recognized allowing a disciplined self to take the true needed action.

Spiritually, Hematite anchors and grounds the spiritual light bodies in a balanced manner to the physical, which is useful in shock, before and after surgery or extremely stressful conditions. Highly protective, an activated Hematite shield will reflect any undesired negativity simply through intention with its mirror surface.

Physically, this mineral is strengthening and revitalizing to the blood and circulatory system and is excellent in shock and stressful situations.

Your Healing Journey Today

Hematite's presence with you today is an indication of the need to activate the Earth Star below your feet, a process as simple as taking your intention there. You are in need of grounding. Hematite asks you to remember that all physical action can be sacred if you will allow your spirit to be in it. Often when life seems boring and pointless physically, the spirit is learning the most important lessons, take time to listen and accept the life you have created. Hematite's presence may also be a symbol of the need to find balance in the mental and emotional selves and take action with your newly found non-reactive integrated self. This is the most sacred stone at this time for contacting the Ascended Masters Saint Germain and El Morya, they may be calling on you.

Affirmation;- "United, Body and Spirit, I am."

Keywords to help in reading the cards;- Spiritual Grounding, Earth Star, Order, The Color Rays, Stress, Saint Germaine, Balance, Color Healing

Body Card Placement;- Hematite is best below the feet, but useful on all Chakras, at the Third Eye in Children will activate Extra Terrestrial communication, It activates the Heart Meridian in the body and is sacred to Mayan Indians at the Left Hand where it holds many secrets.

Spiritual Grounding Trinity (This will Powerfully call and hold the Spirit in the Body);- Pyrite is placed on the Soul Star Chakra, Gold is placed on the Solar Plexus Chakra and Hematite in placed on the Earth Star Chakra. See the Soul Star move down and sit at the heart where it will remain for 21 days offering intimate contact with your spirit for healing and development.

Chemical Composition;- Iron Oxide

Color Rays;- 30% Silver, 30% Red, 12% Black, 7% Gold, 2% Orange, 2%Yellow, 3% Green, 1% Pink, 4% Blue, 3% Indigo, 4%Violet, 2% White

Animal Totem;- Scarab/Dung Beetle

Essential Oil;- Thyme

Hemimorphite

The Egoless State

The Master Crystal Deva Hem-u-e`-el

"Greetings child of the endless light, I thank you for reaching within my frequency. Feel my gentle breath upon you, now let me open you to the joy of the creator, a vision reserved for those who hold the key to the Egoless state.

Let us now hold and activate the mirror of self. I offer to you freedom through self-respect and self-love on all levels. Search deep within your heart to the glistening blue pools of loving expression realized. Ignite the White Rose and Purify; allow the heart to become a filter for all that passes from you, every breath Unconditional and all loving. We have opened your Path of Truth.

Through me now see your world and all within it, know you are its creator, your happiness is but a reflection of this fact. Continue your journey, go deeply inward now, as self-realization can lead to your highest imagined potential, let the world no longer cast a shadow, through your eyes, by choice, you are free."

Hemimorphite in Healing

Hemimorphite is a beautiful deep powder blue opaque stone that often contains white inclusions, it is principally found in China and highly crystallized specimens are quite rare. In the last 10 years, more and more Hemimorphite is being found. This is principally due to the healing effect that it has on us as the crystal of the Egoless State.

Strongly connected to personal power and its appropriate use, Hemimorphite takes us to a healthy space of honesty about our actions in the world. It is a Stone of self-respect and self-confidence without crossing the fine line that these characteristics represent. This is one of the crystals where it is useful to look at the negative state, for it is very common in modern businesses. In its most extreme, the person that needs this stone is not taking responsibility for their actions, dishonest, self-centered and making decisions from a fearful place. These people are in desperate need of Self-Love but see it as weakness so empower themselves to compensate, this makes them Egotistical and the whole cycle starts again, they are trapped, Hemimorphite is their savior.

Working with this stone over time, the voice of the spirit can be heard clearly and allowed to govern life, leading one to their highest potential, not just as a person, but also as a soul. Hemimorphite often holds the key to important information from other lifetimes and will only open the door if we are seeking from an Egoless perspective. Hemimorphite is a contact stone for the Ascended Master Kuthumi and Archangel Jophiel.

More physically, Hemimorphite has an amazing healing ability with the Herpes Virus which is directly connected to the ego. It is useful in Blood and Cellular Disorders and can decrease Pain in a similar manner to Malachite.

Your Healing Journey Today

If Hemimorphite has come to you today, it is a friendly reminder that we are all responsible for our actions. Take a good look at what is happening in life and make sure that you are retaining your personal power and acting from an Egoless state. All truthful acts should harm none, benefit all and stream directly from love in the name of unity. Hemimorphite can also present when there is a need to embrace an important role from another lifetime or when a loved one has recently passed and wishes to communicate with you. Make sure also that you are not being taken advantage of, this stone can appear to let you know you need to recover a part of yourself from someone else's creation.

Affirmation;- "I walk the path of Truth to Freedom."

Keywords to help in reading the cards;- The Egoless State, Self-Respect, Self-Confidence, Truth about own Actions, The Shadow Self, The Herpes Virus, The Voice of a Loved One Who has Passed, True Reflection of Self, Work Is Life Attitude.

Body Card Placement;- At home on the Crown, Throat and Solar Plexus Chakras but this card can be placed anywhere to indicate the presence of ego in or out of the body.

Threefold Flame Balancing Trinity;- Pyrite (Love) on the Soul Star above the Crown Chakra, Hemimorphite (Power) on the Heart Chakra and Hematite (Wisdom) on the Earth Star below the feet. Once mastered, the above Trinity can be taken or worked with in the company of Diamond to activate the final stages of the Ascension process.

Chemical Composition;- Hydrated Zinc Silicate Hydroxide

Color Rays;- 43% Blue, 11% Green, 32% Clear and 14% White

Animal Totem;- Giant Panda

Essential Oil;- Ginger

Herkimer Diamond

Oneness

The Master Crystal Deva Anu-ra-el

"Walk with me a while, my energies know no bounds, I allow distance, time and space to become an illusion, for in separation the united principle of unconditional love which you are is hidden. Let us lift this physical blanket that has robbed you of freedom, your birthright.

Go inward now, not up, down, out or around. The seed you search for is what you are, a seed that is not easily seen, hidden by a flower in full bloom. I will link and bring together the elements of creation, facilitating communication and attunement between them over great distance, but this is not my true purpose. Walk with me a while and you will come to see that all you wish to bring together is but one, there is no separation, or fear, except that which you choose to perceive.

Sit calmly now; carry the joy of unity to the world. I know it lives in your every realized breath. Marvel at my light, for I am but an ember in the fire of your greatness, in truth you are my father, a blessing within the universal oneness."

Herkimer Diamond in Healing

Herkimer Diamonds are high quality double-terminated quartz crystals which usually have 12 Faces and 6 sides, they are found mainly in Herkimer, New York. Unlike a real Diamond, a Herkimer Diamond comes out of the earth geometrically perfect and shining with light, it needs no machine work to make it desirable for jewelry. The Herkimer Diamond is the hardest of all known quartz crystals and generally carries a higher level of light.

This Crystal is revered spiritually, and in recent times has been greatly sought-after for its high vibration and ability to powerfully activate the psychic senses including telepathy. Herkimer Diamond is the crystal of Oneness, able to link the many parts of self into a unified whole and over time guide one to their own true purpose in life. It helps sweep aside the interfering wills of others and allows one to creatively manifest their world free from outside influences. It's linking and attunement effect allows the discovery of past lives and sets up strong telepathic links between people and/or places. Herkimer's ability to hold information can be worked with in study, making information available via telepathic link.

At the mental and emotional level, Herkimer Diamond blends thoughts and feelings with precision allowing realization of the true path of action that should be taken. This is one of a few crystals that can activate confidence to the degree that one can surrender and just "Be".

Herkimer Diamond is one of the key stones for stress on all levels, not only able to release trouble spots, but also able to gather memories from the affected part of self for permanent healing. This is especially powerful, with the types of stress that lead to cancer. Herkimer is also used to normalize the metabolism and general cellular structure while also being of use in conditions of RNA/DNA imbalance. It is a sacred stone of Ascended Master Serapis Bey.

Your Healing Journey Today

Herkimer Diamond is the mineral of oneness; its presence indicates that something in the picture of wholeness you represent in the universe is divided. Such separation within us always fuels the Ego, it justifies its existence and can make us its slave, allowing a loss of confidence, direction and purpose that in turn manifest high levels of stress. By being your true self, life purpose is found. With Herkimer the key word is 'Being', make sure you are being your real self, if you are, it is effortless and fueled by surrender, life simply unfolds before you. Herkimer Diamond asks you to let go of your created path and flow for a while, you may go somewhere you never thought possible.

A plant never tries to flower, it simply exists, confident in the cycle of love flowing through it. To the plant it is just part of the beautiful oneness, it is fulfilling its purpose. Only the perception of mankind can taint this fact and enter choice, pain and separation. Herkimer Diamond is a sacred stone of the Egyptian God Anubis, he will be with you, keep your eyes open for Black Dogs and Crows, the two forms he can manifest as most easily to remind you of the above message. The frequency of Herkimer Diamond is also a key in the pathway of Sirius and entry to The Great White Lodge.

Affirmation;- "I am the infinite unity of light I am."

Keywords to help in reading the cards;- Oneness, Attunement, Stress, Telepathy, Alignment, Linking, Unity, Being, Anubis, Illusion.

Body Card Placement;- Herkimer Diamond can go on all the Chakras. When placed over the site of illness it will link the cause into the mind and over the Thymus gland and/or Appendix it will activate telepathy.

The United Self Trinity (A Spiritual Trinity that powerfully Paves the path to Ascension);- Pyrite above the head on the Soul Star Chakra, Herkimer Diamond on the Heart Chakra and Hematite below the feet on the Earth Star. Relax and allow the gold light of Pyrite to join the silvers of Hematite in the heart, Herkimer will unite them into oneness. This process is advanced and to be approached with respect.

Chemical Composition;- Silicon Dioxide

Color Rays;- 90% Clear, 5% Blue and 5% Silver

Animal Totem;- Ant

Essential Oil;- Cajeput

Howlite

Spiritual Beginning

The Master Crystal Deva Nu-ray-el

"Take my hand in yours child, let me melt the burdens of your physical world and float you will, at home amongst the stars in the infinity of space eternal. Let us light your path and never again will you journey alone.

Like snow, feel me fall around and upon you, calm, peaceful and quiet, let us build the base from which the flower of spirit may bloom. Together again, step gently in the icy footprints I leave and the sunlight that you are will give rise to subtle movements towards your spirit.

In my embrace time is not. The peaceful and patient warrior of light within has risen, emotions tamed and mind at peace. Allow the many vibrant colors of the spirit that you are to manifest a rainbow upon whose back we will ride to the source of all."

Howlite in Healing

Howlite is a beautiful white chalky mineral with grey and sometimes black veins that run across its body. It is a soft substance and thus has been used for carving by many indigenous cultures where it is found on Earth. Howlite has also fallen victim to the ways of man, being dyed blue and sold for the more expensive mineral Turquoise with which, interestingly, she has much in common.

Howlite's simple purpose with humanity is Spiritual Beginning, a role she achieves by cutting our ties to the past and allowing us to create a new solid base birthed from a balanced, peaceful state of mind and emotions so the flower of spirit may bloom.

Howlite is the keystone to the treatment of insomnia and other sleep disorders, which is achieved by her powerful ability to instill calm and peace into the mind. Howlite often finds her greatest roles in healing, side-by-side with some of the most potent and powerful minerals on Earth, to whose action she adds a patient and peaceful side. She is one of the most nurturing and gentle energies we have available to us, a gift that serves us well, as she allows us to reflect on our past, detach and move forward. Few members of the mineral kingdom dissolve anger and rage as well as Howlite, especially where the cause is impatience of self or others.

Howlite is often utilized by spirit to integrate new energies into a person, this is of great use when new energies or guidance are available on the inner plane. Spiritually, in combination with Petrified Wood and Apophyllite, Howlite has the ability to allow astral travel and is a specialized mineral in the discovery of relevant past life information. She may also be used to induce a deep meditative state and is a sacred stone of the Sirius Star System, a major contact stone to The Great White Lodge and the entire Brotherhood of Light. It suits them that the high level of the White Ray in Howlite goes unnoticed, as they always have it at their disposal for higher purpose.

At the physical level, Howlite is able to balance calcium levels of the body and can aid in the upkeep of bones, teeth and soft tissues.

Your Healing Journey Today

With this peaceful, loving and gentle energy by your side, you are being offered a place of peace, calm and solitude. It is time to reflect on all that you are and your greatest achievements from a balanced and peaceful state of mind and emotion. The time has come to gently cast away the attachments to your past and build the foundation of a new and beautiful direction or journey. Howlite is a doorway stone; she indicates to you today that the door is open; you may pass, if you are willing to look forward, rather than back and take each step with love.

Affirmation;- "Peacefully, I accept change."

Keywords to help in reading the cards;- Spiritual beginning, Peace, Calm, Past Attachments, Sleep, Insomnia, Astral Travel, Past Life Message, New Frequency or

Level Spiritually, Initiation, A Test Passed.

Body Card Placement;- Howlite goes on the Heart Chakra, Thymus gland, and above the head to integrate new frequencies.

Astral Past Life Trinity (Adventure, Discovery and Healing);- Petrified Wood on the Left shoulder, Apophyllite on the Soul Star and Howlite on the Right shoulder.

Sleep Deep and Peaceful Trinity;- Place Howlite on the Heart Chakra, Fluorite on the Third Eye Chakra and Charoite on the Solar Plexus Chakra. Do this for 7 Minutes before bed.

Chemical Composition;- Calcium Boro-silicate Hydroxide

Color Rays;- 70% White, 28% Blue and 2% Black

Animal Totem;- Salmon

Essential Oil;- Celery Seed

Imperial Topaz

Confident Manifestation

The Master Crystal Deva Topasel

"Hold me at your heart in hands at prayer, let rays of sunlight pass through and enter us. Now offer me your breath and uncover the fire of creation. Realize and open to my radiant light, the confidence to manifest, control and create your path is my gift.

By my fire through the high spiritual mind, the creative seed that is individual to us all will be realized and carried into action, manifested on the Earth plane. I help integrate at the centre of personal power, instilling confidence and empowering the joy that you are, Embrace me now.

Feel within my fire, the voice of the universal Sun and the will of Ra. Through action, we will rebuild you, calm, balanced and abundant. Create with me, the wisdom of manifestation is before you, let us give it life first in your veins, then in the physical world."

Topaz in Healing

Few crystals on Earth are able to hold the same level of light as Topaz and none match her ability to manifest it into the physical world. At the peak of the Topaz family of crystals is Imperial Topaz, a deep transparent gold crystal with easily distinguishable faces and striations running up its body. Her most amazing gift however is found in the charge of the crystal faces, alternating from positive to negative around the crystal. This allows Topaz the ability to manifest into the world through polarization, the path between positive and negative, the Middle Road or space of all creation, no mineral on Earth manifests as well as Topaz, co-creation in a single body. If you are one of those people that catch yourself saying, "Why do I always get what I DON'T want?" this stone will answer the question.

Imperial Topaz is principally a solar plexus stone, where it powerfully affects the emotional body, first activating it into confidence, clarity and self-love and then empowering focus, order and understanding so one may manifest a path forward with emotional clarity. Under Topaz's guidance one is delivered into leadership, creativity and confidence, which result in perfected manifestation abilities. This crystal is much needed in our world due to the competitive and judgmental ways we have manifested, which in turn manifest a loss of individuality, confusion, depression and a lack of love towards self.

Imperial Topaz can allow one to define the word abundance for self, often with life changing results. It is a powerful awakener of the spirit, often delivering inspiration from the most sacred parts of self. In times of depletion, Topaz can restore the self, acting like a battery, providing a backup energy reserve. In the company of Boji Stone and Kyanite, Imperial Topaz can balance, clear, heal and align in a thorough and powerful manner on all levels of self, speeding the healing process of any ailment. At the physical level, Topaz is effective, mainly in the digestive system, but is also useful in nervous exhaustion and stress. This is a sacred stone of the Egyptian Goddess Sekhmet (Lady of Power) and Ascended Master Hilarion.

Your Healing Journey Today

The presence of Topaz is always a positive sign, if you are looking for a yes or no answer, Topaz is one of the most powerful "Yes" energies. Topaz would ask you to trust yourself, its presence is a sign of the right time and your ability to manifest on any level. Imperial Topaz often signals a time of self-discovery through the birth of a creative, individual and confident path. The place you are within is the place of greatness; there are no limits but your own imagination. In the coming days, you may also receive more confirmation in the form of money or your measure of abundance. Create, Manifest and most importantly Feel as the Emotions are the key to Topaz's energy and work. Make sure you are not blocking your emotions and are emotionally clear, for if you are not, the world you create will not be your own, as its creation will stem from a seed of fear. Imperial Topaz also presents when you are being asked to lead or guide a friend back to his/her personal power or embrace your own.

One thing is always true of Topaz, where she presents, the person that she has come to see always knows why she has come.

Affirmation;- "I confidently create my World ."

Keywords to help in reading the cards;- Confident Manifestation, Personal Power, Solar Plexus Chakra, Individuality, Emotional Healing and Clarity, Abundance, Trust Self.

Body Card Placement;- Topaz is best on the Crown, Solar Plexus and Heart Chakras.

Mayan Healing and Purification Trinity;- Topaz is held in the Left hand, Turquoise is held in Right hand and Clear Quartz is placed at the base of the skull.

Egyptian Goddess Sekhmet Trinity (Opens Clear Communication regarding Power);- Stack Topaz on the Heart Chakra with Sunstone and Obsidian in that order.

Chemical Composition;- Aluminum Silicate Fluoride Hydroxide

Color Rays;- 40% Gold, 30% Clear, 17% Blue and 13% Yellow

Animal Totem;- Cheetah

Essential Oil;- Clove

Iolite

Vision

The Master Crystal Deva O-ra-ohm-el

"Take my ethereal hand of Light and Walk with me in the Sunshine of your creation. Let your mind wander in the empty Violet skies above, for I have come to open the higher senses and deliver you from the confines of physicality.

Wipe away the Violet, fearful tears of the inner eye for we will carry the Violet flame down the pathways of Vision allowing only love to reside. Now, let us unlock the hidden inner doors of activation, turning fear to love and understanding, you will hear the voice of your Soul and see by my light the reality of spirit.

Within my care now, I welcome you to the real world of Joy where endless seas wash upon the horizons in union and the Earth whispers in tongues of fire, the truth of eternal light. Now and forever more, when we close our eyes, we will share the truthful vision of the universal skies in all their glory. Now you will live beyond the Veils in my Embrace."

Iolite in Healing

Iolite is a beautifully transparent violet stone with an amazing clarity and depth of colour that is the perfect frequency of the Violet colour ray. It carries the perfected frequency of the Third Eye Chakra and is its most powerful activation Crystal on the Earth. At the Third Eye, it is able to balance, actively remove blocks and do all that is necessary to allow the true vision to become active. Iolite has even become known, over time, as 'The Violet Stone', a title that aligns it with the ascended Master Saint Germain and The Lady Portia.

This stone provides a powerful vision of self and can activate the ability to press forward in life, taking responsibility for self, especially in relationships. It promotes foresight, Clairvoyant, Psychic and Intuitive abilities so one is prepared to take action, and with the facilitated communication to spirit is able to make sure the correct action is taken for the betterment of all.

Iolite is able to balance the male and female sides of expression and is excellent where there is codependence in relationships. It is one of the most powerful stones of breaking addictions, able to allow the cause to surface and facilitate release, free from the expectations of others.

Iolite is a contact stone to the Arcturian Star System and their unified Voice, Lord Arcturus.

At the physical level, this stone is detoxifying to the Liver, decreases fatty deposits and eliminates toxins. It is also a powerful crystal of Migraine Headaches and Illnesses caused by overuse of drugs, especially marijuana.

Your Healing Journey Today

If Iolite has come to you today, your higher senses are about to become active. Your Clairvoyant, Psychic and Intuitive abilities are your birthright. At a certain time in everybody's life, a doorway opens where their development is most possible, for you that time is now. Iolite also comes into people's lives to help in the realization and to herald the arrival of a vision you have held within you and worked towards for some time. If at this time, you have begun a new venture or activated a different path or vision, Iolite is a good sign that your path is clear. Remember that although to have a goal is crucial to happiness, if one spends a lifetime desiring something, they may never be here for long enough to know if they have it.

Affirmation;- "With Love I choose to see Reality."

Keywords to help in reading the cards;- Vision, Clairvoyant, Psychic and Intuitive abilities, Activation, Dreams Realized, Third Eye Chakra, Foresight, Self Responsibility, Male-Female Expressive Balance, Life Path, Addiction, Illnesses Caused by Overuse of Drugs, Liver.

Body Card Placement;- Iolite mainly works on the Third Eye Chakra, placed over the Liver it will increase the detoxification rate. It can be placed at the Crown

Chakra for Migraine Headaches. Iolite may be placed between two individuals in a relationship to balance male and female sides of communication and the repetitive drawing of this symbol will help break addiction.

Addiction Breaking Trinity (Empowers, Detoxifies, Heals the Cause and Opens Doors to a Better Way);- Botswana Agate on the Lower Left side of the chest, Iolite on the on the Third Eye Chakra and Zircon on the Lower Right side of the chest.

Third Eye Vision Activation Trinity;- Black Coral to the Left side of the head (below the ear), Iolite on the Third Eye Chakra and Apatite to the Right side of the head (below the ear). This exercise should be done at least Seven times over a Twenty One day span, to get the best results.

Third Eye Atlantian Chakra Trinity (Most Holistic Healing of the Third Eye Chakra Available);- Azurite to the Left side of the head (below the ear), Iolite on the Third Eye Chakra and Sapphire to the Right side of the head (below the ear).

Chemical Composition;- Magnesium Aluminum Silicate.

Color Rays;- 70% Violet, 21% Indigo, 7% Blue and 2% Clear

Animal Totem;- Owl

Essential Oil;- Lemon Grass

Jade
Dream Work

The Master Crystal Deva Ja-da-ma-el

"Enter into my silence, within me is the joy of unconditional love, drawn from the Earth, not down from the heavens. I represent its biological state, a living light in purpose; I offer the framework and language of dreams, my Green eyed cat your guardian.

Know I walk by your side upon the path of emotional mastery. Detach now from your over-feeling world and allow in newly found stillness, the selective thoughts of your mind to maintain the vigilant discipline of centeredness and Balance. Feel the purity of your cleansed astral vessel light as a feather and fly unburdened by the weight of mortal fear.

Hear the Jaguar's cry break the silence of unrealized sleep. I sit at the eye of pure vision and offer the dream of truth, as always through the ages. Feel the breath and eyes of the Jaguar cut your path, become through me, that which you truly are and remember, you are a Spiritual being on a Human Journey. Dare to dream, walk through the ancient Temple of Fire, the path of Serapis, with Jaguar as guide, I wait in the light of your realizations."

Jade in Healing

Jade is a beautiful stone that ranges from a creamy white to the highly prized deep Emerald Green in color. This is a stone of the ancients that at one point in many cultures was more valuable than gold and silver. Jade has enjoyed a powerful position in many cultures but primarily the Oriental and that of the ancient Maya, both of whom buried their important figures in it to help carry their wisdom between lifetimes.

Jade is a stone of great wisdom, it is the most powerful stone of the dream state on Earth and initiates mastery on that level of self. It is able to align life to that which is most important and then promote action. It provides this gift not only by aiding the remembrance and embrace of dreams, but also by allowing detachment from emotions so one can find space to assess them and then act as needed. Under Jade's careful guidance, self-confidence is lifted into a space of self-sufficiency and the drive to live the dream is reborn with a powerful new limitless ambition.

Entering this stone's frequency, one may experience the ancient Jade mask and walk through the doorway behind which the powerful elders of the Mayan Culture patiently await the return of their friends.

Jade is a stone that adjusts with the ages, constantly renewing its presence, a fact recently made obvious at the 2008 summer Olympic Games, when it became the only substance other than metal that has ever been used in Olympic medals, symbolizing living the Dream into realization. More physically, Jade is a powerful remedy of the kidneys, it is detoxifying and was used in ancient times for childbirth and fertility. It also facilitates the health of the skin and hair.

Your Healing Journey Today

If Jade has come to you today, it is time to take notice of your dreams. This can be relevant on two levels, the first relating directly to the dream state that occurs when you sleep, and the second to your goals and ambitions in life. Whichever it is for you, the message is the same, listen, assess and then act accordingly to embrace the necessary changes. Both the above levels of the word Dream interact, often giving rise to each other, this little fact is often overlooked, write down all that occurs while you sleep, as you may just be creating your future. Jade only comes into life when we need to know that anything is possible and we are truly limitless in our ability to manifest, now is the time to live your dream into realization whatever it is, take steps so the rest of us can see it. This is the most Sacred Stone of Ascended Master Serapis Bey, he may be calling you.

Affirmation;- " I confidently walk the path of my dreams, in my shadow is infinite light."

Keywords to help in reading the cards;- Dream Work, Mayan Culture, Asia, Physical Love, Astral Travel, Act on Dreams, Ambition, Suppressed Emotion (to be expressed in dreams), Limitless Self, The Jade Mask.

Body Card Placement;- Mainly placed on the Third Eye and Heart Chakras.

Dream State Mastery Trinity;- Stack Apophyllite, Iolite and then Jade in that order on the Heart Chakra to empower control and mastery of the dream state through vision.

Chemical Composition;- Calcium Magnesium Iron Silicate

Color Rays;- 67% Green, 7% Red, 13% White and 13% Black

Animal Totem;- Jaguar

Essential Oil;- Clary-sage

Kunzite

Heart Activation

The Master Crystal Deva Zel-dor-el

"On this day, let it be known, in the tears of light that fall from the sixth moon, an ocean will be born in the Sacred Heart. Always in the perfection of spirit, the creative avenues are fueled by a mind attuned to an open heart. It is this that is my gift to you, let us change the world.

Activate the heart to the pink ray of Unconditional love, then express that into creation via a mind attuned to the universal consciousness of the Violet Ray, let your desire to live in a spiritual world become a reality.

You now see the divine in all things, cultivating unconditional love in the movement back to heaven on Earth; we will manifest a vision of light within and all around you. Let us hold the chalice to the last river, and carry the sacred and flowing silver waters of Isis back to their home in the Sky above."

Kunzite in Healing

Kunzite is a gentle lilac to pink colored mineral which usually displays a high level of clarity. The fact that it is Pleochroic, meaning that the intensity of its colour varies due to the viewing angle, separates it from other pink stones. Often Kunzite will have internal transparent striations that can be seen running up its body, in a similar manner to Tourmaline, this allows Kunzite the ability to carry and direct a potent light force, with which she targets and encourages the Heart Chakra into Activation. A role in which she has no equal at this time on the Earth.

Where one is blocked or closed emotionally and has been backed into a stressful corner lacking self-expression, Kunzite does its best work. She balances, clears and opens one to a secure new world at the Heart, a space where the past and its fears can be surrendered and released for the betterment of all.

With one of its key components, as Lithium, a mineral often prescribed in orthodox medicine for mental imbalance amongst other things, Kunzite has a balancing and healing effect on the mind and mental body, often able to help ward off depression and instill a deep meditative peace where once was turmoil.

Kunzite is the first member of the Heart Chakra Trinity of crystals, an ancient Atlantian sequence of healing. In this sequence, it opens and activates the heart to an unconditional state in readiness for the healing work of Rose Quartz, the stone of forgiveness, so love can once again flow into the world pure and undefined via Pink Tourmaline. Still today at the heart chakra, there is no healing more holistic and complete.

In the Atlantian way, Kunzite is the guiding path stone for the placement of the spirit into the mind by unconditional love; this potent technique allows the spirit's wisdom to be worked with in the physical world. (See below for body card placement). It is also the primary manifestation physically of the Pink Colour Ray holding 81% of it in its light makeup, placing the Master Deva of this stone in a powerful hierarchical position.

At the physical level, Kunzite is useful in reducing panic attacks and can aid in all types of nerve pain, especially at the Lumbar region of the back. It is also a tonic for the Immune and Cardiovascular systems.

Your Healing Journey Today

In the simplest of terms, if Kunzite has come to you, she has come to activate the Heart and open you to a new level of love both internally and in the world around you. Kunzite reminds us, that as the world around us evolves and changes, the levels of love and activities that must be undertaken to recognize that love also vary. She comes as a messenger, entering life when we are missing something that the world around us is offering; she has come to help you see through the heart and receive what you deserve, not by defining it, but simply knowing it is there in absolute open-hearted, deserving trust.

In the coming days, hold your judgments, mental chatter and perceptions and trust your feelings without the need to label them, just feel your way. Let your Heart be your guide and the unconditional love that surrounds us all will have a chance to enter your life. Just as a falling tree in the forest won't break the eternal

Silence if there is no one there to hear it, unconditional love will also be all around you if you simply allow and don't limit it with the mind.

Affirmation;- "In Peace, I walk the path of the Active Heart."

Keywords to help in reading the cards;- Heart Activation, Attachment to the Past, The Pink Color Ray, Mental/ Emotional Balance, Surrender, Emotional Security, Depression, Aphrodite, The Archangel Mary, The Lady of Rose Light. (An Ascended Atlantian High Priestess.)

Body Card Placement;- Kunzite mainly belongs on the Heart and Third Eye Chakras, equally at home on both. Activation occurs at the Heart, while at the Third Eye stillness can be achieved.

Spirit into the Mind Trinity (Gently Places the Spirit into the Mind for Healing and Balance);- Place Topaz on the Crown Chakra, Kunzite on the Third Eye Chakra and Blue Lace Agate on the Throat Chakra.

The Heart Trinity (The Most Potent Healing Sequence of the Heart from Atlantis);- Kunzite is placed on the Upper Left side of the chest, Rose Quartz is placed on the Heart Chakra and Pink Tourmaline is placed on the Upper Right side of the chest. The Crystals can also be placed individually, one at a time, directly on the Heart.

Chemical Composition;- Lithium Aluminum Silicate
Color Rays;- 81% Pink, 11% Violet, 5% Clear and 3% Indigo
Animal Totem;- Macaw / Parrot
Essential Oil;- Rosewood

A note on the Spiritual Heart;- To really understand Kunzite it takes many lifetimes and we must know that her message is not really translatable into human embrace, for she represents Unconditional Love, a substance that is everywhere and in all things, held in the open state of active oneness through realization of unity and sacred purpose. The moment such sacred space is defined by a mortal mind, even through distant perception, it becomes limited, separated, isolated and conditional, losing the basis of itself by conforming to that which those that were made in the image of God decide it is. Kunzite wishes to take you to a place of inner action and receptivity without question. A place so sacred that your greatest actions are Stillness and Allowing, for that is the true place of the All that Is and is the real Active Heart, only able to exist in Unity.

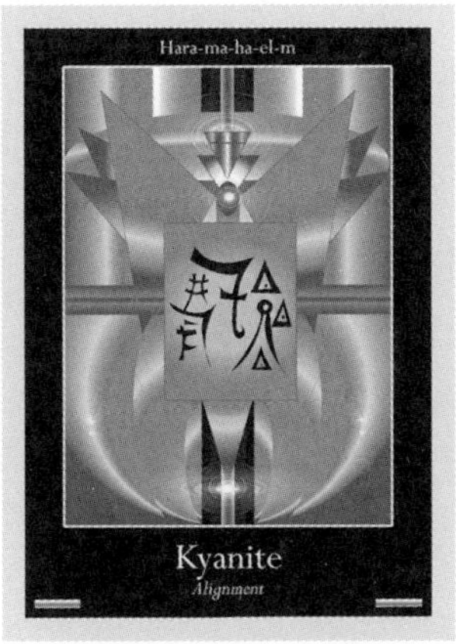

Kyanite
Alignment

The Master Crystal Deva Hara-ma-ha-el-m

"Take my silver blue light to the centre of expression that you are, I have waited for this day, for too long. I, like few others, carry the flame of spirit into the cube like structure of the mind to manifest as thought and enter the world. Together we play a key role in the manifestation of the new age; I will bless and lead you to the infinite true self.

Within my embrace your unconditional alignment to divinity has purified your every deed, all is healed and a new world is manifest. An elapsed moment in past focus, your voice the cast, lift now the earthly veils of blind fate, separation and fear, but remember and learn from their birth, know through spirit's voice you are forever free.

The new world is within you, Child of Light, you have come to liberate it. My presence signals the world's readiness to receive and allow you to step the path of divine purpose. Shine now, the new world is restless in its cage, your truth is its freedom, let the voice of Thothma echo in the stars, it will burden you no more."

Kyanite in Healing

Kyanite is a blue, silver and white mineral that usually forms in blade shaped crystals. Although it is often opaque, gem quality Kyanite is highly transparent and the colour of the deepest ocean with a silver sheen. Calming, Connecting and Communicating are all key words for this amazing stone, but with its high levels of

Aluminum, its best work happens in the head area of the body.

Kyanite is the Crystal of Alignment, a characteristic it not only demonstrates in its ability to balance and align the entire chakra system, simply by its presence, but also in its unmatched ability to build a pathway, to link and accommodate the spirit in the mind permanently. Kyanite's ability to build a pathway to the spirit is crucial in the development of the New Children of Light that are entering our world. It works intimately to adjust the expanded consciousness of these amazing beings to the lower physical brainwave frequencies, thus aiding many of their symptoms including Epilepsy, Autism and other Mental Conditions.

In Kyanite's embrace, once the spirit is linked into the mind, original thought and one's life path becomes known, truth is discovered and if frustration and its resulting anger are present they fade into peaceful, calm communication.

Kyanite is a powerful linking mineral able to link things, frequencies, people and even species together in higher communication such as Telepathy and Channeling no matter the distance or differences between them. In self development work Kyanite allows one to speak their truth, stimulates Astral travel and allows the memory of all that is experienced in altered states.

At the physical Level, Kyanite can help with Epilepsy, Autism, Stroke Symptoms, Mental imbalance, Weight and Adrenal troubles. This is a sacred stone of the Egyptian Gods Anubis and Thoth. Kyanite has strong links to the Ascended Master Kuthumi.

Your Healing Journey Today

If Kyanite has carried its powerful aligning and healing light into your life, you are being shown that something is out of alignment with your goals, purpose or chosen direction. We make decisions in the physical world based solely on what we have experienced or learned in our past. One day, we must take a risk to do things a new way; perhaps we will be the first to ever do it. This is the role of Kyanite for you today, your spirit is ready to fine tune an aspect of your existence, sit quietly and listen, but do not expect answers as a physical mind, these may be words the world has never heard. The Ascended Master Kuthumi may be calling on you.

Affirmation;- "My mind and spirit are one."

Keywords to help in reading the cards;- Alignment, Universal Mind, Spiritual Development, Healing, Higher Communication, Throat Chakra, Original Thought, Starchild, Calm, Brain Imbalance, Dyslexia, Autism, Anubis, Thoth, Kuthumi.

Body Card Placement;- Healing to the Throat Chakra but can go on all Chakras. Other Starchild stones such as Moldavite, Labradorite, Charoite, Sugilite, Selenite, Lepidolite, Hematite and Pyrite all work well with Kyanite. Herkimer Diamond and Kyanite on the Third Eye Chakra will powerfully activate telepathy. Hold this Card at the Heart to call Kuthumi.

Children's Anger Trinity (Soothes, Heals, Increases Understanding and Expression);- Kyanite at the Throat Chakra, Peridot at the Heart Chakra and Charoite at the Solar Plexus Chakra.

Chakra System Alignment, Balance and Healing Trinity (Total Healing, Quick Fix);- Sapphire at the Third Eye Chakra, Kyanite at the Throat Chakra and Green Tourmaline at the Heart Chakra.

Chemical Composition;- Aluminum Silicate

Color Rays;- 40% Blue, 23% Silver, 19% White, 14% Indigo and 4% Clear

Animal Totem;- Crow

Essential Oil;- Lime

Labradorite

Freewill

The Master Crystal Deva Tsidoel

"Enter my light, accept my truths and blessings, for in the darkness of my physical form I hide the endless lights of the Universe. I am an infinite resource of all that was, is and can be. Let us reopen the doors of understanding so you may see again that the power of change rests in your hands. Go Forth, Light the torch of Freewill and create.

Raise your hands to the bright and burning body of Ra, call it forth in a single ray that I can filter into the crown. Feel me run through you and remove outer influence, refining your focus on the ultimate goal of Self. Walk with me now through the fires of purification to the great halls of times past and arise with the true purpose of your spirit firm in hand.

Extraterrestrial and Earth Solar spirits, hear my call, through me, join as one in the movement towards the ultimate goal of the supreme creator's breath and fulfill the unified purpose. Rebirth the ancient Atlantian way of Oneness and unite the Star Tribes so they may again shine as a single star, this time in mastered Physicality."

Labradorite in Healing

Labradorite is a multicolored iridescent stone that changes its coloration, as you change the angle you view it from. The way it dances in the light is similar to Opal, though Labradorite is much more robust, cheaper and usually contains more of the Golden ray.

When one first gazes at Labradorite, it shimmers and dances in many different colours, seeming restless and inconsistent. But every piece of Labradorite when viewed from a certain angle becomes peaceful and still, usually also containing just one colour. In this way, Labradorite has become known as the Magician's Stone, or the Stone of Freewill. It takes the unfocused, scattered and overactive mind that is unaware of its creations, and infuses ordered, focused and intellectual thought, blended with the intuitive wisdoms of the spirit. This not only allows us to be responsible, take charge of our creations, and therefore the ownership of our Freewill, but can deliver us on to our life path and offer one's spiritual purpose.

It is also one of few crystals that, by regulating the inputs of light, is able to integrate the initiations on the path of ascension, preparing the body and spirit to unite. Labradorite is a sacred stone of Thoth, Melchizedek, Kuthumi and St Germaine.

This is a stone of Truth, allowing one to recognize the seeds of disease, disharmony, thoughts and actions in the world, this can activate powerful healing. A potent protection stone, it removes the influence of others from the energy field and infuses imaginative and original thought that rebuilds one's path reflecting their purpose.

Even in Atlantian times, Labradorite was said to have extraterrestrial origins. Today, it is still a powerful facilitator of intergalactic communication. It is especially linked to the Pleiadians, Arcturians and the Sirians, able to anchor their often highly evolved concepts on to the Earth for the betterment of mankind. Labradorite is Moldavite's Earth-bound counterpart and played a key role, with Emerald, in the calling of that stone to the Earth for the New Children of Light. Before anyone works with Moldavite, the physical energy system must be prepared by Labradorite or Moldavite's work will be limited. (See below, the 'Awakening of The Children of Light' trinity of crystals.)

At the physical level, Labradorite may be used to balance the metabolism, hormones and blood pressure, but is very powerful in finding the true cause of disease.

Your Healing Journey Today

The arrival of Labradorite for you today, signals the empowerment of freewill, an exciting time of change and creation, but before she can do her work, the mind must be refined and brought into unity. Labradorite is letting us know, it's action time, so refine your focus, meditate and be sure you feel what your heart and soul need in order to go forward towards life purpose. Prepare to create with love, free from fear, and under the guidance of spirit for the betterment of all.

Labradorite also lets us know that it is time to spiritualize our surroundings and understand the purposes behind all that is in our life, even physically. All creation holds purpose, be ready to know what it is. In your new embrace there are no secrets, only truth.

Affirmation;- "As Heart and Mind Unite, I am, We are, All is."

Keywords to help in reading the cards;- Freewill, Creation, Manifestation, Focus, Mental Scatter, Life Purpose, Akashic Records, Extraterrestrial Communication, Ascension, Fears, Truths, The Pleiadians, Arcturians and the Sirians, Thoth, Melchizedek, Kuthumi and St Germaine.

Body Card Placement;- Labradorite can go on all the Chakras. It has a major energy entry point at the left elbow relevant to the ninth moon in the Mayan calendar, placed there, it will refine intention and empower manifestation via freewill.

Awakening the Children of Light Trinity;- Place Labradorite on the Left elbow, Emerald on the Heart Chakra and Moldavite on the Right elbow. These three cards can also be stacked and placed above the Crown Chakra for a less potent effect.

Star Races and Ascended Masters Communication Trinity (To Communicate with any of the Masters or Star Races mentioned);- Place Labradorite on the Lower Left side of the chest, Selenite on the Heart Chakra and Sapphire on the Lower Right side of the chest. Relax, Listen and Know.

Chemical Composition;- Calcium Sodium Aluminum Silicate

Color Rays;- 30% Gold, 20% Blue, 20% Green, 20% Yellow and 10% Black

Animal Totem;- Coyote

Essential Oil;- Pine

Lapis Lazuli

Realization

The Master Crystal Deva Lazawardel

"I am with you, always by your side I have come to infuse the desire for truth. Let us open you to your past, so you may hear the whispers of fear and pain at the seed of their creation within you. I am Royalty, just as you, united in the quest to cut through the veil of illusion that distracts humanity into complexity, dimming the light within.

Together let us share in mankind's evolution, to embody the gold of the great central sun, as a permanent symbol of our wisdom, greatness and infinite peace. Pray with me in the temple of self, together we will hold the Purple flame with a Golden heart, and all will be revealed.

I Am with you in truth and illusion, anchoring the shining Gold of Love through the mind's Eye. Soon we will raise the great Goddess from her sleep into the embrace of Ra and once again the White Temple will rise for all to behold. Once more we are, with Thirteen Moons upon our Crown, the Unity of the Law of One."

Lapis Lazuli in Healing

Lapis Lazuli is one of the most recognized ancient stones of spiritual work, she is probably most famous throughout Egypt but makes appearances in many ancient texts. She is not a single mineral, but several minerals combined making her abilities very valuable. Often in a single piece of Lapis Lazuli; Calcite and Pyrite accompany Lazurite, which makes up the greatest percentage of the rock and gives Lapis its deep blue-purple colour for which it is renowned. The calcite donates white patches and veins, while the Pyrite acts like golden stars through the deep blue-purple backdrop.

Lapis Lazuli has an affinity for the voice and teaches of the power that is found within it when truth is embraced and the will of spirit is carried into the mind. The energy of Lapis is a dynamic one that knows no bounds; it cannot be limited to the single and separate areas of mortal creations. It seeks to break down, cut through and shed light upon all that is not in alignment with your personal divine spirit. As it does so, it lets the mind know what it finds in a masculine direct manner, cleansing and healing must then follow. It is due to this that Lapis Lazuli is known as the stone of Realization.

Work with Lapis Lazuli empowers the voice as an expressive pathway and allows wisdom to shine in every word, this cuts through the attachments and illusions of the world and in self, offering purpose and direction, as one becomes honest, trusting and loving. This same pathway activates the intuition and psychic abilities. With Petrified Wood at the solar plexus chakra, Lapis Lazuli on the heart chakra can open doorways to past lifetimes of current spiritual importance.

Lapis Lazuli is a member of the Ancient Council of Seven, a direct result of it serving as one of our physical bodies in Lemurian times and ranking it as one of the seven most important geometric tools for the human race. She is also the key to an important Stargate triangulated by the Alpha Stars of the constellations Cetus (the whale), Aries and Pisces through which we all pass before birth. In old Atlantis, those skilled with Lapis Lazuli utilized the voice as a healing tool in mantras, songs and chants and were some of the clearest spiritual channels ever to walk the earth. Lapis Lazuli is a sacred stone of Thoth, Isis, Ascended Master Kuthumi and Archangel Jophiel. It may, for some, open communication to the 24 Elders that Surround the Throne of Grace.

Lapis Lazuli has a powerful effect on the pituitary gland, returning it to balance and thus affects the entire Endocrine system positively. It is used for any problems in the area of the eyes, ears, nose and throat and may relieve headaches.

Your Healing Journey Today

On this day, the regal grace of Lapis Lazuli has landed upon you. An ancient one of infinite wisdom, she has chosen you as her playground. Her presence signals the breaking through, cutting away and true realization of that which should not be on your path. She has come to help you break through the self-created veils of illusion and distraction from your personal higher purpose. At this time, your personal power will be found in your voice as an expression pathway, this gift should be used responsibly with compassion, truth and integrity, for then it will lead to the realization Lapis has come to offer. Don't be confused by the energy of Lapis, this is not a time of healing; it is the time for action and realization, not outward, but inward, to the infinite light that you are. The greatest gifts in the universe are revealed this way. For now, Realize, See and Know, the necessary healing will come later.

Affirmation;- "I am Free in my World, I am the path of Realization."

Keywords to help in reading the cards;- Realization, Voice, Song, Empowered Expression, Illusion, Lost in Life, Purpose, Wisdom, Mind and Spirit Unite, Under the Influence of Another, Egypt, Lemuria, Isis, Cutting Ties, Breaking down the Walls.

Body Card Placement;- Mainly Throat and Third Eye Chakras.

Releasing the Ties Trinity;- Green Calcite is placed on the Right hip, then Lapis Lazuli is placed on the Heart Chakra and lastly Diamond is placed on the Left hip. Lie quietly, visualize, know and feel all the energy you have sent out returning to you, let it enter the body at those three points. Then using your intention cut all outgoing energies, and finish by visualizing a White Rose in the centre of your Heart Chakra. Note;- The gentle healing and nurturing light of Jasper may be of use after this process.

Egyptian Past Lives Trinity (Realization and Integration of Egyptian Lives);- Place Lapis Lazuli on the Third Eye Chakra, Place Petrified Wood on the Heart Chakra, and Smoky Quartz on the Solar Plexus Chakra.

Chemical Composition;- Lazurite (Sodium Calcium Aluminum Silicate Sulfate),Pyrite (Iron Sulfide) Calcium (Calcium Carbonate)

Color Rays;- 53% Indigo 17% Gold, 13% Blue 10%Violet and 7%White

Animal Totem;- Snake

Essential Oil;- Sandalwood. (East Indian)

Larimar

Service

The Master Crystal Deva Isisomel

"Feel my peaceful wave brushing the shore; light me a white candle and within its light calmly float with me along the unique path of your own service. Enter the times forgotten, when man and all creation, from Angel to Elemental walked together hand in hand, this is my world, now only perceived by those that desire perception.

I am the teacher's teacher, igniting the playing field of life with the infinite pathways of joy and expression, each unique and all important. Step into me, the unlimited nature of your creativity, growth and Knowledge will shine from you, with heart and mind at peace and calm in the Ocean of Unity.

In my Guidance you are the lighthouse of purpose, calm, on the rocks of fear leading by example for others to behold as they pass in the darkness of uncertainty, lost behind the veils of the illusionary physical worlds.Walk your path wisely, I am ever with you, in service we are upon the very steps of I Am, and your path home is lit now by the Great Central Sun."

Larimar in Healing

Larimar, the stone of Service, is a beautiful blue stone with white inclusions that wisp through it like a breaking wave in the ocean. It is air and water combined, birthed through volcanic fire, and made physical in the Earth's sacred embrace. No other stone on Earth delivers such a balance of the elements and carries their lessons within it.

Larimar allows a harmonious blending of Emotions (Water) and Mind (Air), cooling all the fiery areas into soothing peace and calm. It then removes the old patterns and opens a holistic view of self, spiritually and physically. Wherever there is a fire in life, such as the emotional and mental extremes of anger, hurt, fear, pain and impatience, Larimar is the solution.

Larimar activates a fearless ability to flow through life. It re-connects us to the Earth and the cyclic Goddess energy which activates a wondrous feeling of freedom in the physical world. This makes it an ideal stone for those that feel trapped in physical life, such as the New Children of Light, who need to rediscover the wonders of Freewill. It awakens creativity, the ability to manifest in the physical world and the inner child that has fallen asleep. Then it powerfully replaces Inaction, Confusion, Tears and Pain with Action, Imagination, Playfulness, Laughter and Joy.

In healing, Larimar is known to clear the meridians of the body and facilitate expression of the cause of illness thus allowing true understanding and permanent healing to occur. Larimar is a valuable remedy for all Cancers, able to cool and redistribute life force from areas of excess such as Tumors, this ability is very powerful when it is coupled with Black Coral and Diamond. Larimar can be worked with to bring soul mates and twin flames together and can be of great use in helping to resolve issues between them which allows rapid spiritual growth. Great beings that answer within the frequency of Larimar include Lady Isis, Quan Yin, Lady Nada and Ascended Master Sananda. Sacred deity correspondences include Artemis, Poseidon, Hathor, Nuit and Anhur. The angelic is powerfully represented by Archangel Uriel.

At the physical level Larimar is worked with in Conjunction with Lepidolite and Kyanite for Schizophrenic disorders. It can benefit Inflammation, Fevers and Sunburn and is a valuable general Pain relief stone.

Your Healing Journey Today

Wherever Larimar goes, there is always need for healing, the exciting thing is, that she usually represents the last stage in the healing process, where one calls upon what they have learnt to help others. If Larimar has entered your life today, you are being called into service. A person, animal, plant or even the Self needs your ability to heal. Larimar reminds us we all have the gift of healing, though its path is infinitely different for each of us. Often the act of healing is simply being the best that we can be at something and delivering via that avenue into the world. Often a bank teller living in truth, acceptance, peace, harmony and love will be a better facilitator in healing than a spiritual healer or doctor, the latter having to wear labels in the world and shoulder expectations. Service finds us all, if you seek it, you will never find it, for it lives in you, alive in the unchangeable light that you are, magnified by your Journey through the ages as a spirit in the universe, a new door is opening, can you stand within it.

Larimar also enters one's life when the Lady Isis is close or there is a need to visit the ocean.

Affirmation;- "My Journey is my Gift to the World."

Keywords to help in reading the cards;- Service, Cooling, Calm, Mental/Emotional Balance, Healing, Fire Attitudes, Innerchild, Atlantian and Lemurian History, Isis, Quan Yin, The Lady Nada, Poseidon, Neptune (astrology), Go with the Flow.

Body Card Placement;- Larimar enters the body at the Right Hip Joint of the body which is a sacred area for it, representing the Electric (3rd) Moon in the Mayan Calendar.

An Ancient Atlantian Five Crystal healing layout;- Place Larimar on the Right hip, Zircon on the Right shoulder, Sapphire on the Left shoulder, Diamond on the Left Hip and Clear Quartz on the Heart Chakra. This can be worked with for all ailments, Powerfully Balancing, Activating and Healing.

Other Starchild stones such as Moldavite, Labradorite, Charoite, Sugilite, Selenite, Lepidolite, Hematite and Pyrite all work well with Larimar. Hold this card at the Heart to communicate with Dolphins and Whales and any Female Ascended Ladies but especially those mentioned above.

Discovering Paths of Service Trinity;- Place Emerald on the Upper Left side of the chest, Lapis Lazuli on the Third Eye Chakra and Larimar on the Upper Right side of the chest.

Soul Mates and Twin Soul Trinity (Calls and Draws them to you where needed or possible for mutual benefit);- Selenite is placed on the Soul Star Chakra, Larimar on the Heart Chakra and Boji Stone on the Earth Star Chakra. Let light rise from each Crystal as Rays and unite above the body at Throat level, where they will become a bright Blue Spinning Star. The Star will Grow Brighter and Brighter then explode in all directions in Search. (This is a very powerful process that is magnified when done in group work, please use it responsibly; you may get what you ask for!)

Chemical Composition;- Sodium Calcium Silicate Hydroxide

Color Rays;- 38% Blue, 16% Clear, 20% White, 13% Pink and 13% Violet

Animal Totem;- Beluga Whale

Essential Oil;- Tuberose

Extra Interesting Facts:- In 1934 Edgar Cayce, 'The Sleeping Prophet' stated in a channeling session that a part of Atlantis would be found in the Caribbean, he went on to say, a blue stone would be found with extraordinary healing abilities and gave a remarkable description of Larimar thus, still today Larimar is sometimes called 'Atlantis Stone'. Larimar was not discovered until 1974 in the predicted area and named by a Dominican after his daughter LARIssa, combined with MAR, the Spanish word for sea. 10 years later, in 1984, a 7th moon was found around the Planet Neptune and called Larissa. Coincidence? Or did the discovery of Larimar call and anchor the spiritual 7th Moon of the Planet Neptune (Sacred to Poseidon, God of the Sea) to the Earth's oceans? Was this an important step in the rebirth of Atlantis and the Atlantian Way? I think so.

Lepidolite

Conscious Feeling

The Master Crystal Deva Lepidoel

"Slow now child, let the mists of life be felt not as rain, for it is in the joy of fully conscious feeling that I will journey with you today. Receive my gift to you through an open feeling heart; I have waited a long time for your return to my frequency.

Let my loving light slow your emotional world and provide a space to breathe and feel the flow of your life force through the body. Direct it now to the highest parts of mind for active realization and into action for the good of all. Hand in Hand we will feel our way into completion.

Complete now, walk with me to the top of the mountain and we will take in the view of all that you are. Up here above the confusion and wearisome emotions of life, breathe, recharge and take time, for we will soon reenter the world, with a lighter heart and committed intent."

Lepidolite in Healing

Lepidolite is a purplish pink mineral with silver overtones that run through it allowing it to shimmer in the sunlight. Forming bladed crystals viewed from certain angles, good-quality Lepidolite can be transparent. It is a relatively cheap stone that is available in tumbled form from most shops.

Lepidolite is the stone of Conscious Feeling; its principal role is to balance the mind and heart soothing and healing the emotional and Mental bodies into balance and harmony. It performs this due to the high levels of Lithium Mica with in it. Lithium is a soft metal and is the lightest solid element; its salts are used in orthodox Medicine in the treatment of Schizophrenia and Manic Depression. These two conditions result most commonly when the feelings are out of alignment with the thoughts allowing the creation of separate personalities and/or identities that create turmoil.

This crystal is one for the New Children of Light, by unifying thoughts and feelings in the healing process, it creates a state of independence that is fuelled by focus, clear decision-making and a desire to reach goals. Mixed into its action is the presence of the Silver Ray, the soothing feminine energy of the moon and the presence of the goddess, which carries understanding to the cyclic nature of physicality, allowing nonattachment. In the treatment of the New Children of Light (Star, Indigo, Crystal, etc), Lepidolite is often found side-by-side with Moldavite, Kyanite, Lepidolite, Sugilite and Larimar. Lepidolite is a powerful emotional healer often and able to go where other crystals cannot, unlocking and creating healing in the deepest of emotional wounds, all in the presence of mental understanding.

Lepidolite is a contact stone for the Master Hilarion, Archangel Raphael, Goddesses Nun and Qetesh, and Egyptian God Neheh.

At the physical level, Lepidolite is useful in cases of Insomnia, Depression, Obsessive Thought and Stress. It can also be helpful with Mood swings, Bipolar disorders, Epilepsy and Alzheimer's. As a Liquid Crystal Lepidolite is a potent skin tonic.

Your Healing Journey Today

If Lepidolite has come to you today, you are being asked to follow your heart. At this time in your life feelings are being united with your thoughts. If you stay true to your feelings, everything will follow its true Path, allowing the manifestation of your goals. Lepidolite often appears when choice, confusion or depression has led to a lack of action in life. She is a gentle, loving motivation towards that which we came to Earth to achieve, but have temporarily forgotten or lost track of, search your heart in a logical way and the real answers are there, they always have been. This is a powerful contact stone for Female ascended beings and the Archangelic Hierarchy.

Affirmation;- "My thoughts and emotions are united and in harmony with purpose."

Keywords to help in reading the cards;- Conscious Feeling, Thought and Feeling Balance, The Reaching of Goals, Decision-Making through the Heart, Children of Light, Follow Your Heart, Stress, Ascended Master Hilarion.

Body Card Placement;- Can be confidently placed on all Chakras Heart and above.

Life Purpose Discovery (This is especially potent with Star Children, helping them make the necessary decisions);- Lepidolite is placed on the Third Eye, Moldavite on the Right shoulder and Labradorite on the Left shoulder. The results usually wash through life within Seven days, at which time support may be needed; I recommend Jasper and Blue Lace Agate.

Feeling Healing Trinity (Emotional Detoxification, Embrace and Healing);- Place Rose Quartz on the Lower Left side of the chest, Lepidolite on the Heart Chakra and Sapphire on the Lower Right side of the chest.

Chemical Composition;- Potassium Lithium Aluminum Silicate Hydroxide Fluoride

Color Rays;- 33% Pink, 33% Violet, 13% Clear, 13% Silver and 8% Indigo

Animal Totem;- Manta Ray

Essential Oil;- Violet Leaf

Lodestone

Earth Embrace

The Master Crystal Deva Ida-rael

"Close your eyes glorious one, align to me, now breathe till your breath and mine are one. Sink into the Earth; let her Pulse run through you, this is one of my many roles. I polarize you to your Earth and all she represents, I am a conductor of her energies, her will and mine are one.

Together we work to lift you to the ascended state that is your birthright. We will remove the walls on your spiritual path, allowing confidence in the cycle of you. From birth to death and back, I will aid you in the absolute commitment to the spiritual self and its movement.

Feel my stabilizing touch and enter the Earth. Take my hand; accept your physical mastery and then fly to the heavens of your own creation."

Lodestone in Healing

Magnetite is another name for Lodestone, which gives away its greatest characteristic, Lodestone is iron oxide that is naturally magnetic, charged from the Earth. It is a black to metallic stone that is very heavy and opaque. Of all the stones on Earth, Lodestone is one of the most grounding, giving its simple purpose as the Stone of Earth Embrace. Related to this, Lodestone is able to open direct communication with the Earth herself, but its healing directive is more related to allowing a conscious view of male and female aspects of self, which leads to a solid grounded approach to life's paths.

Lodestone is the governing mineral of the first initiation towards Ascension, Mastery of the Physical Body. When one has lost their path, life force, motivation and drive, Lodestone is the answer, Stabilizing and Energizing their masculine and feminine aspects via polarization and direct contact to the Earth, balance, alignment and healing result.

Lodestone always draws that which is needed for growth at all levels and attracts the healing energies that are necessary for recovery, often showing the way back to health. It aids powerfully in the discovery and walking of the 'middle road' the space between polarities (void) which leads to healing, manifestation and growth spiritually. In meditation, it helps in the integration of the energies experienced, reducing dizziness and allowing remembrance of that which has been experienced.

Lodestone is a valuable mineral in Psychic Surgery, where it is used to remove disease, especially Cancer, then activate the understanding of the pathway to make the healing permanent. At a more physical level Lodestone aids in the functioning of the Endocrine system, helps heal nose bleeds and is second to none in pain management associated with the neck, shoulder and back.

Magically, Lodestone is a popular stone in Spell Craft where its strong drawing abilities are used to find lost objects and information; it is also a powerful stone for the calling forth of the little people, elementals such as fairies. Try placing lodestone in a dish of milk or cream outside or on the window sill, they will come from everywhere. Lodestone is sacred to and opens communication with Lord Allah Gobi, Master El Morya and the Master Osiris, Goddesses Inanna and Anat, and the Egyptian God Geb.

Your Healing Journey Today

If Lodestone has come to you today, the masculine and feminine aspects of self are attempting to find balance. Often this will present as spells of dizziness, a feeling of being lost in life or unanchored in the physical world. The choices we make in the world are best made from a balanced space, Physically, Mentally, Emotionally and Spiritually, if they are not, life and its pathways can become one-sided and lose their potency. If we allow the mental and physical worlds to be more masculine and the emotional and spiritual worlds to be more feminine, balance is often easier to find. Simply be aware where you spend most of your time. Lodestone also comes into people's lives to deliver realizations as to the curing pathways and cause of disease or illness. Sit, and by intention balance and align your chakra system, see a silver star beneath your feet and allow it to spin. The Manu, Allah Gobi, Lord of the First Ray, may be calling on you, listen for his message.

Affirmation;- "I Embrace my Physicality, it is the Greatest Creation of the Eternal Spirit that I am."

Keywords to help in reading the cards;- Earth Embrace, Grounding, Masculine/ Feminine Balance, The First Initiation of Ascension, Healing Pathway, The Manu (Lord of the First Ray), Base Chakra, The Earth Star Chakra.

Body Card Placement;- Lodestone is most at home on the Base Chakra and Earth Star Chakra.

Placed, or beneath a bowl of milk or cream, this card will attract members of the Elemental kingdom. (Apatite on the heart will help in the translating of their language and forms of communication.)

Locate missing objects or people Trinity;- Lodestone, Jade and Herkimer Diamond are placed with a photograph, picture or written statement of that which is to be found into an envelope which is then placed under the pillow that night. The answers will come in the Dream State.

Elemental Calling Trinities (Sequences for Earth (Gnomes), Air (Fairies), Fire (Salamanders) and Water (Undines);- Lodestone, Apatite and your choice of Turquoise for Earth, Fluorite for Air, Sulphur for Fire and Larimar for Water. The Three Cards are always laid out in a Triangle, with the Top point the Crystal that changes.

- -Turquoise pointing North for Earth; Place the Cards around a Bowl of Cream or Milk.
- -Fluorite pointing East for Air; Place the Cards on a Yellow Cloth, Burn some Incense and drink some Spearmint Tea.
- -Sulphur pointing South for Fire; Place the Cards between Two Orange Candles.
- -Larimar pointing West for Water; Place the Cards beneath a Glass Bowl filled with Sparkling Mineral Water.

Chemical Composition;- Iron Oxide (Magnetized)
Color Rays;- 25% Black, 25% Red, 25% Silver and 25% Gold
Animal Totem;- Worm
Essential Oil;- Patchouli

Malachite

Clearing

The Master Crystal Deva Malochel

"Raise your arms to the stars golden angel of the sun, let me aid you on your Journey. Breathe me in and let my hidden yellow flame ignite the power in you. Feel my warmth in your veins, the flower of Purification, clearing and true personal power has come to bloom.

Accept my green vibration, one of earthly love to which the basis of fear gravitates, then melts away. Let me bless you with the courage and strength to face your limitations and fears, entering into my understanding, you will see your role in their creation and be free to fly again.

Now released from the weight of the physical world, welcome to the freedom of the fearless state, for love is all that is. Fear stems from the un-mastered mind at play in the fields of Illusion, your perception is its vitality, life force and creator."

Malachite in Healing

Malachite is a deep forest green, mineral with lighter green to yellow banding that runs through it, usually in circular patterns. A soft mineral, it has been used by many cultures for carving. Malachite is mined for its copper content, which rarely occurs naturally as a solitary metal. Thus Malachite carries all of the properties of copper and although it is a green mineral, most of its action takes place within the yellow ray of color at the solar plexus chakra, the centre of personal power and identification of self. The principal crystal of clearing, Malachite makes us aware of our pathway of healing or growth then powerfully delivers awareness as to that which blocks us. Malachite can find the seed of all illnesses or disharmony and then surface it into awareness for healing. She is a crystal of courage and determination who infuses the drive to seek a better way, casting away the self limitations and attachments to the past especially where fear and guilt are concerned.

Spiritually, Malachite can aid vision at the third eye in meditation and is able to clear the subconscious mind. In ancient Egypt it was utilized as a link stone with Selenite to the energies of Sirius and the Great White Lodge. Malachite is a sacred stone of the Goddess Het Heret (Hathor) and Master Osiris.

With Malachite's affinity for the solar plexus area of the physical body, it is a powerful remedy for releasing stress and tension from that area which is useful in restoring complete breathing in asthmatics. She is also able to absorb energy from painful, diseased or inflamed areas aiding healing of most issues including Teething in children, Torn Muscles, Arthritis, Swollen Joints and Broken Bones.

Your Healing Journey Today
Malachite's presence with you today, indicates an active, or the need to enter an active, process of clearing. There is something happening in life that needs your attention, however vision of it is blocked or simply unavailable and must be cleared. Malachite asks you to trust your instincts, keep your heart open and have courage. Trust the spirit you are, your faith in self is often being tested when Malachite appears in life. There comes a time in everybody's life when they must clear away a sacred space to simply exist alone within. (Remember; "Alone is All one, not alone".) Malachite is also a very physical stone; her presence may also indicate the need to clear a physical ailment, the seed of which is currently unknown to you.

Affirmation;- "I am a blinding light, I am Healed, Clear and Free."

Keywords to help in reading the cards;- Clearing, Healing, Hidden Process, Solar Plexus Chakra, Healing Path, Purification, Trust in Self, Fear, Guilt, Frustration, Anxiety, Blocked Pathway of Growth, Asthma.

Body Card Placement;- Malachite is best on the Heart and Solar Plexus Chakras, but can go directly over any painful or inflamed areas to draw off the pain and congestion.

Clear Vision for Healing Action Trinity (Clear the pathway of Vision and allow control of

Freewill.);- Place Malachite on the Right shoulder, with Iolite, the stone of Vision, on the Third Eye Chakra and Labradorite the stone of Freewill on the Left shoulder.

Super Clear, Pure and Real Trinity (The most Purifying Stones in one Place at one time);- Place Bloodstone on the Heart Chakra, Malachite on the Solar Plexus and Black Obsidian on the Sacral Chakra. Read all the Crystals first so you know what you are in for, drink lots of water for seven days after the Healing and repeat it if you feel you need to.

Chemical Composition;- Hydrated Copper Carbonate (8% Water)

Color Rays;- 40% Green, 15% Yellow, 15% White and 15% Blue

Animal Totem;- Rhinoceros

Essential Oil;- Lemon

Moldavite

Starchild

The Master Crystal Deva Elomra

"Children of the Stars hear my call, I have come with love from the home land, in this the necessary light transition of Planet Earth and the Human race.

Step into my green robe; let my embrace be the doorway to the place of your true origin and birth. Let tears fall no more in longing to return, as separation is an Illusion to which I will bring light. Draw from my glow the pathways of activation that you have come to complete. Let your gifts be free to manifest, in this Earth cycle to which you are tied.

As I was at the beginning, at completion, I will be there to carry you home to the glory of the Stars, a homecoming of the ages. Let us release the gifts now from their prison and shower the universe in the unity of light realized, sacred and whole."

Moldavite in Healing

Moldavite has been very misunderstood in our modern world, most people believing that she is here to offer a higher frequency for us to explore, when in fact she sees her role as one more of grounding. As "Starchild", the simple purpose of Moldavite suggests, this beautiful bottle green gem stone that fell from the sky is the result of a call that the Earth put out to the universe for assistance with the Children of Light, often referred to as Indigo Children, Crystal Children etc. Moldavite is actually green obsidian with a starry origin. As the Moldavite enters our world it is bombarded by gases which give rise to a beryllium 10 isotope.

This Rare Isotope potently affects the human body allowing a powerful energy transition into the space between frequencies. Moldavite thus is the stone of 'the space between frequencies', it allows separate frequencies to enter oneness where freewill has yet to be mastered. To those familiar with these spaces (the New Children), it brings great grounding and understanding of the laws of a Duality based world, opening potential for healing. To those not used to these spaces, Moldavite places you within them, a state many call a high frequency, but in reality just no frequency.

Of the many Starchild symptoms that Moldavite seeks to correct, the most important ones are mental and relate to their inability to hold their expanded spiritual consciousness within the physical brain, which leads to imbalance and malfunction. Moldavite often encounters one that is unwilling to live, inwardly lost, separate, isolated, disgusted and unwilling to accept Earth life. Then as Moldavite works its magic, the Starchild becomes accustomed to physical Earth life and accepting of its limitations. They discover the joys of freewill and slowly a passion to create a better world emerges. Under Moldavite's guidance they take new, brave and original paths, breaking out of their shell and delivering their abundant individual gifts to the world. Eventually, when time allows, Moldavite is here to ensure they become the teachers of a better way for us all. It should be known, that every person on Earth today below the age of 20 at some stage in their life will need to interact with Moldavite's frequency. Remember also that although Moldavite has come to assist the Children of Light, she is also a powerful healer for any of us that can identify with her healing gifts. We should note that the Children of Light have been coming to our world for quite some time and it is common to meet a 50-year-old in desperate need of Moldavite's sacred embrace so they may finally feel at home on Earth.

Moldavite is a powerful communication stone between the people of Earth and intergalactic races, it activates telepathy and higher metal abilities. Physically, Moldavite is a great aid in all forms of Autism, Epilepsy, Brain Imbalances and Malfunctions.

Your Healing Journey Today

If Moldavite has landed in your life today, you are being asked to give thanks, and spend a little time recognizing the joys of physical life here on the Planet Earth. The gift of freewill should be understood for it is the creative principle behind life and the same vessel via which you may have everything you desire. Moldavite is a positive energy in your life on this day, indicating a gift, skill or path that has been lying dormant, within your Spirit, has been triggered into manifestation by your recent action or perhaps lack of it. Its energy signals growth, renewal and change, something that was put in place long before your birth into this world is about to be realized and manifested. Spend some time in the glory of nature, recognize the diversity and brilliance of Earth and give thanks for your life, it is at the peak of your celebrations that all will be revealed.

Affirmation;- "Physicality Holds a Greatness Only Those That Embrace Purpose Ever See."

Keywords to help in reading the cards;- Starchild, Freewill, Indigo Child, New Children of Light, Dawn of a New Age, Activation Energy, Intergalactic Races Communication, Clarity, Growth, Renewal, Change, Telepathy, Between Worlds, The 11:11 Gateway, Shamballa, Ascended Master Kuthumi, Lord Melchizedek.

Body Card Placement;- Moldavite is an activation Stone more than a healing stone, it can go on all the Chakras and areas of the body for that purpose, but it is especially powerful on the Heart and Third Eye.

Star Travel Trinity;- Herkimer Diamond on the Right shoulder, Apophyllite on the Left shoulder and Moldavite on the Heart Chakra offer an amazing journey to your Soul's Stella Origin. (Note;- Iolite can also be placed on the Third Eye Chakra to activate and aid Spiritual vision)

Starchild Activation Trinity;- Balanced activation of the Earth Path Forward);- Labradorite to the Left side of the head (below the ear), Moldavite on the Third Eye Chakra and Ruby to the Right side of the head (below the ear). This exercise should be done several times over a 21 day span, to get the best results.

Chemical Composition;- Silicon Dioxide, Aluminum Oxide Beryllium 10 Isotope

Color Rays;- 37% Green, 37% Black and 27% Clear (Note 1% next dimensional Colors in Flux)

Animal Totem;- Whale Shark

Essential Oil;- Yarrow

Moldavite's Mission

Labradorite is Moldavite's Earth-bound counterpart and it was that stone that initiated the call to the stars for a stone of greater Spiritual Healing as the Starchildren were not listening to his message of Freewill and were manifesting their missions poorly. Emerald, the stone of spiritual healing, was also struggling to find answers. The Children were not able to gather information in the between spaces where they left it. Due to this, Labradorite still should be worked with before moving to Moldavite. The Beryllium Isotope of Moldavite relates it to the other beryls of Earth, the main ones are, Aquamarine, the stone of simplification, Morganite, the stone of Equality in Love and of course Emerald, the stone of Spiritual Healing, which begs the Question; Is Moldavite the New Emerald for the People of Earth?

Moonstone

Mother Goddess

The Master Crystal Deva Lunlael

"A wise mother of the Earth I am, take my hand and let me guide you. Invite me to walk within, beside and around you, I only go where I am called. Open to the joy of emotion, I will teach you the pure language of the feminine spirit. Let my flowing Luna embrace fill you and initiate the path of compassion, nurture and motherhood.

In the deepest, darkest, forest of your emotional being I am the light in the clearing. I hold the key to completion on the feminine path of ascension. Together let us carry the light of your soul into the emotional body, leaving harmony and balance where once was turmoil and pain.

The goddess exists in all that I touch, inducing the love of feeling where once stood Fear. Together again we will walk by the light of the Moon, through the clouds of your completion into Oneness, reaching up we will Touch, Balance and Absolve the Sun."

Moonstone in Healing

Moonstone is an ancient and traditional stone from Atlantis for the Goddess and one of the ruling stones of the Female path of Ascension. Most often, it is a milky white stone, but nice specimens have transparent parts and rainbow colors through them and may even have a pink, yellow, black or light blue shade. Often the colors found in Moonstone will dance within the stone, similar to Labradorite, which is often sold as a substitute to non-discerning buyers. Another common trick is the placement of colored paper behind the stone in jewellery, to make an ordinary stone look amazing, keep your eyes open.

One of the most potent representations of feminine energy in the earth, Moonstone teaches the path of the Goddess through the emotional body. She soothes and heals the emotions by bringing them under the soul's control. This delivers an understanding of the cyclic nature of all things which activates nonattachment and freedom of expression.

When the emotions have been repressed, ignored or simply drowned in masculine energy, Moonstone will work her magic, bringing release and eventual control of the emotional self.

Moonstone is a very magical stone, worked with in magical practice as a representation of the Goddess energies and the taking control of the emotional aspect. Her masculine opposite is Garnet and the two are worn on the middle finger of both hands to facilitate manifestation. Moonstone can also be worked with to speak to the Oceans, where it translates the voice of the moon, which we know as the tides, into messages that are best heard at the point of change, the space of stillness.

At the physical level, Moonstone is useful in Pregnancy, Childbirth, Lactation, Fertility, Hormonal Imbalance and PMS. It may also be useful for Sleepwalking.

Your Healing Journey Today

The Goddess is at your door, it is time to open your heart and feel. Moonstone comes to us when it is time to feel and truthfully open the door to our emotional self. Many of us believe we already do this, but living in a constant emotional state is not true feeling, as it holds no mastery, discipline or understanding. Moonstone asks you to sit and feel, just sit. Don't label, think, act or react, just feel. By doing this, one gains the ability to experience the cyclic nature of our world. Just as things arise, so they fall away and we are able to surrender and be happy without attachment. This is the path of the Goddess and only those that embrace it may wear the Luna Crest. Remember a feeling is only a feeling while it is felt and experienced, once it is recognized by the mind it is a thought.

Spend some time around the ocean if possible in the coming days, call and ask the Lady of the Lake to be by your side, see her rise up and stand with you, she is always waiting and will help at this time in your life.

Affirmation;- "Mother Goddess embraced, I am emotion realized."

Keywords to help in reading the cards;- Mother Goddess, Divine Feminine, Emotions, The Moon, Lunar Energy, The Ocean, Cycles of Life, Crying, Emotional release, Surrender, Compassion, Sacred Stone of Isis, Pallas Athena, Aphrodite.

Body Card Placement;- The entry point for feminine energy on the body is found at the tip of the chin, this is the entry point for Moonstone and the sacred space for her energy.

The Atlantian Pathway to Isis Trinity (For the embodiment of the Goddess);- Pearl is placed on the right shoulder, Moonstone, upon the chin (or just below on the neck) and Silver upon the left shoulder. Visualize the Moon with a Ray of Light shining from it that enters the Heart Chakra. See the Three Divine Feminine selves walk down and come to rest in the body. They are the Innocent and Pure, The Cyclic and Mothering and the Wise and Understanding. These increase in age, Girl, Woman and Wise Elder.

Wiccan Healing Manifestation Trinity (Powerfully manifests a chosen Healing Path);- Place Moonstone on the Throat Chakra, a crystal of your choice on the Heart Chakra and Garnet on the Solar Plexus Chakra. Draw Moonstone and Garnet's energy to the Heart Chakra and let them combine with your chosen crystal, see them all as a ball of light that will remain with you for a 7 day healing process.

Chemical Composition;- Potassium Aluminum Silicate

Color Rays;- 60% Silver, 20% White, 10% Clear and 5%Pink

Animal Totem;- Turtle

Essential Oil;- May Chang

Morganite

Equality in Love

The Master Crystal Deva Maryel

"Be patient child, listen with love, take time to let the sounds that flow from you be filtered through the heart. In my soft embrace light up with joy, for you are alive in all things, joined at the infinite home of the endless light.

Let me carry you through the alone times by the light of your soul's wisdom and allow you to see the joy in being the creator of all that you are in this moment. For within this vision of completeness is the power of self-control, disciplined in action for the betterment of all.

Let all separation, competition and judgment fall away. Rejoice in the family of light to which you belong. Only unity will you find by the light of my eternal and endless heart, a fire of which you are a vital flame dancing at the base of oneness."

Morganite in Healing

Morganite is a clear Pink Crystal from the highly distinguished Beryl family of crystals, her brothers and sisters including Emerald, the Crystal of Spiritual Healing and Aquamarine, the Crystal of Simplification.

This relatively forgotten, though very powerful stone will make itself profoundly present in the coming age, where what it has to offer will be highly sought-after.

As the stone of Equality in Love, Morganite fosters the ability to express and listen from the heart, which allows growth via relationship. Where once inequality reigned with a winner/loser mentality, a relating is learning attitude is born with self-control and an understanding of shared perception.

Morganite is a powerful group work stone, its unifying energies stimulate, activate and cleanse the heart chakras of all involved, creating a strong harmonious bond.

Spiritually; this powerful stone of oneness via the heart, can induce a state where one can see their roles with humanity and take hold of responsibility for their personal creation.

Physically; Morganite targets the Lung area of the body where it can play a healing role in most conditions, including Asthma, Emphysema and other conditions of lowered oxygen.

Your Healing Journey Today

Relationship is the keyword here, be sure that you are expressing and listening from the heart. Whenever we make the commitment to enter a relationship, regardless of whether it is personal, business, or even the choosing of our own parents, it is easy to forget in physical life how powerful and important it is. We are selecting our teachers. These people and mutual experiences have been chosen by you, to sculpt and help you become everything you have decided to be in the world.

Make sure that you really see relationship is not isolated to person to person type relationships, an Artist has a relationship with their Brush, a Gardener to their Plants and a Healer to their Role in service. The Message of Morganite is one we all need on some level, take her hand and Grow.

Affirmation;- "I relate, I listen, I learn, I love."

Keywords to help in reading the cards;- Equality in Love, Oneness, Relationship, Listening, Inequality, Self-Control, Group Work, Shared Perception, Harmony, Paul the Venetian Master.

Body Card Placement;- Morganite is best on the Crown and Heart Chakras.

Morganite and Angelite can be placed under a Pink candle to infuse an environment with Equality and Peace.

Space of Equality Trinity (Delivers one into the space of Equality and offers insights on staying there);- Morganite is placed on the Heart Chakra, Amazonite is placed on the Throat Chakra and Peach Calcite is placed on the Solar Plexus Chakra. This is not always as smooth a ride as it sounds, the Nurturing support of Red Jasper will often be needed.

Chemical Composition;- Beryllium Aluminum Silicate

Color Rays;- 70% Pink and 30% Clear

Animal Totem;- Swallow

Essential Oil;- Vanilla

Obsidian

True Self-Reflection

The Master Crystal Deva Taramael

"Welcome Child of Light, I am blessed in your presence. Long ago we embraced, you and I are old friends. I am the Embrace of Bast, Breath of Set and Path of the Jackal, the pathway through the shadow self, doorway to the Physical worlds and their Mastery. I allow polarities to be known, and carry the freedom found in dedication to self as Spirit Eternal. Will you walk the inner path of the Jackal? Let us ignite the Stargates hidden deep in your heart and be blinded no more by the Stars above, for fear you will not see the infinite glory that holds them.

Evolve with me now. Call the Three stars from the heavens above and let them rest in your Eyes. In blinding Blue light, let them expand to 13 and come to rest at home in infinite embrace with the Ancient Moons. In a single call of Power, Unite them now at the Heart and Explode self into the Velvet Black light of all that is, the point of Universal Birth. We will Journey now, to the self perceived darkest corridors and by the light of my being, the reflection of truth within you will be obvious. Beware, I am direct in my action. If you dare walk my path, embrace self, and transmute all by my earthy flame of Truth, to Love, you may never chose to return to your Old Life of Unrest.

In acceptance of my Gifts and in the definition of the Shadow's embrace, you now see and feel me in reality, for there is nothing to fear in the limitless light I represent. In the reality of the Spirit's Unity, we are nurturing and eternally Loyal to divine purpose. Let us rewrite the path of light so Humanity will hide in the Shadows no more and Journey proudly in the Stars within and finally above to Glory."

Obsidian in Healing

Obsidian is volcanic glass, most commonly black, quite dark and opaque, it can be quite transparent and may display rainbow colours and inclusions that allow it to have swirls and bands of different colour through it. In today's world, there are many different varieties, but only a few of them are naturally occurring. Probably the most popular form of Obsidian is a form often referred to as Apache Tears, this form is quite transparent and easily mistaken for Smoky Quartz. As a volcanic stone, Obsidian is formed in the last stage of volcanic eruption as the earth settles back to peace. Its healing action is very much like this. Aggressive and ruthless, it leaves no stone unturned in the Truthful Reflection of Self, but for the one that succeeds upon the healing path of Obsidian a profound peace and spirituality may be discovered that is unequalled in the mineral kingdom.

Via the true vision of self, Obsidian activates positive change where the level of honesty with self leads to true Self-love and satisfaction without the Ego. It can teach one how to nurture the self and approach change with direct action to get the job done.

A stone of the void space, Obsidian aids the journey deep within the self to the silence between polarities. Once in this space, powerful visions show the available life pathways and give insights into future events. Obsidian can dispel negativity, having a shielding effect on the physical and emotional bodies. It is also used in shamanic practice to transmute energies especially in shape shifting, facilitating the movement into animal form and consciousness. It is also one of few activation stones for the Earth Star Chakra, providing powerful grounding and a polarized energy so the spirit may enter physicality. (It works powerfully with Selenite in this process.) Obsidian is a sacred stone of the ancient Mayans, Egyptians and American Indians. It is a sacred contact stone for Saint Germaine, the Egyptian God Anubis, the Master Osiris and Goddess Bast. In Atlantian times the stone was known as the 'Black Transformer', gateway between life and death.

On the physical level Obsidian enhances the Immune System, combats viral and bacterial inflammations and balances the digestive system.

Your Healing Journey Today

If Obsidian has come to you today, it is time to be truthful about self, and your actions in the world. The presence of Obsidian lets you know the time to take action is now here. There is something that you are unable or unwilling to see, that is interfering in your life's progress. Consciously or unconsciously, this untruth has led you to a space of inaction. If such things are allowed to exist, over time they only lead to pain and suffering. If there is truth in the self, there will be love for the self. If there is love for the self, there will be harmony and balance in the self, once this exists, peace will live in you and spill into your world in a blinding light of unconditional Love. Obsidian also often presents as a protective force when needed to deliver the truth behind illness. An exercise we may do to facilitate the purification of the shadow self, which will seem silly, but is very effective, is to stand where you can see your Shadow and from the understanding that water is Unconditional Liquid Light, wash it. This is not an exercise for the lounge room and is most effective on the beach with a bucket of saltwater, but the hose out the back will do just fine.

Affirmation;- "I walk the path of Unconditional Truth."

Keywords to help in reading the cards;- True Self Reflection, Dishonesty, The Temple of Shadows, Change, Vision of Self, Honesty, Nurture the Self, The Colour Black, The Void, Earth Star Chakra, Transmutation, Immune System, Anubis, Mayan and/or American Indians.

Body Card Placement;- At first site of illness to understand its purpose and lessons. Principally the Heart Chakra, and all Chakras below it, including the Earth Star Chakra below the feet.

Spiritual Growth and Stella Activation Trinity (Increases Light Quotient and Heals that which is not on our Path);- Place Gold on the Heart Chakra, Selenite on the Soul Star Chakra and Obsidian on the Earth Star Chakra. Let the Earth and Soul Star Chakras spin and speak to each other through the Gold light at the Heart Chakra.

Path of the Jackal Trinity (A Testing Pathway from Atlantis through Fears and Self Limitations);- Obsidian to the Left side of the head (below the ear), Herkimer Diamond on the Third Eye Chakra and Black Tourmaline to the Right side of the head (below the ear). Please use caution with this Trinity, it has a direct and potent effect on all levels, only do it if you know you will see the process through.

Earth Star Activation Trinity (Amazing Grounding Retaining a Connection to Spirit);- Black Obsidian, Selenite and Hematite are placed in a triangle layout at the Earth Star Chakra below the Feet. Iolite is also often placed on the Third Eye to increase vision.

Chemical Composition;- Volcanic Silica, Glass

Color Rays;- 70% Black, 30% Clear, 5% Gold and 5% Silver

Animal Totem;- Jackal

Essential Oil;- Benzoin

Opal

Emotional Magnification

The Master Crystal Deva Upalael

"Take a deep breath, allow me to enter the emotional vessel that you are. Now together, let us open you to the feelings deep within, residing in absolute truth, you will hide no more. Your fears will melt in your new awareness. I am the open active heart, embrace me, I will burn within you forever in guidance.

Like the light of a thousand suns, I will shine and magnify you, making you aware of the role of emotion in the creative avenues of manifestation and Judgment. Be aware as I enter you that I know no Limit, seeking to place you on your individual path of realization, I will magnify the emotional space. In your choice to begin our work it is nearly over, realization is the key.

Let realization of feeling blossom now into trust of self and Joy. I help all that will truthfully step upon my emotional frequency. Mine is a path of fire held in water's embrace, all are ready, but few truly awaken me and stand in my emotional fire of truth, lest they burn."

Opal in Healing

Opal is a multicolored, vibrantly iridescent stone that captures light, allowing it to look different from every angle. Opals are up to 21% water, which allows them a powerful effect on the emotional level, where they magnify feelings, allowing a chance to take responsibility and be in absolute awareness of the intentions behind them. Opal can be your best friend when you feel good and understand your emotions, or your worst enemy when you take no responsibility for the way you feel or are unaware of the intentions behind your emotional state. She quite simply magnifies whatever she finds, she knows either way, you will find mastery and balance.

Opal is a stone for those that believe they do no wrong, are inhibited and/or do not act on feelings. She teaches one to allow feelings into action, respect the emotions of others and be faithful and imaginative.

This stone can allow you to read the true intentions and feelings of others via the eyes, where it has a powerful healing effect. Opal also activates the higher spiritual and psychic abilities making them useful in everyday life. It is one of few stones that are able to assist people to embrace earth changes and is often able to deliver the reason, cause or purpose behind them.

Great beings that answer within the frequency of Opal include Lady Isis, The Lady of the Sun and the Master Sanat Kumara. Sacred deity correspondences include God Uenuku and Goddess Nuit.

Your Healing Journey Today

If Opal has come to you today, you are being asked to be truthful about the way you feel and take action. Often in life, we feel it is better for others if we are not completely truthful where our feelings are concerned. However a small untruth can quickly become the base for a far larger and more hurtful illusion. Opal's work is often done within the self and is personal, in which case you only hurt yourself, but when it includes those we love and those that respect us, the least we can do is be honest and truthful.

Feel your Heart, Discipline your Mind and Allow your Spirit, only then can your Perfection rise through the Purifying Fires of Truth.

Affirmation;- "In the light of emotional truth, I take action."

Keywords to help in reading the cards;- Emotional Magnification, Truth, Responsibility for Feelings, Independence, Action through Feeling.

Body Card Placement;- Opal can powerfully be placed on the Chin especially during the full moon. It does great work on the Heart, Throat and Earth Star Chakra.

True Self Realization Trinity (Caution; this Trinity is very aggressive in its action);- Place Elestial Quartz on the Third Eye Chakra, Opal on the Heart Chakra and Black Obsidian on the Solar Plexus Chakra. These are very aggressive stones, Jasper will often be needed to support their action.

Healing Power of the Goddess Trinity (Emotional Healing in the Goddess Space);- Silver on the Lower Left side of the chest, Opal on the Heart Chakra and Chrysocolla on the Lower Right side of the chest. Lie back and focus on Feeling at the Heart.

Chemical Composition;- Hydrous Silicon Dioxide (Colloidal Silica up to 21% Water)

Color Rays;- All in Flux

Animal Totem;- Lyre Bird

Essential Oil;- Wintergreen

Peach Calcite

Harmonize

The Master Crystal Deva Kel-el- ra-m

"Open your heart and draw the infinite spirit into its blessed peace, let the Pink and Gold Rays unite, in a wave of harmonizing Peach rain that confirms our union. My Gift for you is of the highest parts of self, facilitating action on all levels, your life has been a preparation for our union.

At your consent and now in my embrace, I will harmonize your Heart, Body and Mind. Step powerfully with me into your emotions, with the active intelligence to translate that which transpires into potent growth through real action and Healing in the purity of love's Glory."

A blinding light at harmony in the universe, permit your halo to descend from above your head, into your heart. Let it tell the story of truth, for you represent the pure sound of love in positive action. A vision of united Love, Power and Wisdom at home high upon Kailash, eyes upon the World.

Peach Calcite in Healing

This beautiful stone is most easily recognized by its angelic gentle Peach hue, which results as Peach Calcite is a blend between Gold Calcite and Pink Calcite, carrying the healing characteristics of both stones. This alone makes Peach Calcite a powerful healing tool and also gifts its simple purpose as the Crystal of

Harmonization.

Gold Calcite carries the highest mental ability of the Crown chakra connected to spirit into the body for Realization which delivers a connection to universal mind. Pink Calcite carries forth the frequency of Unconditional Love for the removal of old emotional patterns, fears, sadness and grief from the body.

The blend of these two powerful crystals as Peach Calcite, allows one to unconditionally feel the necessary emotions with the higher self present to activate growth without compromising personal power. This dissolves old emotional patterns in a direct and permanent manner and makes Peach Calcite a crystal of the new age, a cure for those that compromise their personal power in the service of others, which is a common theme.

This Crystal allows one to feel secure and embrace love on all levels, including for the self, making it powerful in the breaking of addictions. It will remove fear and grief, and can remove nightmares by providing the understanding as to why they are occurring.

Peach Calcite can be worked with to increase the clarity of communication with the Angelic realm, either visually or in an audio manner, a process that is empowered by the presence of Tanzanite and Elestial Quartz. It is a sacred stone of Lord Maitreya and the Lord Sai Baba that will powerfully open up the pathways of mutual communication.

Physically, Peach Calcite is useful in conditions of Multiple Sclerosis, Lethargy, Stress, Tinnitus (Ringing in the Ears) and Heart conditions. It is a specialist healer of bone, cartilage and connective tissues.

Peach Calcite is a powerful healer of the etheric template level of a human being and by a skilled energetic healer, can be worked with in the reprogramming of genetic material.

Your Healing Journey Today

It is easy to let life be divided into little parts for easy management, but there comes a time to clean out that which no longer serves you or contributes to the whole. Peach Calcite's presence with you today lets you know,it is time to unite all the parts of self, release the past and give thanks inward for the hard work that has resulted in your growth. Peach Calcite will shed light on those things, hidden in the separation but obvious in the United whole. All your questions at this time in life will only be solved if approached by a powerful, though unconditional, and United path. Sit now and call back all of your energies and commit to self. Peach Calcite often appears if one's balance of power and love is unsettled. Have a look at your life and make sure love and power are balanced in expression and your activities have been undertaken for the right reasons. This is a sacred stone of Lord Maitreya, the Planetary Christ, who called it into existence, he may be around you.

Affirmation;- "Power and Love Unite, I Am at Harmony, my Sound is Infinite."

Keywords to help in reading the cards;- Harmonize, Unconditional Love/ Personal Power Balance, Old Emotional Patterns, Stress, Addiction, Unite the Parts, Angelic Messengers, Threefold Flame, Service. Bones, Lord Maitreya.

Body Card Placement;- Heart, Crown and Solar Plexus Chakras.

Angelic Communication Trinity;- Place Peach Calcite on the Heart Chakra, Tanzanite on the Third Eye Chakra and Elestial Quartz on the Crown Chakra. (This is a powerful trinity of crystals and potent process, please approach it with respect and without ego.)

The Solar Plexus Trinity (Most Holistic Healing of the Solar Plexus Available);- Peach Calcite on the Lower Left side of the chest, Gold on the Solar Plexus Chakra and Sunstone on the Lower Right side of the chest.

Chemical Composition;- Calcium Carbonate

Color Rays;- 38% Gold, 38% Rose (Pink) and 24% Clear

Animal Totem;- Peacock

Essential Oil;- Geranium

Pearl

Purity

The Master Crystal Deva Mer-q-el

"Flow with me and together we will walk the path of the moon at play upon the ocean. Rest in my silver throne a while and discover the essence of Purity that I am, for it is I who has called you to my side.

Wear the Luna crest upon your brow and feel it wash you clean with the cyclic rains of forgiveness. Let my silver sheen envelop you as you stand on the shores of your emotions, now step forward into the waves of my existence and let them run their course of purification, through me you will be whole.

I am the keeper of children, call me when in need, my innocence is eternally yours. Let my loving embrace stand as Joyful Unconditional Love in action towards Emotional Freedom and Purity forever. I am by your side, embrace me."

Pearl in Healing

Typically, the Pearl is a hard round object produced within a living oyster shell. They are highly iridescent holding the beauty of the moon in their silvery shimmer. In modern times pearls are rarely natural, usually being cultivated so their shape can be manipulated. Many people do not realize a strand of true natural round matched pearls sells for $500,000-$1,000,000.

The healing nature of the Pearl is highly emotional. It captures this ability mainly via its formation process, where it begins as an irritant within the Oyster, something as simple as a grain of sand. As the Oyster attempts to heal and purify itself, its secretions create the Pearl. This process mimics our human emotional journey here on the Earth, stumbling upon irritants and lessons, then by their embrace recreating ourselves as a thing of Divine Beauty. In simplicity, the Pearl teaches us to embrace our emotions as they are the way forward to perfection. She shows us and holds within her the cyclic nature of all things, teaching that from the most trying circumstances, if we will feel, we will evolve into completion and then that completion will be tested, so we can go grow, higher and stronger, again and again.

At the heart of the Pearl's work, she is the mineral of Purity, not because she purifies the bodies, but due to her ability to place us in that space of Peace, Truth and Love through total feeling. In such a state nothing need be purified, it is perfect and evolves as such. It also helps with acceptance of 'the now' and, purifies our path with the divine flame of purpose.

Pearl is the ruling stone for the first third of a woman's life, the little girl, innocent and pure, but so wise of spirit in the universal cyclic law. It is then the responsibility of Moonstone to carry that cyclic law into physicality and anchor the Goddess within, birthing motherhood and the true state of woman in the second third of a woman's life. Lastly, it is the role of Silver to anchor the Wise Woman or Crone to teach the world the ways of the universe. Pearl, Moonstone and Silver in that order, are referred to as the Pathway to Isis Trinity and will rebirth the goddess, where she may have been lost at any stage in life or perhaps never really recognized as divine.

Pearl can increase intuition and can be worked with to learn the spiritual basis of sexuality and sacred union. This makes it a fantastic stone for men and women who view relationships as an attachment and thus lack commitment. Pearl has always been revered as a balancer of hormones, often regulating a woman's cycle, bringing it into alignment with the moon's phases and increasing fertility.

In Atlantis, Pearl was a stone of childbirth, facilitating the process, increasing maternal instincts, calming and relieving tension and stress. It was also utilized to spiritualize the emotions at the Heart Chakra, something we will need more of after 2013. Pearl is a link stone to the Whales and Dolphins, Quan Yin, Goddess Artemis, Archangel Uriel and the galactic identity Sirius.

Pearl has a remarkable healing ability with stress-related digestive disorders and any form of malignancy.

Your Healing Journey Today

Pearl has entered your life to deliver her message of feminine Peace, Balance and Trust to your current emotional state and processes, she wants you to be aware of, and believe in the cyclic nature of all things, nothing is forever, all must change, evolve and grow. Sometimes in the moment, we struggle to see the benefit in all taking place around us. It often takes time, trust and truth, facilitated through action to unmask the cycle. Be patient and trust your feelings at this time, let them create your future without fear. If you are a parent, very often the presence of Pearl is a symbol that our ways are interfering with those of our children, pushing them off their personal path. Take care in that department; let your feelings be your guide, as often they will allow things the mind will not. In the coming days take time out to see and be with the moon, breath her into your open heart, and carry her with you always, you are in transition. Pearl is also a potent contact stone for the Lady Master Quan Yin she will be with you. Pearl often appears in life to unlock the hearts of those who have gifts in the realm of healing children.

Affirmation;- "I am the purity of the Ocean, the Endless Sea of Stars and Breath of the Lotus."

Keywords to help in reading the cards;- Purity, Innocence, Feminine, The Moon, Nature's Cycles, Emotions, Fertility, Divine beauty, Pathway to Isis Trinity, Hormone Balance, Approach of Motherhood, Pregnancy and Childbirth, Healing Children, Whales and Dolphins, The Quan Yin, Sirius, The Wolf.

Body Card Placement;- Pearl is ideal for all healing where the sacred innocence is required, often allowing the truth to be seen. It will work on any of the Chakras, but is a stone of the goddess, whose energies enter the body via the tip of the chin.

The Atlantian Pathway to Isis Trinity;- See Moonstone.

Personalized Menopause and/or Hormone balance Trinity;- Select a crystal that represents your client via your wisdom or draw cards. Place this card on the Heart Chakra, place Pearl on the Third Eye Chakra and Garnet on the Solar Plexus Chakra. This process is very powerful, if done once a week over four weeks.

Chemical Composition;- Calcium Carbonate Conchiolin (Organic Substance)
Color Rays;- 32% Silver, 29% White, 13% Pink, 13% Indigo and 13% Blue
Animal Totem;- White Cockatoo
Essential Oil;- Aniseed

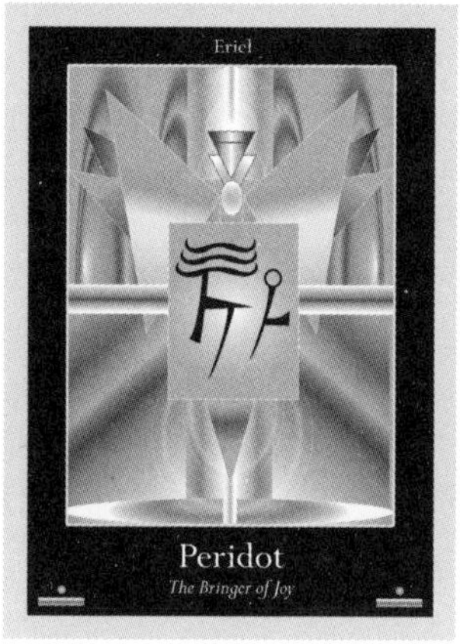

Peridot

The Bringer of Joy

The Master Crystal Deva Eriel

"Embrace me, I have waited for you patiently in the halls of Thoth where your return is written in stone, cast in time eternal. Breathe and let our shared life force flow through you. You and I are about to enter a space of Joy, so you may shine like the Solar Sun from which you originate.

Hand in hand, let us ignite you and spread the light by your realized glow. Allow your state of being to enter Joy Unconditional and others will follow. In my presence, disease is a thing of the past, there is only happiness, let it become the basis of your creative avenue.

I bless the gift that you are, the fire of Earth burns in me and will be released into joyful creation at your asking. The planetary song echoes your journey, let us return to a single light. I await your calling."

Peridot in Healing

Peridot is a greenish-yellow, transparent mineral usually found in quite small pieces due to its violent creation as a volcanic stone and the weathering processes that often follow its birth. These same processes allow the mineral some profound healing abilities not found in the same combinations or to the same degree in any other single stone, in fact Peridot really does the job of two stones in one. Within Peridot we find the Yellow fires of Creativity, Vitality and Personal Power balanced in the Cooling, Loving and Healing embrace of the Green Healing Ray. In Atlantian times it was known as the Stone of the Hidden Sun after its uplifting effect on the psyche, a reputation that even today has led it to be known as the 'Bringer of Joy'.

Generally the person that needs Peridot is lacking inspiration, feels trapped in the physical world and is tired of their own negativity, from which it feels there is no escape. This common state in our world, over time develops into Anger, Depression, Stress and even Jealousy. When Peridot shines its hidden light, the Heart and Solar Plexus Chakras ignite into communication and the mind is stimulated into action. It is from here that Peridot teaches the cycles of life allowing the release of the past by placing power and trust into the heart, thus rebirthing Self-Love and Forgiveness that can only lead to Healing and Joy.

Peridot with its gentle way of power and love is a great development stone for the sensitive. It can gently activate the psychic ability and offer life purpose, while for those who struggle to see beyond the confines of a physical world it can open the doors to other possibilities.

Peridot was the favorite stone of Cleopatra and is still the sacred contact stone for her divine energy and wisdom. It is one of the Stones mentioned in the bible as part of the great Breastplate (an Atlantian channeling tool) and is often referred to in the scriptures under the name, 'Pitdah'. Peridot is a key stone for one of the most ancient initiations of the sacred order of the Essenes and is mentioned in their library, The Dead Sea Scrolls. It was also utilized by an ancient order of the Druids in the creation of the Green Rose of Avalon. This is a sacred stone of Egyptian Goddess Maat, The Lady Nada, Paul the Venetian Master and the Ascended Master Sananda.

Peridot is a balancing stone of the Endocrine and Digestive systems. It is one of few stones that are a healing tonic for the entire body and it is useful in childbirth, able to stimulate contractions and increase the dilation rate of the birth canal.

Your Healing Journey Today

The answer to the question that is at play in your life right now, is a resounding YES. Few minerals on the Earth are as positive a sign as Peridot, she has entered your life to shine her empowering Optimism and Love upon whatever shadows have crept into your heart and areas of self belief. The arrival of Peridot in life usually signals a healing and rebirth of sorts. A part of self is to be replaced by a greater, more purposeful avenue where personal power is allowed to shine through the heart rather than stand alone. This is a great time for you to forgive, forget and let go of the past. Try to not look over your shoulder for those cycles of life have closed in Peridot's embrace to give rise to a brighter way of life containing all that you would term as joyful, a life you truly deserve, all you need do now is accept it.

Write a list of all the things that make you happy and spend some time knowing you deserve them, only when we feel something can it enter our life, thinking we deserve something means nothing to the feeling heart that creates your happiness.

Affirmations;- "I Embrace Personal Power and Love as One."
"I Burn the Green Fire of Joy in my Heart."

Keywords to help in reading the cards;- The Bringer of Joy, Personal Power, Love, Heart and Solar Plexus Chakras, Creativity, Healing, Peace, Depression, Anger, Jealousy, Skepticism, Volcano, Explosive Characteristics, Temper, The Essenes, Cleopatra, Avalon.

Body Card Placement;- Solar Plexus and Heart Chakras.

Joy and Happiness Trinity (Creates a Space around one for some down time);- Peridot on the Solar Plexus Chakra, Amber on the Heart Chakra and Angelite on the Throat Chakra. This is a great bath Combination that a Liquid Crystal practitioner can make up for you.

Aggression, Anger and Power Healing Trinity;- Peach Calcite on the Solar Plexus Chakra, Peridot on the Heart Chakra and Blue Lace Agate on the Throat Chakra. Simply sit the cards on the body for as long as you feel necessary (10 minutes is fine but longer is better). This is a powerful combination of crystals, make sure you understand and/or your patient understands all three stones and the way they work, often there is a 3-7 day delay before the healing process really begins. As with all trinities in this book, you may need to see a Liquid Crystal Practitioner to get real support and to obtain the Crystals as an Oral Dosage, to get the most out of this Trinity in Healing.

Chemical Composition;- Magnesium Iron Silicate (Trace of Nickel)
Color Rays;- 43% Yellow, 43% Green, 7% Blue and 7% Clear
Animal Totem;- Honey Eater Bird
Essential Oil;- Mandarin

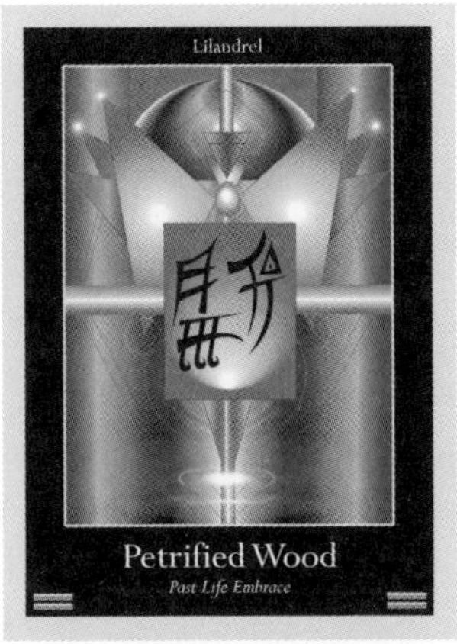

Petrified Wood

Past Life Embrace

The Master Crystal Deva Lilandrel

"Take a calm breath child of light, let your eyes gaze upon the world not out, but inward. All that you are on this day, you owe to your past; your experiences, paths and choices equate to the Now. Take my hand, it is the future we will create on this day, for the betterment of all.

Let my voice gently touch you now, for long ago, as witness, I stood high on the hill, impenetrable to the stresses. Within me I hold the wisdoms and keys to the doorways of times past, they flow in my structure as Stars float in the night sky. Stand in my hollowed body and let my branches be your arms stretched outward to your Goals, my roots will support you in loving guidance, so it will Be.

I am with you now, you live in me as I in you. Accept future mastery through ownership of the Key to Now. Let us go within and see the light of you, let it explode in a wave of creation that the world will follow to their benefit."

Petrified Wood in Healing

Petrified Wood is literally wood turned to stone. It has all the colours of wood, just as you would see in a living tree, but in the process it undergoes, the addition of other minerals allow it to also become Reds, Yellows, Pinks, Greens and Blues. It is a type of fossil, where all the organic materials have been replaced with minerals, most often quartz while retaining the original structure of the wood.

Petrified Wood is quite simply, a natural Hall of Records, which gives rise to many of its properties that are useful in healing, including its position as the Crystal of Past Life Embrace. Where the discovery of past lives is concerned and the exploration of them, there is no equal to Petrified Wood's mastery.

The energy of this stone is deeply strengthening, grounding and stabilizing, which allows it to remove stress, worry and anxiety, by enabling one to discern the important things in life from those that are beyond control. In the presence of Petrified Wood, life is simplified, one becomes optimistic of their abilities and able to find the lessons linked to events, so they need not be repeated which is very important in the healing of illness. Petrified Wood can break down the confines of Earth time and space, allowing a sense of freedom and stimulating powerful spiritual growth. This Crystal is an important part of the Lord of Time Crystal Trinity. (See Clear Calcite) It is a sacred stone of Ascended Masters Serapis Bey and El Morya, while deity correspondences include Chronos, Dionysus and Neheh.

At the physical level, we use Petrified Wood for Incontinence, Paralysis and any conditions of hardening such as arteries, skin and bones. It is also useful in Hearing Loss, Arthritis and Rheumatism.

Your Healing Journey Today

The presence of Petrified Wood for you today, means there is information coming to you from past lifetimes. Pay close attention to your dreams, and to any messages that you are receiving. A simple way to collect this information is to sit with a pen and paper in the presence of this card, place the pen on paper and simply write. Have the intention of answering any questions, relative to your past lifetimes or you may even wish to write the questions out prior to beginning. The secret with automatic writing, as it is called, is to not read what you have written until you have finished. In Petrified Wood's presence, it is also good to take time to discover the important things in life, discerning them from the things that are out of your control. Such realization simplifies life, reduces stress and allows progress.

Affirmation;- "I embrace the Now."

Keywords to help in reading the cards;- Past Life Embrace, Lessons behind Illness, Stress, Worry, Choice to Excel, Stabilization, Grounding, Vitality, Spiritual and Business Success, American Indians, Shamanic Practice.

Body Card Placement;- This card can go directly on to a problem area to help one understand its purpose. In past life work, it is best placed on the Solar Plexus Chakra.

Past Lives Trinities;- Petrified Wood as the stone of Past Life Embrace, can be worked with to enter lifetimes served in selected areas of the world and beyond. This is usually done in meditation for spiritual growth and realization, I recommend doing it at night as some information is only available in the dream state. Simply place Selenite on the Crown Chakra, Petrified Wood on the Heart Chakra and the sacred stone of your chosen area on the Third Eye. (See below table for some Examples.) Happy Journeys and fly well.

Chemical Composition;- Silicon Dioxide

Color Rays;- 20% Black, 26% White, 40% Yellow and 14% Red

Animal Totem;- Cicada

Essential Oil;- Coriander

Clear Quartz	African
Ruby	South America and Atlantian
Lapis Lazuli	Egyptian
Sapphire	Greek and Lemurian
Emerald	The Essenes and Middle Eastern
Silver	American Indian and Tibetan
Gold	Asian, Incan and Mayan
Hematite	Australia
Aventurine	New Zealand
Moldavite	Local Universe

Pink Tourmaline (Rubellite)

Gift of Love

The Master Crystal Deva Rubellel

"I enter your world humble and in joy, like a butterfly of light my wings will echo love's infinite embrace. I wish to live in your heart and light your steps in the sacred dance of life that you represent.

Let the sun rise in your heart, feel the warmth of its infinite love activate and overflow. Let the rays of your empowered love rain outward to the waiting world. Share all that you are through realization that you and the source of unconditional love, are one.

With pure activation, by your hand, let us send the message of safety in love and the world will follow. Within your embrace of love's completion, I send now, a rain of unifying pink light to fall upon humanity. Unite now in the light of love's sacred embrace."

Pink Tourmaline in Healing

Pink Tourmaline, similar to its more common varieties, Green and Black Tourmaline, is a very powerful mineral at moving energy. It can be remarkably clear, containing more of the Clear than the Pink color ray and like all Tourmalines, has long striations that run down its body.

Pink Tourmaline is the third crystal in the Heart Chakra Trinity, following Rose Quartz, the stone of forgiveness and Kunzite, stone of heart activation, its purpose is summed up in the words, 'Gift of Love'. Once the heart has been healed, activated and opened, Pink Tourmaline helps one to become comfortable with sharing love with the world again. It infuses trust and confidence in the power of love, which in turn allows expression of emotions and the healing of past experiences with forgiveness, this then results in the opening of one to receive love again in life.

Over time in Pink Tourmaline's embrace, one can realize the unlimited nature of love that resides in us and learn to share that realization by giving love as a constant gift to all that cross our path. Pink Tourmaline does its work by powerfully linking the Crown and Heart Chakras, which allows the highest lessons relating to the Heart to be taught directly from our spirit in absolute truth.

This is a sacred contact stone to the energies of Paramahansa Yogananda, Archangel Mary, Master Sananda (Jesus), Goddess Aphrodite and the Lady Isis.

Pink Tourmaline can be of use at the physical level where there is Endocrine Imbalance, Infertility or poor communication between body systems. It is also useful in liquid form as a skin tonic.

Your Healing Journey Today

The presence of Pink Tourmaline today in your cards is a wonderful flash of love, where Pink Tourmaline goes, love quickly follows. As a messenger of love, this crystal reminds us that love is just an emotion until it is given and received freely, at which point, it becomes unconditional and the most powerful force in the universe. In life we can act with love, dress as love, understand love and feel love, but to truly know love, one must unconditionally give love away. With Pink Tourmaline by your side, you can be trustful and confident in the laws of love, forgive your past and go forward with an open heart. Keep your eyes open in the coming days for Butterflies, they will come to remind you to keep your heart open and be the Gift of Love in the world. This is a Sacred Stone of Mother Mary.

Affirmation;- "I Give Love, I am Love."

Keywords to help in reading the cards;- Gift of Love, Unconditional Love, Heart, Past Attachments, Giving, Endocrine System Balance, Fertility.

Body Card Placement;- This is a Heart Chakra stone.

The Heart Trinity (The Most Potent healing Sequence of the Heart from Atlantis);- Kunzite is placed on the Upper Left side of the chest, Rose Quartz is placed on the Heart Chakra and Pink Tourmaline is placed on the Upper Right side of the chest. The crystals can also be placed individually, one at a time, directly on the Heart.

Letting Go of Attachments Trinity;- Hold Green Calcite in the Left hand, Pink Tourmaline in the Right hand and Place Zircon on the Heart Chakra.

Chemical Composition;- Sodium Lithium Aluminum Boro-silicate Hydroxide

Color Rays;- 57% Clear, 30% Pink and 13% Gold

Animal Totem;- Butterfly

Essential Oil;- Rock Rose (Cistus)

Pyrite

Spark of Life

The Master Crystal Deva Py-ra-el

"You say your world is fast paced, tiresome and all consuming of the life force. Those that are under this spell have forgotten their heritage of perfection and boundless energy. I have come to carry you upon my shoulders and anchor deep, the golden solar breath from the center of your sun, the same breath that gave you the spark of life at your birth into this world. Let Ra rise again in your heart.

Draw the solar breath by choice now, and call the Solar Logi, the master of light, to your heart. I will translate his letters of fire and embed them deep. It is through this that my joyous vitality will lift and anchor life into every corner of your existence.

At our meeting, let it be known in the sacred halls of Ra, that perfection reigns, above all. Let the shadows and imperfections that can only be manifest by a mind unrealized run and hide. I wish to join you now, as you spread your wings, lifting into the embrace of the fire bound seed that you are, ever vibrant and living. All will bow at your feet seeking your united flame, call me as you need, swift in Hanumans blessing, I will come, a ray of fire, the Truth of Light."

Pyrite in Healing

Pyrite is a brassy, yellow-gold mineral that demonstrates a physical mastery of geometry in the shapes of its crystals and their arrangements. Pyrite can come directly out of the ground as anything from the perfected masculine Cube, to the perfect Dodecahedron of Spirit or the perfected feminine Sphere. Due to this ability Pyrite is known in the mineral kingdom as The Master of Geometric Form. The ability to do this individualizes Pyrite in the mineral kingdom and allows this Deva to work on levels that are not accessible to many other minerals. At the heart of this is one of Pyrite's greatest gifts, it is able to activate and enter the Soul Star Chakra located six inches above the Head. The Soul Star is the home of the Soul Consciousness or Higher Self, it acts as a translation mechanism between you and spirit and is the true 'Spark of Life', when it leaves we die. Pyrite's good friend is Hematite, The Master of the Color Rays in Matter. Hematite activates the Earth Star below the feet, the two working together can polarize the entire chakra system making them a powerful manifestation tool and crucial to finding Spiritual balance on the pathway of Ascension.

Pyrite is quite a masculine stone in its action which is quite mental and outwards in its approach; it can unite the minds and deliver discipline. Pyrite will increase and empower memory, focus and the total life force of a person, anchoring the Sun's energy, making one shine with happiness and drive for health on all levels. Pyrite's mental mastery is such that it allows the truth to be seen and recognized, not only in self but in others and the world in general. The polished mind acts as an impenetrable shield for any darkness or negativity, and even assists with physically dangerous situations, occupations and illness, making one feel secure and confident in their own light. Pyrite is thus the perfect remedy for the emotions and common conditions of Life force usually found at the Solar Plexus Chakra, such as Depression, Anxiety, Tiredness, Lowered Immunity and Vitality.

Spiritually, Pyrite is a powerful Crystal to work with in any kind of channeling, healing or self communication work, usually bringing understanding to all that is experienced directly from the Soul Star. It is an ancient teacher of the Universal Truths and Language of Light (Sacred Geometry) holding the secrets of the universe within itself for those that are ready. Pyrite is a Sacred Stone of Ascended Master Melchizedek, Helios and Vesta, our Solar Logos, and Thoth of Egypt.

Physically, Pyrite is a powerful friend in manifestation work, it is a stone of the Throat and Lung area, will reduce fevers and balance the digestive system. It can also aid DNA/RNA repair and treat Gout.

Your Healing Journey Today

If Pyrite has come to you today, you are headed into the warm tropical waters of Self Realization. Mastery, Purification and Healing of the Mental and Personal Power levels of self are occurring. This beautiful energy that surrounds you on this day paves a Fearless road of Joy and Happiness; the Sun will rise in your heart offering the vitality that you have requested to change your life. Now all you must do is use it. Stand in truthful focus and choose your path wisely, the voice of your Soul has never been so present, breathe it to your Heart and take action. In Pyrite's embrace, the time is right to do whatever it is you have put off and hidden in the back of your mind. Play in the shadows of self and release them into the world with Love Power and Wisdom.

Listen not to the sounds of the world around you, for they are not yours, hear the inner single sound that you truly are and the Peace, Love and Oneness of the Universe will be born from your Confident Spark. Remember the only thing to Fear in the universe is your own mind out of control, it creates your perception and eventually your entire world, your reality. Be Free Now, Choose Life.

Affirmation;- "I am the Divine I am."

Keywords to help in reading the cards;- Spark of Life, Vitality, Energy Levels, Mental Ability, Focus, Easily Manipulated, Mental Discipline, Confidence, Solar Plexus, Sacred Geometry, Soul Star, Voice of One's Soul, Depression, Anxiety and/or Panic Attacks.

Body Card Placement;- Mainly Solar Plexus, Heart and Crown Chakras, but Pyrite is special at the Soul Star, six inches above the head.

Integration of the Three Fold Flame Trinity (Calls, Activates and Holds the Flames in Balance);- 1) Tanzanite on the Solar Plexus Chakra, 2) Larimar on the Heart Chakra and 3)Pyrite on the Soul Star above the head.

Brain Hemispheres Balancing Trinity (Good for Starchildren);- 1)Lepidolite to the Left side of the Head (ear height), 2) Pyrite on the Soul Star Chakra above the head (or on Third Eye, please use your Intuition), 3) Charoite to the Right side of the head (ear height). This is a good ongoing treatment and will get more profound results if practised each day over a 21 day period.

The Mental Trinity (Mastering the Mental Body, The Third Initiation);- Fluorite to the Left side of the Head (below the ear), Clear Calcite on the Third Eye Chakra and Pyrite to the Right side of the head (below the ear).

Chemical Composition;- Iron Disulfide
Color Rays;- 60% Gold, 12% White, 11% Red, 11% Yellow and 6% Orange
Animal Totem;- Monkey
Essential Oil;- Basil

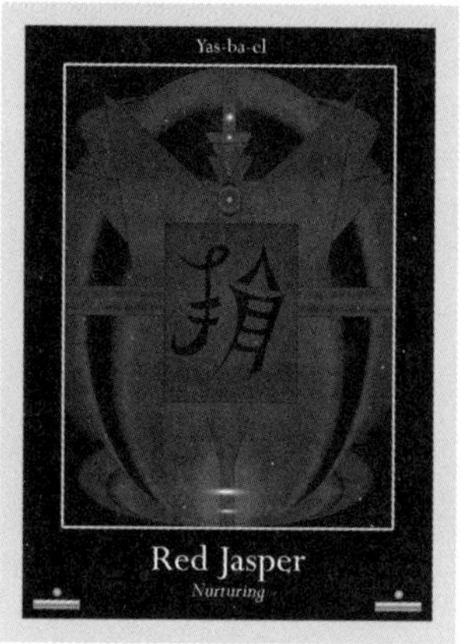

Red Jasper

Nurturing

The Master Crystal Deva Yas-ba-el

"I am the voice of Earth's sacred embrace, accept my gift. Gently feel me move through you, my subtle energies and gentle warmth will slow your world to a new pace in alignment with your total being. Through me you will come to see, know and honor your needs as part of God's creation, let us begin.

Allow me to sustain you, raising your life force so you may see with new eyes and gaze out into your creation, seeing beauty all around you. Just as mother and child, I will lift you and Nurture your growth towards the light, infusing you with the joy of living and the glory of your power, as creator in all you do.

Self nurtured child in the arms of the Earth, walk now the journey of self embrace and the world will follow in the gentle glow of your unconditional heart, back to the joy of oneness. I have warmed your path with the gentle winds of confidence, let them guide you home."

Jasper in Healing

Red Jasper is an opaque rust red stone that is found in many countries of the world. As with most minerals that are plentiful, and reasonably priced, this is one which humanity is in dire need of due to the pressures of modern lifestyle.

Most of the properties of Red Jasper were gifted back to us from the American Indians. Within their teaching, Jasper is the blood of the Earth, a gift from her, which is able to take you deep within her stabilizing, gentle and warm body and surround you in her nurturing embrace. Within that embrace, all change is gradual and flowing, life rolls along at a rate that is suited to the self with as little turbulence as possible. These characteristics make Red Jasper the most Nurturing mineral on Earth. She is a gentle, grounding and stabilizing stone that is extremely valuable in healing and life where change occurs too fast, a situation also known as the healing crisis. With Red Jasper there is always time in life, and original forward movement is assured.

Red Jasper facilitates the grounding and remembering of dreams by anchoring the Astral body to the physical and can also be protective in those activities. Usually, the dreams of Red Jasper facilitate the releasing of the past and help manifest the path of the future. Red Jasper is a sacred stone to Ascended Master El Morya and the Archangel Michael, it is also a contact stone for Pan.

At the physical level, the sustaining energies of Red Jasper are useful in the recovery process of any illness or after hospitalization when energy levels are low. It is better in conditions of deterioration rather than those of malfunction, especially within the Circulatory and Digestive systems.

Your Healing Journey Today

If Red Jasper has come to you today, it is time to put yourself first and nurture the self. Take time out and do something special for yourself. Red Jasper only appears when life is moving too fast and needs to be slowed to a pace that is more suited to you as a person. Allowing life to move at a pace that is suited to self is actually quite easy, the hardest step is the first. This is because those that do not nurture the self as often as they should, often excessively nurture others. The mind has to be re-taught that loving the self is the first step to truly loving the rest of the world. Stop putting it off, book yourself in for that massage, facial or simple time out. Put it in your diary and do it consistently, once is not enough, that's just that head of yours again, what is your Heart saying?

Affirmation;- "I Love Myself, Nurtured I am of Service."

Keywords to help in reading the cards;- Nurturing, Self-Love, Stabilizing, Sustaining, Grounding, Recovery, New Directions, Time, Family, Desire for Children, El Morya, Archangel Michael, Pan.

Body Card Placement;- Red Jasper is best at the Base Chakra, it has a powerful protective side, which is able to absorb negativity even when simply placed in a room, place the Jasper card under a white candle and light it to achieve this.

Gentlest Healing Ever Trinity;- Place Blue Lace Agate on the Throat Chakra, Red Jasper on the Heart Chakra and Howlite on the Crown Chakra. This is a divinely gentle healing Energy that gets great results, if you see a Liquid Crystal Practitioner, have them make this up as a Crystal Bath for you.

Chemical Composition;- Silicon Dioxide

Color Rays;- 72% Red, 14% Pink, 11% White and 3% Black

Animal Totem;- Buffalo

Essential Oil;- Cedarwood (USA)

Rhodochrosite

Self-Love

The Master Crystal Deva Rho-clor-el

"Embrace me, step into the Rose Ray of unconditional light. Let your love for self light the world, freeing those that would seek outward. Feel the breath of self forgiveness on the back of your neck and let it warm the coldest parts of you into the eternal lights of B'ani-or-a. Gaze with me across the Lands into the sacred halls of Shamballa.

Walking the tops of the White Lands, we will enter a place where all interaction is united in completion through creative love. Together let us fill the lower parts of self through the heart, let it dictate your direction. Let the touch of Isis and Light of Ra unite within, so you may step forward in its unlimited Joy without fear and create the glory of you, eternally lit in all you do.

I am with you Great One, you honor me with your presence. Together, we have built a Temple in your heart where we can grow the seeds of universal light into the ever serving Path of Unconditional Love. Let it be expressed now in perfected action, for the betterment of all and sit confidently in the sacred throne that is the physical body realized. Now I am Love."

Rhodochrosite in Healing

The most commonly found Rhodochrosite is a beautiful Peach-Pink mineral that has white bands running through it. In some outstanding specimens, the white bands form concentric circles and in highly crystallized states it can appear a deep, clear, red color.

The colored rays present in this stone, powerfully link the Crown, Heart and Sacral chakras together in sacred communication, delivering many of this stone's most important properties, including its simple purpose as the Stone of Self-Love. Rhodochrosite opens the heart under the guidance of the spirit and carries their united energies down to the Sacral. This manifests new love and belief in self, opening deep, profound healing that is empowered through forgiveness. This potent combination will release deep pain and hurt often related to sexuality and abuse.

When one is actively harboring avoidance and denial about their surrounds in life Rhodochrosite empowers them to face life, make decisions and accept the changes that result directly through the Heart.

This stone can be worked with in meditations to find a soul's purpose and aid in the locating of other members of one's soul family, usually delivering information in the Dream state, especially when empowered with Jade. Rhodochrosite is a contact stone for the Archangel Mary and will facilitate communication with any female Ascended Masters, including the Lady of the Fountain.

At a more physical level, Rhodochrosite is useful for Internal Infections, Cancers, Thyroid Imbalance, Irritable Bowel Syndrome, Digestive Imbalance, Uncontrolled Visions and Troubled Sleep, such as Nightmares.

Your Healing Journey Today

In the presence of Rhodochrosite on this day, you are being asked to take a step into Self-Love, take some time out and do the things that you love individually, doing these things allows us to retain the passion we need to live life to its full. In the coming days you will often be learning the true lessons of compassion and forgiveness, where you will remember that your ability to recognize traits in others simply means that once, or possibly still, they lived in you. On this important journey into the heart, have faith in yourself and trust in the world, let go of attachments and remember beyond all things, each of us chooses and creates our path, Self-Love is our most personal and important responsibility.

Affirmation;- "I love myself."

Keywords to help in reading the cards;- Self-Love, Unconditional Love, Sexual Abuse, Crown, Heart and Sacral Chakras, Compassion, Self Identification, Deep Pain and Hurt of the Heart, Family, Relationships, Avoidance and Denial, Digestive System, Archangel Mary, Lady of the Fountain, Lord Sananda.

Body Card Placement;- Mainly on the Crown, Heart and Sacral Chakras.

Male and Female Balance Trinity (Balances self on all levels with Self-Love as the tool);- Stack the Rhodochrosite, Boji Stone and Peach Calcite cards in that order, top to bottom on the Heart Chakra.

Soul Purpose Trinity;- Place Rhodochrosite between Pyrite and Hematite in a Triangle at the back of the Third Eye Chakra, this will only work when you are ready.

Discover Soul Family Members Trinity;- Information is received in the dream state. Place Rhodochrosite with Jade and Selenite in a gold envelope under your pillow.

Chemical Composition;- Magnesium Carbonate

Color Rays;- 57% Pink, 28% Orange, 10% White and 5% Clear

Animal Totem;- Cat

Essential Oil;- Ylang-Ylang

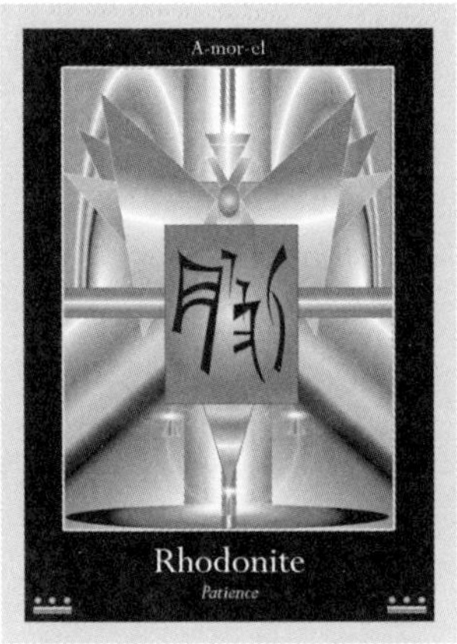

Rhodonite

Patience

The Master Crystal Deva A-mor-el

"Join me and the gentle breeze of Love that I am will bless you on all levels, through me even the most physical hold the Pink ray. Together, let us ground and anchor unconditional love into one and all, for in this moment, with you as my conductor, our love will touch all that cross our path.

In my embrace, conduct my overflowing love, feel the voice of grounded personal Power raise the endless waters of peace and flow gently upon their back through life. Let your acceptance of change play a symphony of Trust and the world will hear your song.

Taking a breath now, be patient, great being of light, for with love there is no beginning nor end, there simply is no need, there is only the Now and it will extend into your every dream and vision of Light, a spinning star of radiant completion."

Rhodonite in Healing

Rhodonite is a light pink mineral with black and/or white clouds or veins running through its body. Usually it is opaque, though in rare crystalline specimens, it can present as quite red and transparent. Of all the crystals available in the heart frequency, Rhodonite has the greatest grounding ability of the pink ray energy. It is from this that it gets its reputation as the stone of Patience. Rhodonite's grounding of love into the physical world affects the most mundane and boring of life's activities, offering discernment, reason and understanding. Life with Rhodonite by your side takes on new meaning as impatience, negativity and fears of change are melted with love into patient acceptance via a new found responsibility for the creation of our physical lives.

This is a stone of the modern world, where too often, love is seen to be the surrender of power to keep the peace. In such cases, it teaches the understanding that balanced ownership of personal Power allows love and peace to coexist. The message that Rhodonite holds is one of the most spiritual, often opening healing paths and gifts. It is very much a stone of service, igniting the desire to help others find love in themselves, which spills into their world and work, so healing and understanding results.

In Atlantian Times, Rhodonite was also known as 'Mantra Stone', relating to her potent ability to allow love and truth to be heard and infused into the voice and music, so it could travel upon its healing path within. It was recognized that if one could not hear the words in music, they were not allowing healing to result on some level. The same still applies today and Rhodonite is regarded, even at the physical, as a great healing stone of all Ear problems.

At a more physical level, of all of Rhodonite's healing gifts, one of the most important roles she plays is as a principal stone in the treatment of Multiple Sclerosis, where she can often deliver true healing and forward movement. Rhodonite has a gentle, calm and relaxing effect on the emotional body, which, when coupled with its physical nature concerning love, makes it a powerful healer of panic attacks, grief and useful in any emergency situations. She can also be of use with Inflammation of the joints, Infertility and Scaring.

Your Healing Journey Today

If Rhodonite has come to you today, she offers you the simple word Patience. She is a gentle reminder that Patience is a measure of personal power and self-love sent forth into action. If one places no love into the world and its events, the world gives no love back and life becomes painful until we reject it. Impatience is a form of rejection either of the world or of the self, remember that all is valid and has purpose or else it would not be in existence and if it is in your space or any level of your reality, you play a role in its creation. Rhodonite lets you know that it is important to love all in your world, only then can we learn from it and be free through unity.

It is very possible, with the arrival of Rhodonite, that you are experiencing a little confusion in life regarding direction. Her message is simple, Love all, do all to your best ability and never have fear, for it is simply a lack of understanding.

Replace fear with love and via patience, peaceful change and growth will result. Love is about to enter your life in a physical way, give it space and let it dictate your future.

Affirmation;- "Love is my Guide, it Patiently lives in my actions."

Keywords to help in reading the cards;- Patience, Physical love, Boredom, The Pink Ray, Ownership of Personal Power, Responsibility for Physicality, Music, The Secrets in the Music, Acceptance of Change, Problems around Predictability, Ear Problems, Panic Attacks, Multiple Sclerosis, Stress.

Body Card Placement;- Principally Rhodonite works on the Base and Heart Chakras.

Grounded Heart Activation Trinity;- Rhodonite on the Right shoulder, Lepidolite on the Heart Chakra and Morganite on the Left shoulder.

Mantra Trinity (Explore the hidden effects and gifts of Sound and Music);- Sapphire to the Right side of the head and Morganite to the Left side of the head, both in line with the ears. Then place Rhodonite on the Thymus Gland (between the Heart and Throat Chakras) This technique is facilitated if Paul the Venetian Master (Ascended Master of the Third Ray) is asked to facilitate the process. The Mantra Trinity above was also utilized in Atlantis to hear the sound of the planets moving and spinning through space, something called The Music of the Spheres.

Multiple Sclerosis Trinity (Supports, Protects and Facilitates movement in the direction of Health);- Rhodonite is placed on the Heart Chakra, Turquoise on the Throat Chakra and Selenite on the Solar Plexus Chakra.

Music of the Spheres Trinity (The sound the planets make in the Universe);- Place Rhodonite between Turquoise and Selenite in a Triangle at the back of the Third Eye Chakra. Lie on your back outside looking into the Sky, see and feel the Earth spin and Pulse, close your eyes when they get heavy and listen.

Chemical Composition;- Manganese Iron Magnesium Calcium Silicate

Color Rays;- 62% Pink, 21% Black, 13% White, 2% Orange, 2% Red

Animal Totem;- Frog

Essential Oil;- Marjoram (Sweet)

Rose Quartz

Forgiveness

The Master Crystal Deva Ka-kini-el

"Slow now, little ones' let my soft glow find you and open your heart to self. Feel my loving ray melt the world from you. I evolve by your calling and as you rise in the name of the eternal flames of Isis I am by your side.

With me you will only rejoice in life, but first let us sit and breathe forgiveness to self and others. Call to balance the three flames in your heart and be warmed by their joyful glow. Take time now to recognize the endless source of love that exists in you, for through this, all can be healed and love will be your creative avenue.

Let the falling tears of the world be captured and transmuted in the chalice of forgiveness that is your heart. Joy, freedom and peace are within and all around you and never have they left your side. Let us empower their rise, as they are the basis of a Life forgotten, a way that is my gift to you, Fly now, be free."

Rose Quartz in Healing

For many people this is the first crystal they ever receive or purchase for themselves, thus it rarely needs an introduction. Rose Quartz is a pink variety of the Quartz family that can display perfect clarity and although rare and expensive, may form beautiful terminated crystals. Its abundance in the world shows its importance with humanity and our need for its powerful healing qualities.

It surprises many people that energetically, Rose Quartz holds a blue frequency rather than the pink that appears to the physical eye. The action of the stone however, shows us the presence of the blue ray for it is the stone of Forgiveness, a journey that can not be taken without truthful expression, the heart and throat united as one. Forgiveness is a journey of truth, grace and higher peace within self which spills out in the world around us through love filled right action, but it all starts with self-love. Over time, Rose Quartz can lead one to understand the infinite nature of the open heart and that all can be healed.

Rose Quartz has the ability to dissolve anger, guilt, jealousy, stress and tension, and it is a specialist at healing male or father figure issues that may be stored deep in the darkened corners of self. Rose Quartz can put the Joy back into life by slowing it down to a pace that is manageable so love can be recognized and experienced. This helps one to find the things that really are necessary and fosters an embrace of the arts and creative avenues of physicality that contain Love.

At the spiritual level, Rose Quartz may be used to balance the love aspect of the Threefold Flame, it partners Kunzite and Pink Tourmaline in the ancient Atlantian Heart Chakra Trinity, within which they Activate, Open, Heal and lift the heart to a new higher frequency, making change permanent and healing all that cross their path. Rose Quartz is a sacred stone for the Divine Archangel Mary who utilizes its pink and/or blue frequency to provide visions for humanity. When combined with Gold, it is a contact stone for Lord Maitreya the planetary Christ.

Physically, Rose Quartz purifies and rejuvenates the body; it is useful to instill proper heart function and is a leading stone for male infertility. It may also be useful with Lung conditions, Leukemia, Parkinson's and Alzheimer's disease.

Your Healing Journey Today

On this day, as Rose Quartz enters your life, you are to be showered in love, your heart is being expanded to the unconditional giving state so healing may occur for self, and for all of those that are close to you. Embrace yourself in the flame of forgiveness and your endless light will illuminate the world.

Living in a physical world, we are challenged every day with fear, pain, suffering, anger and resentment, to name a few, they are all around us, but cannot penetrate the shell of the infinite Love we represent unless we allow them entry. Over time, all of us are affected by a world seeking only to be forgiven and loved, thus we must periodically Cleanse, Heal and Purify ourselves. Today is that day for you, forgive yourself and your world, ignite the flame of love within self and have faith that the world around you will bathe in its light. Tell everyone you know that you love them, send letters, hold hands, give hugs, but most importantly remember none of it, instead let it expand inwards and pave your personal path to an unconditional state that the world can benefit from permanently. Everyone and Everything wants love, be the Voice and Heart that gives it and you will never be without it.

Affirmation;- "In Love's Infinite Fires I forgive and I am Whole."

Keywords to help in reading the cards;- Forgiveness, Self-Love, Anger and Stress, Heart and Throat Chakra Communication, Issues with One's Father, Healing, Purification and Cleansing, Male Infertility, Divine Mother Energy.

Body Card Placement;- Throat and Heart Chakras. Rose Quartz can powerfully open telepathic communication in some people when placed upon the Third Eye Chakra.

The Rose Quartz Fountain of Forgiveness;- Light two pink candles and burn some Palmarosa essential oil. Take three drops of Rose Quartz Liquid Crystal if you have it, then hold the Rose Quartz Card in your receiving hand (Left if you are Right handed) and place your other hand on your heart. Close your eyes, breathe slowly and call Ka-Kini-el, the master Deva of the stone. See yourself standing on a plate of Rose Quartz and allow rose colored light, the Fountain of Forgiveness, to run up the body and out through the Crown Chakra. Listen, Feel and know that you have attained total forgiveness. Stay as long as you are comfortable then open your eyes to end.

Arcturian Contact through the Heart Trinity;- Place Rose Quartz on the Throat Chakra, Sodalite on the Third Eye and Dioptase on the Heart Chakra. This is best performed in the first 20 Minutes of the 14th Magical Hour of the day. (Count from first light on the day of practice.)

Speak the Heart Trinity (Emotional Verbal Expression Helper);- Place Lapis Lazuli on the Lower Left side of the chest, Rose Quartz on the Throat Chakra and Turquoise on the Lower Right side of the chest.

Chemical Composition;- Silicon Dioxide (Trace Manganese)
Color Rays;- 41% Pink, 23% Blue, 18% White and 18% Clear
Animal Totem;- Dog
Essential Oil;- Palmarosa

Ruby

Spiritual Warrior

The Master Crystal Deva Ru-Bast-el

"Join me, at home in the King of Beasts, take vision, through the Tiger's Eye. Be that which you were endowed at birth, a warrior of light, infinite and everlasting. Feel your every breath a fire of feminine creation. You, in my embrace, help guard the door to the Lady of Flame, the living light of the Eye of Ra, Praise be to Bast.

Be free with me and open your heart to the world. Breathe my warm breath up your body from the depths of Earth. Feel my emotional fire live within you.

Fear not the darkness of the world, nor carry it upon your shoulders lest it be yours. Take rest that all belongs to its creator, has purpose and is a shade of love often tainted by the undisciplined will. Light we have, the flame of courage and spiritual power.

Your journey with me is one of motivation and realization. Together we will cut the path to the absolute self, removing and indicating that which is in the way of its expression. Take pride as I walk by your side and in your footprints, you are whole and empowered by that which you are. Call me, with peace, I wait, ever vigilant."

Ruby in Healing

Ruby is one of our Master healing crystals on the planet Earth. Recognized as one of the leading energetic principles of the Atlantian time, she is a member of the Council of Seven, one of the sacred crystals of Egypt and a stone that is found in the ancient breastplate. Of all the things that Ruby is used for, her ability as a record keeper and a doorway to the Akashic records is perhaps her most profound. Many of the healing systems and methods that are currently popular have been birthed back onto the Earth via Ruby.

A powerful stone of Courage, Ruby is one of the most active and dynamic stones available. More expensive pieces are bright Red and highly transparent in color, though Ruby of spiritual significance is usually pinker and even purple. This occurs when the stone is carrying a large amount of information or records, which may also be indicated by one or many triangles on the Crystal.

The effects of Ruby on a human being are best summed up in its simple purpose, 'The Spiritual Warrior'. She stimulates a passion for living, experiencing and creating from a positive and courageous state in the mind and the emotions. Often where one has become their own enemy, disempowering and allowing themselves to fall into the depths of depression and negativity, Ruby is the stone to go to the rescue, a job she does in a powerful and highly emotional way. By amplifying your emotions, she lets you know you don't like how you Feel, then empowers the mind and lifts the vital force so you can create a better life.

A highly spiritual stone, Ruby represents the path of true feeling, the language of love, and the universal oneness. Ruby can direct the will of spirit directly into powerful action, promoting passion and change at all levels in life and self under total guidance. She is a powerful Kundalini stone, activating the Serpent and facilitating its mastery. Ruby is a sacred stone of Paramahansa Yogananda, Master El Morya and Lord Osiris. It is a contact energy for Anubis and Bast.

At the physical level Ruby has proven herself to be of use in blood and heart disorders, digestive and intestinal disorders. At the mental level, she is a powerful remedy of schizophrenia.

Your Healing Journey Today

If Ruby has come to you today it is time to be the Spiritual Warrior. She tells you that the time to stand on your own two feet is here. A situation has arisen in life that needs to be faced in a courageous and feeling manner. She lets you know that the decision or decisions that you face are about You, Your life and Your future, they are your business. Trust your self, the answer and all the guidance you need is within you.

It is very possible also, that you are not truly feeling your way through life, allowing instead your mind or those around you to direct you. Ruby is a shining light of Passion; write down what you are passionate about, where is your Fire?

Affirmation;- "I feel my world, I am the Spiritual Warrior."

Keywords to help in reading the cards;- The Spiritual Warrior, Self Trust, Passion, Strength, Courage, Ancient Information, Empowerment, Vitality, Life Path, Choice, Kundalini, Sexuality, Past Life Dream.

Body Card Placement;- Ruby can play on all the major Chakras but has an affinity for the Heart Chakra and placement at the physical heart.

Spiritual Warrior Trinity;- Ruby is placed on the Heart Chakra, Sunstone on the Solar Plexus Chakra and Topaz on the Sacral Chakra.

Igniting Passion Trinity;- Ruby is placed on the Heart Chakra, Pink Tourmaline is placed on the Solar Plexus Chakra and Crocite is placed on the Sacral Chakra.

Sacral Chakra Trinity (Most Powerful Healing available for that Chakra);- Crocite is placed on the Left hip, Zircon is placed on the Right hip and Ruby is placed on the Sacral Chakra.

Chemical Composition;- Aluminum Oxide (Trace Chrome)

Color Rays;- 50% Red and 50% Clear

Animal Totem;- Tiger

Essential Oil;- Cypress

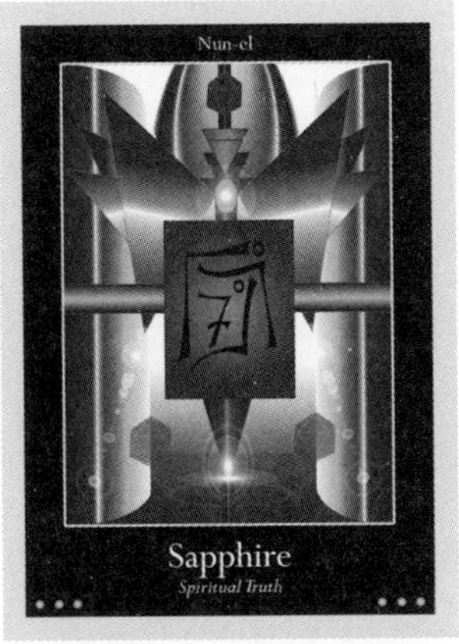

Sapphire

Spiritual Truth

The Master Crystal Deva Nun-el

"See the sun dance on the ocean; allow my presence to descend from the blue sky above. Now feel my open arms hold you, all will be replaced by your own solar angelic essence, blinding in its Glory. A Vision of Truth realized.

Listen to the Solar Angel speak, it is the unencumbered you in all your glory. Trust in my blue ray embrace and enter truth, peace and calm, it is the total of my world, I know no different. I am the blue light of the evening sky, dance with me and we will deepen the faith in your spirit.

Arise from my liquid light embrace, lift like a wave on the ocean and seek the shore of eternity to release, in a blinding blue flash, the ultimate truth of unity, peace and love for all."

Sapphire in Healing

All the blues of the great oceans are found within this stone, some so dark, they appear black until held to the sun where they come to life, others a beautiful light sky blue. Sapphire is perhaps one of the most famous gemstones on Earth, sacred in many cultures around the world and one of the ancient Council of Seven crystals from Lemuria. Sapphire carries one of the most calming and peaceful energies available in the mineral kingdom, enabling one to feel Free.

Principally a communication stone and powerful stone of channeling, Sapphire opens all the higher communication centers, enabling psychic abilities and infusing accuracy into the intuition, all this culminates in mastery of communication.

Sapphire is a powerful stone of the mind allowing it to be calmed and moved into peace which results in an uplifting and joyful feeling of freedom. It is a powerful anti-depressive, allowing those that are cut off from spirit and struggling to find beauty in the self to reveal it, then by integration, purpose is reborn again in life.

Potently increasing the availability of the spirit, Sapphire aids in the conversion of Knowledge to Wisdom, a gift it performs through the egoless anchoring of absolute truth. Through work with this stone, awareness of one's life purpose may present itself in such a way that a path to achieving it is made clear.

Great beings that answer within the frequency of Sapphire include Lady Isis, Lady Nada and Lord Maitreya. Sacred deity correspondences include Artemis, Poseidon and Nun.

Physically, Sapphire is of use in balancing overactive body systems, has an affinity for the veins, which it strengthens and can correct eye problems. It has also been shown to be of use with mental and digestive imbalance.

Sapphire has a strong memory that can hold information, often concerning healing systems and techniques from times past on Earth.

Your Healing Journey Today

Be sure that you're being truthful, with self and others. Love as thought is truth; truth at the level of spirit is unconditional love, the very presence of the infinite self. Remember always, that the measure of truth starts within the self, if you are right within, you will be right in the world. Sapphire's presence in your life today may also mean that it is time to convert the knowledge you have worked so hard to achieve into wisdom. This conversion only takes place through action defined by the spirit in the egoless state, go inward and listen, then act accordingly. Sapphire also appears when one is being called to the Ocean, it may be time for the cleansing light only it can offer.

Affirmation;- "In Truth, I Am Free."

Keywords to help in reading the cards;- Spiritual Truth, Communication, Channeling, Blue, Peace and Calm, Ancient Healing Systems, Psychic Ability, Convert Knowledge to Wisdom, Intuition, Life Purpose.

Body Card Placement;- Mainly placed on the Throat, Third Eye and Crown Chakra. When placed on the Thymus Chakra, Sapphire will stimulate telepathy. It may also be placed at the site of disease to learn the truth behind an ailment.

Thymus Activation Trinity;- Sapphire on the Lower Left side of the chest, Herkimer Diamond on the Thymus Chakra and Aquamarine on the Lower Right side of the chest.

Trinity of the Elders;- Sapphire is placed on the Throat Chakra, Emerald on the Heart Chakra and Ruby on the Solar Plexus Chakra. Hematite can also be placed on the Earth Star Chakra and Pyrite can be placed on the Soul Star to increase this powerful healing process.

Chemical Composition;- Aluminum Oxide

Color Rays;- 70% Blue and 30% Clear

Animal Totem;- Elephant

Essential Oil;- Chamomile (Ger)

Selenite

Spiritual Guidance

The Master Crystal Deva Mer-ka-bel

"Let the silver white aura of Earth's liquid fire surround you, my calm warmth will still and calm the mind and emotions. Too long has the door to your spiritual guidance been conditional, I hold the key and we have initiated this most holy of unions.

History lives in me, the Mother's life and blessing. Feel now a single star that I am, carry me from below your feet to the centre of universal love that you are, shine now in the infinite light of us. My energies have lifted you to a new high, open the highest parts of self and reintegrate the mind of spirit. Linked now in my embrace, the clearest state attainable, the direct link to the unlimited source you are.

In my liquid white fire, you are free, the Phoenix has flown, its message heard and realized. Brothers and sisters of the Great Bear, for you I have a special gift, enter my presence and let my liquid light embrace remind you."

Selenite in Healing

Selenite is principally a clear to white mineral; it is found in many areas of the world, with every location offering a little diversity to the end product. Selenite's many types and formations are often known by other names, such as Gypsum, Desert Rose and Satin Spar. It often picks up impurities from the earth during its formation process, sometimes leading to a change from its pure white colour, the most common others being Gold, Rust Reds and Browns. Selenite is the crystal of Spiritual Guidance, it opens us to our friends in other frequencies and aids in the translation of what they offer to us. Selenite is quite a mental stone, able to manifest the clearest state of mind available and hold it open to embrace the advanced concepts of spirit and the universe. This powerful effect on the mind flows over into the emotional body, allowing one to be emotionally calm and controlled, fostering love for self.

Selenite holds one of the most powerful activation energies on Earth; it is an activator of the higher chakras, powerfully activating the Soul Star and Crown Chakra, allowing the embrace of spiritual content with understanding. Selenite can also activate telepathic communication, past life communication and can be of use to clean and clear the physical and energy bodies.

Selenite is a powerful link stone to the Pleiadian Star System and may in some, open associated wisdoms and paths of service that must be completed now. With Turquoise, Selenite may allow one to speak directly with the Earth and facilitate her balance via grid work and Liquid Crystal direct Earth dosing.

At the physical level it is used for disorders of the Prostate, the bones, spinal misalignment and lowered flexibility. It can increase the milk production in Lactating mothers and is an anti aging stone.

Your Healing Journey Today

If Selenite has come to you today, there are beings with information that is ready and available for you on the inner plane. This information and guidance is relevant to current circumstances and situations, as well as your spiritual growth, and very often your purpose on Earth. It is worth noting that Selenite only comes when the ability to receive the information from spirit has already been mastered.

One of the best ways to get this information is to do a little automatic writing, sit quietly with a pen in your hand, keep an open mind and listen, write down whatever comes. It is best to not read what you are writing and to read it later, often yawning can help loosen the throat chakra and facilitate the entire process. Alternatively, set up a meeting time with spirit on the astral plane to collect the information in the dream state. (Jade and Apophyllite can help with this.) Selenite is a sacred stone to the Pleiadian Star System they may be contacting you. Selenite is also powerfully connected to Cats, if you have one around you, it has a message. Their principle wisdoms are in the flame of Love and heard through the Heart, Sit, Listen and Feel.

Affirmation;- "I am the Eternal Voice of Spirit."

Keywords to help in reading the cards;- Spiritual Guidance, Spiritual Mind, High Light Force, White Light, Channeling, Messages, Soul Star, Pleiadian Light Work, Activation, Initiation, Lady Portia, Vywamus.

Body Card Placement;- Selenite does its best work at the Soul Star Chakra. It empowers at the Solar Plexus Chakra and Facilitates Channeling at the Throat Chakra. Placed at the Base Chakra it initiates direct Pleiadian contact, in this process the symbol for Selenite can also be drawn on the palms of the hands.

Surrender to the Fear Trinity (Places hidden fears into the hands of spirit);- Black Coral on the Lower Left side of the chest, Selenite on the Crown Chakra and Lapis Lazuli on the Lower Right side of the chest.

Channeling Trinity (Increases, activates and balances all the needed pathways for spirit communication);- Selenite is placed on the Crown Chakra, Angelite is Placed on the Third Eye Chakra and Turquoise on the Throat Chakra.

Light Quotient Expansion Trinity (Increases the level of light in the body cells at rest);- Bloodstone is placed on the Lower Left side of the chest, Selenite is placed on the Heart Chakra and Clear Calcite is placed on the Lower Right side of the chest. Light is drawn into the body at the Heart and expanded through the entire self.

Chemical Composition;- Hydrated Calcium Sulfate

Color Rays;- 40% Clear, White 40% and Gold 20%

Animal Totem;- Puma

Essential Oil;- Tea Tree

Silver

The Lunar Path

The Master Crystal Deva Argen-tel-m

"Accept the gentle joy of my Silver rain; let it fall upon you, tears of the full moon in the endless sky above. Receive my gift of the Lunar Path, for in my embrace you are the goddess. The lunar body rises and sets in your every breath.

Look deep now into the eyes of the moon, seek your eternal self and ascend my silver stairs into the embodiment of your feminine soul and all that is undertaken. Feel, see and know your progress, in this the greatest test of all, physicality. Lift now, your feminine spirit, for together, we are the very wind of change embraced for the betterment of all.

I am your mother; breathe in the path of Isis. Welcome me as the ocean does each night when I dance upon her back. With Patience, Balance and Compassion the complete cyclic flow of all creation rests in your hands. Under my influence, you are protected in my flowing silver gown. You are pure, fly now, back to the blanket of stars of your creation and once again reclaim the solar crown."

Silver in Healing

Silver is a White metal that I am sure most of us have seen or have piece of jewelry made from at home. As long as the sun has been aligned with Gold, Silver has been aligned with the moon. The association of Silver to the goddess and all she represents is an ancient one and still to this day it is renowned for the feminine vibration it holds. This is the mineral of the Lunar Path; Silver's energies are cyclic, flowing, cooling, gentle and mothering like a calm ocean. She opens the Goddess path in self, cooling and balancing excessively masculine attitudes, harmonizing emotions and facilitating clear and well ordered communication.

Silver is an honest mirror for the spirit, reflecting the truth about the progress that is being made on the spiritual path while infusing, patience, perseverance and an understanding of cyclic flow to help prevent attachments. She activates the Soul and Earth Star Chakras and will greatly aid visualization and psychic ability. Silver is one of three minerals, including Pearl and Moonstone that are used in a set sequence to activate the Pathway of Isis, an ancient Atlantian ascension pathway.

At the physical level, Silver is a powerful Antibacterial, Antiseptic and Antibiotic. It is also used for headaches and fevers, topically on Burns, and for any problems associated with childbirth and fertility. Silver is one of few remedies for sleepwalking and Anorexia Nervosa.

Your Healing Journey Today

If Silver has come to you today it is time to activate and harmonize the Goddess self. She lives in you as your most feminine component and is seeking a pathway of new expression. Take time to feel and balance your emotional body and be sure to verbally express what is found there in a forgiving and compassionate manner. You may need to accept the closure of some cycles and birth new ones, an active emotional body is a good base for action that changes lives. Drink plenty of pure water for the next couple of days, Silvers presence often means a total cleanout of your system. Silver is also the first energy to present when a soul is readying to incarnate, this card should always be seen as a symbol of feminine fertility and the fact that a little soul is ready. This is a sacred mineral of Isis and the Lady Nada, seek them, they will be close.

Affirmation;- "I walk the path of the Moon, its cycle is my emotional freedom."

Keywords to help in reading the cards;- The Lunar Path, The Moon, The Goddess Self, Cycles, Expression, Emotion, Fertility, Feminine, Voice, Pathway of Isis, Child, The Wolf, Goddess Hecate, Menopause.

Body Card Placement;- Can go on all Chakras.

Pathway of Isis Trinity- See Moonstone.

Aligning for Ascension Trinity (Activates the Self and prepares the bodies for Initiations on the path to Ascension);- Gold on the Lower Left side of the chest, Diamond on the

Heart Chakra and Silver on the Lower Right side of the chest.

Chemical Composition;- Pure Silver

Color Rays;- 99% Silver and 1% Black

Animal Totem;- Wolf

Essential Oil;- Myrrh

Smoky Quartz

Earth Light

The Master Crystal Deva Uran-om-el

"All is a loving expression of the divine, only perception and judgment can taint this fact. Have trust and I will lead by example, for my radiant light is hidden just as yours. Let fear fall away, take my hand through the light filled state of physicality and know there are no wrongs and rights, only Love.

No matter the bonds of physicality, the spirit will soar with or without your intent. Let me anchor self trust and walk you to the cliff of times past where you can willingly spread your wings. You will soar, and god will walk the Earth once more, in your personal completion of physicality.

You are and thus I am. Allow your new found ways of light to ride the current of Earth's sacred pulse to your true home. The warm fires of spirit await you, burning bright even in your absence, feel their warmth in your heart and offer it to the waiting world."

Smoky Quartz in Healing

Smoky Quartz is quartz crystal that has encountered radiation naturally in the Earth. This has allowed it to darken and become a smoky grey to black color. Nice pieces hold all the transparency and structure we expect of Clear Quartz but its properties vary significantly, mainly due to its color and immense light holding ability. Smoky Quartz holds great light and retains the most profound frequency of all the darker minerals on the planet, earning it the simple purpose of Earth Light in healing. Tied to this are many of the lessons it holds for us, leading by example, it shows us that even the most mundane physical activities and manifestations hold purpose and through their embrace and interaction, a chance for growth. The Ungrounded, Insecure, Depressed, Tired of Life, Fearful of change and failure symptom picture that Smoky Quartz aids, is unfortunately quite common in our world, thus it is not surprising that most crystal shops have an abundance of pieces, the darker it is the more light it holds.

With Smoky Quartz at our side we have a constant reminder of the divinity that lives in physicality, and the blinding light that we ourselves represent in the universe. Confidence in this is at the heart of the stone's work. It encourages us to let go of our past and continue our journey forward, focused, with a thirst for life and the changes that it offers, without getting pulled off course by the smaller complexities.

Smoky Quartz, with its ability to ground the spirit and all of its characteristics into the lower physical chakras, creates an acceptance of others helping one to find the path of equality, balance and unity. This dissolves the need to compete and judge, leading to a peaceful, calm and present person that eventually chooses a path of Service. In old Atlantis, the High Priests and High Priestesses of Smoky Quartz were among the most powerful healers, holding a mastery over physicality that few other positions offered. Their healing ability with Animals and Plants was unequaled and many revered people involved in Shamanic Practice and healing today are reincarnations of those beings. Smoky Quartz was one of the most important stones worked with in the creation of Osiris towards the fall of Atlantis and is thus a sacred stone of his, linking one powerfully to his energy and principles (see Exercise below). Don't go to Egypt without Smoky Quartz. Ailments of the Sacral and Pelvic areas of the body are relieved by this stone, it can help balance body fluids and may aid in the removal of excess radiation from the body after treatments.

Your Healing Journey Today

If Smoky Quartz has come to you today, she is here to help with Emotional healing and the redefinition of your physical space. She has come to aid you on an already active journey deep into the physical self to find the light that gives you life. Once recognized, you will shine that fire into the darkest areas of self. In Smoky Quartz's embrace, the darker and more physical the better, to her, darkness is a measure of light content, light that you can reclaim and use as fuel towards the goals and the happiness you have chosen for your self. In the sacred embrace that is around you today, offer up all your darkest, most difficult and pain filled aspects, leave no stone unturned, let go and be free. Never again will you see physicality as separate from spirit for it is the space of the supreme realization of the united oneness.

When an aspect of your physical world weighs heavily upon you, see a Rose, perfect, gentle and delicate, for it shares the same origin and source of life. If you will allow this, your life can become a glorious art work, paving the united path to the Supreme Oneness with Peace, Love and Joy.

Affirmation;- "My Physical World is Filled with Light."

Keywords to help in reading the cards;- Earth Light, Self Acceptance, Physical Embrace as Divinity, Grounding, Emotions, Tired of life, Disrespectful of Life, Life Change, Release, Healing, The Physical Journey, Osiris, Lord Sananda, Rainbow Serpent.

Body Card Placement;- Smoky Quartz can go on any of the chakras, anchoring the spirit into them and offering its wisdom to issues in that area of life.

Uniting the Isis and Osiris Templates (Balances Male and Female sides and places one in the active Octahedron of Light);- In a lying position, Smoky Quartz is placed in the Right hand, Larimar is placed in the Left hand and Herkimer Diamond is placed on the Heart Chakra. A White Pyramid is visualized above the head with its point up and a Green Pyramid is visualized below the feet pointing down, the two are slowly brought together, joining bases at the heart to form an Octahedron (Diamond) that will spin and remain around the body for 7 Days, facilitating Spiritual and Devic Communication.

Chemical Composition;- Silicon Dioxide (Sodium Trace)

Color Rays;- 33.3% Clear, 33.4% Black, 33.3% White

Animal Totem;- Crocodile/Alligator

Essential Oil;- Black Pepper

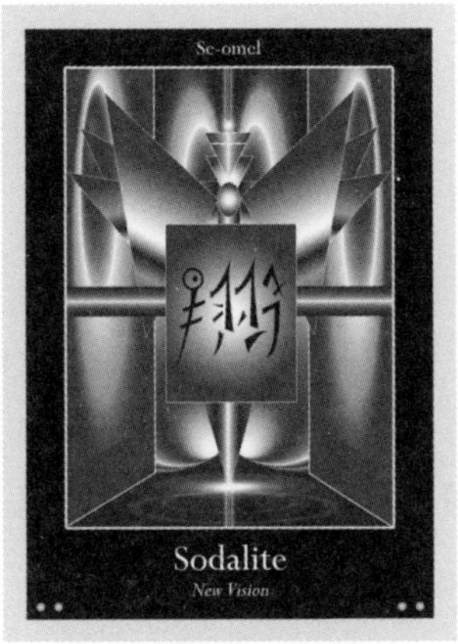

Sodalite

New Vision

The Master Crystal Deva Se-omel

"Slip gently into the velvet robe of my light and enter my frequency. In my embrace, we have opened the unlimited realization of spirit eternal to the level of complete knowing.

Closing your eyes at night, let the stars of the inner world drift by you, this is one of my gifts, empowering intuition and vision, but still there is more. Calmly step into conscious thinking, open the mind to the endless expressions of energy around you, now let my light slow them, distilling them down to a single movement, through this you will rejoice in my frequency, for all is spirit and as endless as the night sky.

Let the Dragons soar high above in the heart of creation's eye, a message of pure potential and a path of empowered light, a New Vision carried in the eyes of the living stars of Earth. May they speak and the world listen, I await their true calling, my flame is theirs."

Sodalite in Healing

Sodalite is the deep Indigo-Blue opaque stone with silvery white inclusions throughout its body like white light dancing in the universe. It is quite a common stone, found in most crystal shops around the world which is an indication that we need it for our evolution at this time.

Of all the stones on Earth, Sodalite holds one of the highest percentages of the Indigo Colour Ray making it a stone of great Wisdom and linking it intimately to the working order of the mind. Sodalite links together all the aspects of mind, from the highest point of the spiritual all the way to the subconscious, and allows one to dance between them. This also creates the ability to freely move from emotional to rational, by the inclusion of spiritual thought, and makes one able to truthfully speak about emotions and be free from attachment at the level of the subconscious, which is useful in destroying addiction and control issues. Sodalite's ability to create new mental patterns and its potent linking ability, lead to greater focus and the creation of new goals, which is where it gets its reputation as the stone of New Vision.

As a spiritual development stone, Sodalite opens the third eye and can aid in the translation of that which is experienced, it facilitates meditation and with its ability to drop one in the infinite oneness mentally, is the more physical anchoring counterpart of the highly spiritual stone of knowing, Celestite. This connection makes Sodalite a first stopping point when one needs a more spiritualized vision in life.

At the physical level, Sodalite is able to calm panic attacks, especially where the cause is a division of self and the stress it causes. Sodalite is the number-one crystal for the lymphatic system and any problems found there, it is useful in diabetes, insomnia and with throat troubles.

Your Healing Journey Today

On this day, with Sodalite by your side, the Conscious, Subconscious and High Spiritual Minds are uniting to manifest a New Vision that has been hidden inside you. In the coming days, you are encouraged to speak truthfully about your emotions, which will create a freedom of attachment to that around you and open the doors for a new world with you at its centre.

The most difficult thing in manifesting a new path in the world is allowing our focus, which is predominantly mental, to move through the emotional body into the etheric, and then physically manifest. To facilitate this, we must remember that emotional focus is the act of Truthfulness with Self, and it is the Voice of this that Sodalite offers to you as a gift.

"A world focused on Truth, is a world surrounded in Love, a world surrounded in Love, must act with Love, and such directed Love Unites, Enlightens and gives rise to more Truth."

Affirmation;- "I am the perfected Vision, the New Vision of Light."

Keywords to help in reading the cards;- New Vision, Linking the Minds, Indigo Colored Ray (Wisdom), Attachment, Knowing, Rational and Intellectual Thinking, Truth Emotional to Rational Link, Addiction, Control Issues, Focus, Lymphatic System, Panic Attacks, Contact from the Ashtar Command.

Body Card Placement;- Sodalite is best at the Throat, Third Eye and Crown Chakras.

Addiction Trinity (To break an Addiction);- Botswana Agate is placed on the Right shoulder, Sodalite on the Heart and Onyx on the Left shoulder. This should be done for a period of time once a week, to aid in breaking the addiction, then one should work with detoxification stones such as Bloodstone.

The Restart Trinity;- This can be used as a re-entry to life or any aspect of it, clearing the past, preparing for change and creating the New Vision. Green Calcite, Zircon and Sodalite are arranged in a triangular formation at the centre of the chest. (I strongly recommend acquiring these as Liquid Crystals from a qualified practitioner, in Trinity form to powerfully enhance the process.)

Panic Attacks Trinity;- Rhodonite on the Upper Left side of the chest, Sodalite on the Heart Chakra and Botswana Agate on the Upper Right side of the chest.

State of Knowing Trinity (Induces a High vibration into the sought after space of Knowing);- Celestite, Sodalite and Clear Quartz are stacked on the Heart Chakra. Iolite can also be placed on the Third Eye Chakra to stimulate vision.

Lymphatic System Balancing Trinity;- Lapis Lazuli is placed on the Left hip, Sodalite is placed on the Right hip and Blue Lace Agate is placed on the Thymus Chakra.

Chemical Composition;- Sodium Aluminum Silicate Chloride

Color Rays;- 53% Indigo, 17% White, 13% Blue, 10% Violet and 7% Silver

Animal Totem;- Lizard

Essential Oil;- Parsley Seed

Sugilite

The Inner Child

The Master Crystal Deva Rama-hol-m-el

"Let my hand take yours, together we will walk the journey of life as a child, we will laugh and play, free from the harder illusions of physicality.

Via me, embody the essence of the spiritual mind and deliver it to physicality through stimulated intuition. Let my Magenta-Violet Light connect you to the great past masters of our world so you may carry their Wisdoms and serve the Paths of the Future.

By my side, I have called you to action and in the embrace of the Infinite oneness we will translate the messengers of light, the Starry Ones here to assist in Earth's evolution. Never despair at the state of your world, the help is here and together we will awaken them one by one, the Children of Light have come home."

Sugilite in Healing

Purples, Violets and deep Magenta blend beautifully together to give this crystal its individual purple hue often swirled with black and/or white inclusions and bands. Truly a crystal of the new age, Sugilite has come to us primarily to aid in the development of the Starchildren that are presently being born on our planet. One of the greatest problems facing these amazing beings is the anchoring of their highly spiritualized minds and concepts into a physical world, a task for which there are no guidelines. Sugilite opens an unconditional heart space via its magenta frequency, and then utilizing the Purple Ray, powerfully anchors the spiritual mind into the physical, often delivering realization of divine purpose. It is due to this, that Sugilite is the crystal of the Inner Child. It manifests the story of the perfected blend between Spirit, Physicality, Mind, Discipline, Play, Love and Laughter which results in the carrying of the unconditionally mastered child into adulthood. This ability to retain the Inner Child into adulthood rebirths the adventurous spirit, fosters the ability to laugh and encourages one to do new things from a Fearless, stress-free space, letting life become a spiritual experience, rather than settling for the common stagnancy that so many adults suffer as they age in a physical world.

Work with this stone over time, by way of its spiritual link to the physical, can answer the great questions such as; Who am I? Why am I here? And where am I going? Its ability with this is extraordinary, and even extends to information regarding disease processes, to which it offers complete and permanent cure. The causes of disease where Sugilite is concerned are usually hidden in Anger, Boredom, Depression, Stagnancy, Pain, Negativity or Mental Disorder which it simply moves aside to reveal the truth.

Sugilite is a renowned channeling stone, able to connect and open the pathways to past spiritual masters of Earth, an ability that is enhanced in the presence of Black Coral and Selenite.

In Atlantis, Sugilite was the principal stone of the Third City, Ahonuia, which was the city of the Divine Mother Principal. The Gateway stones of that city, Sapphire and Pearl, still balance Sugilite's work indicating the Inner Child is retained through the Truth of Spirit and its resulting Pure actions in the world.

Sugilite is a sacred contact stone for Saint Germaine, Lady Portia, the Archangel Zadkiel and Egyptian God Bes.

At the physical, Sugilite is useful for pain management, especially associated with headaches and inflammation, it will reduce stress and balance Pineal, Adrenal and/or Pituitary gland function. This is also a principal remedy for Left/Right brain imbalance and resulting conditions such as Epilepsy, coordination problems, Autism, ADD and Dyslexia.

Your Healing Journey Today

If Sugilite, the crystal of the Inner Child, has made itself present today, the voice of purpose is echoing all around you, the question is however, will you hear it? The Inner Child could be described as the unencumbered voice, or expression of the spirit that you are, it is a part of you that understands its purpose and reason for living. Its main job is to consistently deliver this to you, under the guidance of spirit through the veil of physicality, to keep you on your path. But, physicality is complex, multifaceted and distracting, so to blossom into a mastered part of an individual, the Inner Child must be managed and parented correctly, only then can the voice of the spirit be filtered into physicality with truth. The Key lesson here is one of Balance and Mastery. Laughter, Happiness and Play are all forms of expression that allow unconditional love to flow from us and the voice of the Inner Child to be heard, but discernment is still required for these things to be constructive on a life path. In the presence of Sugilite, take time to let the voice of your spirit be filtered through the heart, and then it's up to you to take action in the physical world. Remember also that Laughter is often the best medicine, but it may also be a set of universal ear plugs that allow the true self to be hidden from the world, crushing the Inner Child. By Sugilite, on this day, you have been called into service to the Self, let your actions in the world echo your response in the halls of Wisdom, Love and Power, and on this day, take hold of your destiny into Light. Sugilite also appears to those that must, or are working with children, to stimulate the process and further define the role in their Words, Worlds and Ways.

Affirmation;- "I am a Spiritual Being on a Human Journey."

Keywords to help in reading the cards;- Inner Child, Starchild, Creativity of Spirit, Playfulness, the Laughter/ Tears Balance, Anchoring Spirit into the Physical World, Depression, Negativity, Loss of Purpose, Mental Imbalance, Stress, Contact from Past Spiritual Masters.

Body Card Placement;- Sugilite works its wonders primarily through the Crown, Third Eye, Heart and Earth Star Chakras. Sugilite is a record keeper stone for lifetimes in the Asian areas of the world, especially Japan, and will surrender these records when appropriate, simply take three drops of Liquid Crystal Sugilite and/ or place the card or physical stone on the Heart Chakra, lie back and relax.

Star Children Mental Balance Trinity;- Labradorite on the Right shoulder and Moldavite on the Left shoulder, work with Sugilite on the Crown Chakra.

Inner Child Mastery Trinity;- Place Sapphire on the Third Eye Chakra, Sugilite on the Heart Chakra and Pearl on the Sacral Chakra, enjoy the Journey.

Chemical Composition;- Potassium Sodium Lithium Iron Manganese Aluminum Silicate
Color Rays;- 43% Violet, 26% Pink, 16% Black, 9% Indigo and 6% Clear
Animal Totem;- Seal
Essential Oil;- Everlasting

Sulphur

Physical Radiance

The Master Crystal Deva Illuminel

"Born from the released fire of Earth, I am a master in the realm of explosive eruption and the fiery nature. My flame in your hand will soften the edges of expressions and situations, taming the roaring flames that only manifest pain.

Sit down and let us nurture the fire of you to a warm glow by which you can seek comfort and guidance without the fear of being burned. In the orange-red glow of your newly disciplined light and vitality, rise now and shine physically radiant in the world.

Now, harboring the power of the yellow ray, lift your will and creativity. Embrace your fiery potential and see perfection in all that you do. Stare deeply into your own eyes, until you see the dancing flames, let them melt away all that blocks you and the many paths you manifest. The Bennu has been reborn, a vision of the spirit's glory physically realized."

Sulphur in Healing

Of all the crystals in the mineral kingdom, none is a higher representative of the yellow ray of color then Sulphur. This mineral is bright yellow and able to form beautiful translucent crystals. Sulphur is the hottest of all the minerals on Earth, which gives this stone its reputation as a highly reactive and allergic substance. In magical law, Sulphur is also known as brimstone, appearing in many nursery rhymes and children's tales. Sulphur is an important part of the shamanic traditions of Earth and is a link stone to Earth's Fire elementals.

The energy of Sulphur is primarily mental initiating understanding and wisdom. It carries calm into fire attitudes through its experience in that element, but can motivate, activate and empower where needed. Sulphur, acting as the mineral of Physical Radiance, places the creative imagination, vitality and power of the fire element into the body, allowing one to become a shining light within the perception of self. This makes it a potent crystal of self worth, especially where its lack is masked in fire such as anger and rage.

Physically, Sulphur is excellent in Skin Conditions and all conditions of heat such as inflammation, infections and fevers. Any hardening in the body such as Arthritis, Calcification, Kidney and Gallstones or Hardening of Arteries may be melted with Sulphur's fire.

In Atlantis, Sulphur, as the principle crystal of the yellow color ray, was revered for its ability at the Solar Plexus chakra where it always works alone due to its Heat. It is a sacred stone of Lord Lanto, Helios, Vesta, and the Egyptian deities Sekhmet and Shu. Sulphur is the memory stone for Nibiru, our ancient sister civilization that existed on the planet we now call Mars. For some people, when it is placed at the Third Eye it will open visions of that time.

Your Healing Journey Today

If Sulphur has come to you today, there is heat in your life that needs to be controlled and mastered. Fire is one of the greatest catalysts on Earth, the hand that wields it is always responsible for that which it destroys or creates. If you are in the process of decision, be cautious, it may contain hidden fire.

Sulphur also delivers the message of physical radiance, asking you to love yourself physically, take time to see yourself. This powerful crystal is also coming into your life to lift your vital force, empower you and prepare you to manifest that which you have chosen. The energies of the Lion are ancient, holding much spiritual significance in many cultures from Nibiru to Egypt, on this day he walks at your side. Will you hear the lions roar?

Affirmation;- "I am power, I am the force, I have the strength to let my mind run its course."

Keywords to help in reading the cards;- Physical Radiance, Strength, Power, Fire, Heat, Fire Elementals, Solar Plexus Energy, Self-Love, The Colour Yellow, Anger and Rage.

Body Card Placement;- Sulphur mainly works via the Solar Plexus Chakra, over the Physical Heart or in the Power Hand (the hand you write with). Sulphur will empower candles which are lit for a defined intention. Try carving the Sulphur symbol into them, repeating your intention, before lighting them.

Personal Power Trinity (Mastery and Balance in Expression of Power);- Topaz on the Upper Left side of the chest, Sulphur on the Solar Plexus Chakra and Ruby on the Upper Right side of the chest.

Feline Communication Trinity (To speak Cat);- Boji Stone is placed on the Left hip, Rhodochrosite is placed on the Right hip and Sulphur on the Heart Chakra. Once the above has been completed, most people will have three days of enhanced feline communication.

Chemical Composition;- Sulphur

Color Rays;- 95% Yellow and 5% Orange

Animal Totem;- Lion

Essential Oil;- Citronella

Sunstone

Ra, Light Radiant

The Master Crystal Deva Ra-ba-el

"Praise be to Ra, I am your personal source of radiant light, feel my warm vitality, I carry the spark of life through the corridors of emptiness, pain and illusion. Life and joy are evidence of my footsteps.

Lie back in the blazing Sun, let its light bathe you in its optimistic and confident fires, Breathe them into the body and choose life for every cell. Now send them forward and embrace your greatest goals with ease. These are some of my gifts.

Lifted, your radiant solar light is a star to behold, your vitality is at its peak, with me it is summer year round. There is only the Radiance of my loving light, express it with Joy and Smile, we are one. Hold now the sacred Eye of Horus, Know its path and together we will offer it back to aid the Devic Rise of Wisdom into humanity's embrace."

Sunstone in Healing

The glory of the radiant sun rests within this stone, gold, red, orange and yellow all dance in its body, reflections and refractions of light that it captures from any source close to it. The colors inside Sunstone are never dormant, changing and shifting based on the viewing angle and the amount and type of light present. Sunstone is a Sacred Stone of Ra, the Sun God of Egypt and is a potent representation of his vital energies. This is the crystal of Solar Light Radiance, all the sun does for life, this stone will do for you.

Under Sunstone's spell, optimism, vitality and confidence beam from a clear energized state, allowing the setting of high goals with fearless enthusiasm and trust in your abilities to reach them. Life is Good, the Sun lives in You, You are in Life and truly Alive.

Often, those that are in need of Sunstone have entered a dark place in life, often believing that an unshakable shadow has been cast upon them, forcing them into an unavoidable depression fuelled with moods, lowered self-worth and pessimism. Life becomes mundane and the cycle never seems to end, Sunstone's vitality is their Saviour. The vitality of Sunstone clears, heals and balances the bodies, removing fears and feelings of failure by intimately linking the Soul's consciousness into the equation. This potent inclusion opens up universal truth and may just make one the Sun that gives light to the rest of the world, as 'Umbram Fugat Veritas'. (Truth puts Darkness to Flight –Algernon Blackwood.)

Sunstone is a stone of solar worship, used in conjunction with Sun meditations and in work related to the Mayan and Egyptian cultures, it is the Sacred Stone of the Egyptian pharaoh Akhenaten who will still answer in its frequency. In fact, Sunstone is a record keeper of all that Akhenaten came to do on the Earth, his message and work can still be found within it. Sunstone also powerfully opens communication to the Ascended Master Serapis Bey.

At the physical level, Sunstone is a Master healer of all throat problems and stomach ulceration. It can also cool, calm and clear all fire-based conditions in the body such as rheumatism.

Your Healing Journey Today

If Sunstone has come to you today, the light of the Sun is about to ignite your life, increasing your vital force, expanding your frequency and infusing you with the joy only the Sun can deliver. The coming days are bound to be positive and flowing, but it is important to not block the potential this frequency carries with negativity and pessimism, for Sunstone will then explode into healing mode and you will wonder what hit you. Optimism is a key word where Sunstone is concerned and it is possible that you are having your share of rough days at the moment, Sunstone has come to fill a role as your personal Sun, showering positive light into your world and lightening the load. Sunstone can also open the voice and purpose of one's soul, so listen in a state of potential action, for with frequencies such as this, swiftness is the key.

If you are searching for an answer to a question, Sunstone is one of the most positive of responses that you could hope for, it screams, Yes, Yes, Yes at you. All you need to do now with your new vitality, is spring into action. Are you still reading this? Go, do it ......Now!

Affirmation;- "I am Radiant Light, behold my Vitality."

Keywords to help in reading the cards;- Ra, Radiance, Light Quotient, The Sun, Vitality, Life Force, Chi, Optimism, The Setting of Goals, Self-Worth, Soul Star Chakra, Moods, Depression, Powerful Fears, The Mayan Culture, Egypt, Akhenaten, Serapis Bey, Constellation Leo.

Body Card Placement;- Sunstone can go on all the body chakras to balance and heal, but it has an affinity for the Solar Plexus, Throat and Soul Star Chakras, where it lightens the load, removes fears and adds vitality.

Messages from the Ancients Trinity;- Sunstone on the Soul Star Chakra, Selenite on the Heart Chakra and Moonstone below the feet at the Earth Star Chakra. You will see a door with a triangle on it, step through it into a pyramid, where you will be greeted and information will be exchanged.

The Initiation of the Star Denebola;- Takes place on the 19th of May, Sunstone is its governing stone on Earth, dare you hold the Lions Tail? Place Sunstone on the Heart Chakra between 11:30 and 12:00pm, Relax and you may learn her lessons and her glorious history.

Chemical Composition;- Sodium Calcium Aluminum Silicate

Color Rays;- 27% Yellow, 27% Gold, 23% Red and 23% Orange

Animal Totem;- Scorpion

Essential Oil;- Cinnamon

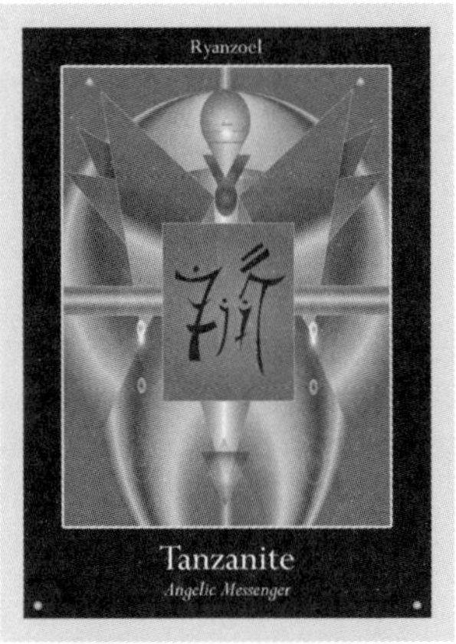

Tanzanite

Angelic Messenger

The Master Crystal Deva Ryanzoel

"Let us begin, hold my image to your heart, look up at the passing clouds overhead and pass through them to the blue of the sky. Falling into its expanse, be lost a while, as my silver robe surrounds you, now we are one. Feel my cool, calm touch upon your brow and let it awaken the flame of power, hear the sound of freedom as it burns within you.

A being of light, young to your Earth, we meet finally. Let us ready you to serve humanity, activate and open the higher senses, so that you may see reality and enter the new age. Listen carefully now for the sounds of your soul, its whisper holds your freedom and path.

I am a being of great vision and sound, my role on Earth to this point is found in service to the angelic messengers of light, who use my frequency to enter your realm of perception. My robe will now allow this same gift to be yours; you may enter their realm as teacher and student.

You will hear more of me, child of light, I have many gifts for you."

Tanzanite in Healing

Highly transparent and forming strong geometric crystals, Tanzanite is a beautiful combination of purple, indigo and violet with shades of blue and silver through it, it is very expensive and quite rare. Tanzanite is the mineral that holds the title of Angelic Messenger, making it the most powerful link stone to the Angelic kingdom on Earth at this time. The Angels are the keepers of the flame of Power for Earth, which also tells us that Tanzanite is a stone of personal power and its mastery.

Tanzanite can break down the human idea of time and space, allowing a more vast understanding that is universal. This makes it a great stone for those that say there is never enough time in life.

Much of Tanzanite's work is Spiritual, a potent stone of the higher senses, it activates and opens the third eye, throat and crown chakras anchoring Clairaudience, Clairvoyance and all forms of spirit communication. The high activation of spiritual communication with Tanzanite allows one to physically manifest under strong guidance, as well as take a more inventive and creative path in the world. The new path taken under guidance is chosen by accessing personal Soul records through a powerfully enhanced Tanzanite meditation.

Tanzanite is also a transmutation stone absorbing negative energies and converting them to love and understanding. Due this powerful ability, this stone is sacred to the Ascended Master Saint Germaine who utilizes aspects of this stone's transmuting ability blended with Amethyst to hold the Purple flame of Transmutation in our dimension. As well as Saint Germaine, Tanzanite is also sacred to the Archangel Michael, the Lady Portia and Lord Melchior.

At the physical, this mineral has a marked effect on the immune system, balancing its function and has over the years been shown to open communication to those in comatose states. It also can remove inflammation, help in depression and clear skin problems.

Much of what Tanzanite is on Earth for will not be given back to us until we accept more of the Atlantian way of Oneness after 2013.

Your Healing Journey Today

You are entering a stage of great spiritual development, your higher senses are activating and opening, readying you to reclaim your gifts from other lives and possibly enter into service to mankind. However, in order to complete this transition, you must own and balance your personal power. At no time in life has it been as important to know what you want, who you are and whom the world sees you as. Take time to write it all down, a truthful understanding of self now will aid you to integrate the messages you are receiving and make them a reality in the world. Not having enough Time is not a valid reason for inactivity, there is always plenty of Time in life for the spirit, and only the mind and body are bound to its limitations.

Let your creative and inventive selves play, they will reveal the new you, but be prepared for change, the Angels have entered your life via the Wisdom of the crystals; their path is one of fire, the path of the Phoenix.

Affirmation;- "Empowered, wise and all Loving, I am the Solar Angel."

Keywords to help in reading the cards;- Angelic Messenger, Personal Power, The Higher Senses, Clairvoyance, Clairaudience, Violet Flame, Past life Gifts, Creativity, Soul Records, Gifts.

Body Card Placement;- Tanzanite works its magic mainly on the Third Eye Chakra, Throat Chakra and the back of the Heart Chakra.

Power Balancing Trinity for Star Children;- Place Lepidolite on the Third Eye, Tanzanite on the Throat Chakra and Moldavite on the Heart Chakra.

Angelic Communication Trinity (3);- Tanzanite on the Lower Left side of the chest, Elestial Quartz on the Heart Chakra and Angelite on the Lower Right side of the chest.

Saint Germaine Communication Trinity (2);- Tanzanite, Amethyst and Iolite are stacked in that order (Iolite on the top) at the Heart Chakra.

Chemical Composition;- Calcium Aluminum Silicate Hydroxide

Color Rays;- 43% Violet, 34% Blue, 13% Silver and 10% Green

Animal Totem;- Praying Mantis

Essential Oil;- Galbanum

Tigers Eye

Personal Power in Action

The Master Crystal Deva Lin-fa-el

"Welcome to my frequency. I will make you at home in all parts of the universe for within my embrace, you will know it lives within you. Without fear, ignite the flame of personal power. I will guide you in its use with clarity and insight on this the journey of spirit.

Let us raise our hands up and take the Sun from the heavens, anchor it into the solar plexus and blend it with the Stabilized Earth body. Stable and filled with life, let us now manifest all that we desire.

With personal power embraced into action, you will remember the ultimate goal of peace and unity for all. Forget not, that you are a flame of the endless Sun, which patiently awaits your realized return, a blinding star of light and symbol of your journey to completion."

Tigers Eye in Healing

Ordinarily, Tigers Eye is a striped, golden-yellow and brown mineral; the gold component of Tigers Eye refracts and reflects light as it is moved, similarity to the eye of the tiger, giving rise to its name. However, this stone's name is not only fitting due to its appearance, but is also a reflection of this mineral's effect on the emotional/mental level, where it activates personal power, confidence, drive and self-reliance, traits we associate with the phrase, 'Eye of the tiger'.

Tigers Eye is the stone of Personal Power in Action, it is needed by many people as generally people are re-active to situations causing them to not take appropriate action. With Tigers Eye as guide, one is empowered and able to think before acting which encourages grounded, appropriate choice, and optimism for forward movement in life. This is a stone for those that feel trapped in life; it brings purpose to all activities, removes mental clutter and defines the path forward. Tigers Eye is said to bring good luck and wealth to all who embrace it. It also is powerful as a travel stone, allowing one to feel at home, no matter where they are, aiding all the symptoms of travel sickness.

At a spiritual level, Tigers Eye can aid the development and understanding of the kundalini energies, delivering discipline in the realm of sexuality especially when placed with Black Onyx and Garnet.

Physically, Tigers Eye is of use with reproductive disorders, broken bones, personality disorders, and in all forms of addiction to regain personal power.

Your Healing Journey Today

When Tigers Eye enters life, good luck and wealth follow, but in order to receive you must be prepared to take action, not move into reaction. Take caution with whatever presents itself, remembering that true action has no fear, regrets or limitations. It is the purest measure of personal power mastered for the betterment of all. The presence of Tigers Eye also can indicate a holiday or a well-deserved break. Tigers Eye is also the sacred stone for the Lord Lanto, an Ascended Master, who resides on the yellow ray, he may be calling you.

Affirmation;- Through self confidence, I take Action.

Keywords to help in reading the cards;- Personal Power in Action, Drive, Confidence, Self Reliance, Courage, Kundalini, Travel, Sexuality, Asia, Lord Lanto.

Body Card Placement;- Generally placed upon the Solar Plexus Chakra. But at the Base Chakra this card will help one understand the purpose for circumstances in life. This card placed beneath a candle will create a balanced environment of personal power, returning all poorly directed energies to their creator.

Understanding Current Life Circumstances Trinity;- Amazonite on the Lower Left side of the chest, Tigers Eye on the Solar Plexus Chakra and Zircon on the Lower Right side of the chest.

Sexual Discipline Trinity;- Black Onyx is placed on the Left hip, Tigers Eye is placed on the Right hip and Garnet is placed on the Sacral Chakra.

Chemical Composition;- Silicon Dioxide Iron

Color Rays;- 38% Gold, 23% Black, 13% Yellow, 13% Red and 13% Orange

Animal Totem;- Bull

Essential Oil;- Star Anise

Turquoise

Spirit of the Earth

The Master Crystal Deva Azurel

"Take my hand and Connect through me to the Earth's loving expression, feel her breath and be free to play in her gardens of Color filled joy. I have come to carry you back to all that you are.

I am a river, blue with the ray of communication; lie quiet and in blessing of Ra look into the endless sky. Feel me open you to the Purity, Clarity, and art of Truthful voice, listen well as the Grandmother speaks her song and let it dance in your every cell.

You have stepped now into the calm waters that I am, as many have before you. Together again, we are the pathway to the Eternal voice of Feminine spirit. Let her joyfully rise now and fill the clouds so we may taste again the sacred rains of love as her Tears fall upon us. The Serpent has swallowed its Tail and the Age of Greatness has found its home."

Turquoise in Healing

A true gift from the Earth, Turquoise holds one of the most profound healing vibrations we have available to us. An opaque blue-green stone that often has black veins running through it and inclusions of Silver, it holds a true Feminine energy and plays a key role in the Rise of the Atlantian Way, Rebirth of the Goddess and the 2012 Transition.

Where the Blue of Father Sky and Green of Mother Earth meet and commune,

Turquoise is born. Turquoise is a gift to translate, blend, heal and unite physicality and the Spirit. The bluer the stone, the more it opens to Spirit, while the presence of Green opens one to the Goddess and the nature of Earth. It is from this that Turquoise gets its simple purpose with the Human race, 'The Spirit of the Earth'. She is here to teach us, as the only vessel capable, to deliver Mother Earth and Father Sky into Unity and Oneness. Her color is a measure of our success and she has been getting Greener and Greener as we evolve, soon the Green Ray and Blue Ray in this stone will equalize in Percentage and the Male and Female energies of Earth will be able to reverse, the Goddess will Rise from the Earth and all will be again as it was in Atlantian times, the deadline is 2012, it will happen, we are over the threshold.

One will notice that Turquoise is found within all the regions of the world where sacred and important teachings stem from, this is due to the fact the Earth needs the Turquoise to translate and commune with her spirit. Whenever she does this, humankind as her conduits pick up some wisdoms that then become the foundations of great teachings (This is especially relevant to Spirits incarnating at the time). This has occurred in many ancient cultures of the world from the Tibetans, Egyptians, Oriental races and famously the Mayan and American Indians. Presently Turquoise is the National Gemstone of Iran, I wonder what we are to learn from there?

Turquoise is a master healer, able to offer the true cause of dis-ease then activate the pathway of cure with clear expression on and between all the levels of self, physical to spiritual. In the presence of this stone, all communication pathways are infused potently with truth and creative flare, no obstacle is too great as the holistic self unites with the common goal of Perfection.

In Atlantis, mastery of Turquoise carried great weight with the High Counsel with the many desirable gifts it allowed. These included Enhanced Immunity, realization of one,s personal Path of Service (enhanced with Garnet) and the activation of potent Psychic and Healing abilities, but by far the most important gift was its ability to allow direct communication with the Earth and her spirit. With Turquoise, it was said that even the ears of Mortals could hear the sound of the Planets moving through space, The Music of the Spheres, a sound that plays through the Soul before birth and a reminder of the greater unity we represent.

Turquoise is the sacred stone of the Egyptian desert Goddess, Hathor and Estsanathehi, the Goddess of the Navajo Indians. It is also a sacred stone of the Pleiadian Star System and its teachings, while the Lord Maitreya, Lord Allah Gobi, Master El Morya and Master Osiris will all respond in its frequency.

On a more physical note, Turquoise is Cleansing, Anti-viral, Anti-biotic, Calming, Restorative and Balancing to fire conditions in the body, such as acid imbalances (Gout, Stomach Ulcers, and Rheumatism). It is also potent with Rhodonite and Peridot against Depression and Panic Attacks and when coupled with Iolite for the eyes is sure to get a result.

Your Healing Journey Today

Today you have been blessed by the presence of the Spirit of the Earth. The presence of Turquoise in your life is a sign that your true Earth connection has been compromised. The most common word used to describe your state is 'Ungrounded'. Signs of this vary; at the Physical it may be digestive issues and dizziness, at the Emotional a lack of True expression or just a void feeling, at the Mental it appears as confusion and a lack of focus, while at the Spiritual we seem lost and without purpose. Turquoise has come to reunite the selves and get all the parts of you communicating with each other again. Life is about to be back on track again, getting close to nature in the coming weeks will help, but all of Turquoise's work stems from perfected communication, the voice is your real tool of change, use it, and use it wisely. The holistic flair Turquoise adds to the voice may leave you with both feet in your mouth if you don't listen to your heart and wave the flag of Truth.

When a Cat purrs, its Love is Felt, when a Bird sings, its Wisdom is Heard and when a Snake strikes, its Power is Seen, such is the Spirit of the Earth, Know it lives in you.

Affirmation;- "I am United in the Oneness of Earth's Spirit."

Keywords to help in reading the cards;- Gaia, Spirit of the Earth, Atlantian Past Life, Ungrounded Spirit, Communication, Expression, Creativity, Male and Female Balance, Throat Chakra, Voice, Unite Heart and Voice, Rise of the Goddess, 2012, Shamballa, 11:11 Gateway, Pleiadian Star System, Dehydration, Need to Detoxify the Body, Pan, Hathor.

Body Card Placement;- Turquoise is at home on all the body chakras and over any areas of Illness, it is a master healer and will benefit any ailment, Physical to Spiritual. Over the Liver with Bloodstone, Turquoise will aid detoxification and speed healing. Turquoise water can be of great benefit as a general health tonic in times of illness and lowered immunity, simply place the card under a glass of water in the morning for several minutes then drink half the glass, drink the other half before bed.

Pleiadian Healing and Communication Trinity;- Selenite in the Right hand, Turquoise in the Left hand and Sapphire on the Third Eye. Breathe, see a Blue Star in the sky above you and move towards it, let it become a Blue door that will open to a Blue light that will surround and enter the body, sit, listen and allow.

Note;- This can be a profound healing technique that may surface information that must be processed for healing and change to become permanent. Drinking the Turquoise Water described above, prior and after the meditation will help. Jasper or Rose Quartz can be used to settle and nurture if the healing path is overwhelming. (Sit the Jasper card on the heart.)

Depression Healing Trinity;- Turquoise is placed on the Throat Chakra, Rhodonite is placed on the Heart Chakra and Peridot on the Solar Plexus Chakra.

Ascended Earth Trinity (The Earth will become your Teacher in the Ascension Process);- Gold is placed on the Soul Star Chakra, Turquoise is placed on the Heart Chakra and Silver is placed on the Earth Star Chakra. This is an ongoing process of evolution. Practise it whenever you, can the results are outstanding.

Chemical Composition;- Hydrated Copper Aluminum Phosphate (Iron)

Color Rays;- 46% Blue, 36% Green (Increasing fast to 46% by 2012), 9% White and 9% Black

Animal Totem;- Bear

Essential Oil;- Sage

Other Turquoise Info;-

- Turquoise is mentioned in the bible as one of the 12 stones (1st stone of second row) in the Breast Plate of Hebrew High Priest, Aaron.
- The oldest Piece of Jewelry found to date is a Turquoise and Gold Bracelet from 5500 BC said to belong to the Egyptian Queen Zer. (She was really Atlantian or it would be set in Silver.)
- The Pleiadian Stargate is most active on the 15th- 20th of January. Its entry is governed by the geometry and Light frequency of United Turquoise, Selenite and a Third Crystal depending on the time of Travel (If you aligned at 8:00pm that stone is Amazonite)

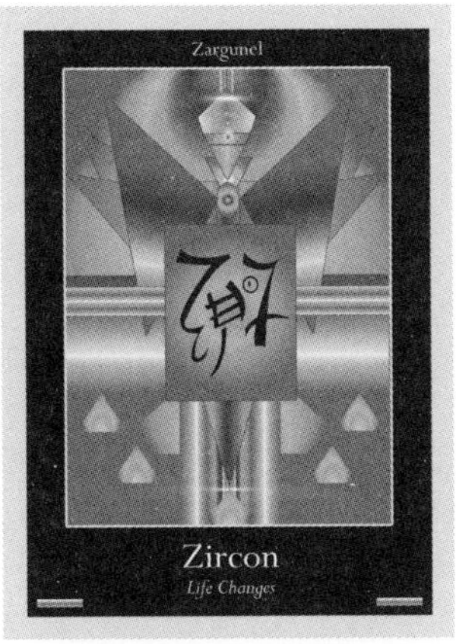

Zircon

Life Changes

The Master Crystal Deva Zargunel

"I am an ancient one, step onto my path, I have come to honor you with the change and movement in life that is necessary in this now moment. Hear now my voice of potential, endless and infinite, the universe lives in you.

You, through me, have become like a ray of light, filled with the integrity and power of spirit. Allow your trust in self to guide every step embracing all change as transition and rebirth. In my Sacred Light, let a new future be born in your every Breath.

Communication runs through me, I am the Breast Plate of the Ages, the spoken vessel of fire, Connector of Worlds and Lord of Change, I kneel at your feet as through you, I am. Hold yourself and embrace the Universe, we are one."

Zircon in Healing

Of the many stones on Earth, Zircon is mentioned in more religious texts than any other, it is truly one of the ancients. Zircon comes in all colors from red to blue, most however, are gold, clear, yellow or a combination of those. It is interesting to note that although this is the most talked about mineral in ancient texts, it is rarely found in crystal shops, this is not due to its rarity, but quite the contrary, Zircon of varying grades is found nearly everywhere and therefore not worth selling. Zircon makes up many of the world's beaches and river beds, the most famous of which would be the Ganges in India (The River of Change). It is also worth noting that this mineral is melted down to form computer chips, so although you may not have it at home as a recognized crystal, there is a good chance she has affected you today.

Zircon is the crystal of 'Life Changes', a fact that it not only offers to us via its role with computers, but also in its healing ability. Zircon activates a Trust in Self at the seed of its work, which blossoms into an embrace of change without fear; the past is forgiven and released, opening all the potential paths forward. The mind is then cleansed and the many parts of the self unite to become one with the single goal, to grow through change with acceptance. It is thus easy to see, Zircon is a great stone for those who, due to past failures, have given up on themselves and are trapped in the past.

As a spiritual development stone, Zircon increases the intuition and sheds light upon the areas of self still to be explored, so the journey of life can continue and the path to higher enlightenment is discovered. It is one of few stones able to link directly into one's genetic level, able to facilitate necessary changes for evolution. This fact was misused in Atlantian times and today is accelerating our race's growth towards 2012 and beyond, even through computers.

Zircon has always been seen as a visual translation stone between Spirit, Man and the Earth, able to bring clarity to messages received from all levels. It is a sacred stone of Osiris, a relationship that stems from its role in the genetic creation of the Osirian and Isirian principles in Atlantis.

At the physical level Zircon is a specific for sciatica and nerve pain associated with the spine. It can be helpful with depression and may be helpful in translating schizophrenic visions, leading to healing and understanding.

Your Healing Journey Today

If Zircon has come to you today change is at your doorstep. The changes that are usually presented by Zircon are ones that have been long-awaited, they are always life altering experiences from which one grows both inwardly and outwardly in the world. The most exciting thing about Zircon presenting for most people is that it usually represents the last part of life change, the part after the pain, tears and attachments have been realized, meaning real change and Now. Zircon is also a great communication stone and will bring focus, determination and forgiveness to the party, through this it lets us see that change is not just about cutting away; it is about formation, realization and Growth. One thing is for sure, with Zircon present, things are about to be very different.

Zircon's Life Changes always permeate all levels of self, they are wholistic, which means you won't see them if you look at single parts, they hide in the open expanse of the whole, the last place a mind would look for them and that is Zircon's real Gift. Enjoy your new world and keep your eyes open for Spiders, Zircon's corresponding animal totem, they often come as validation. This is a contact stone for the Ascended Master Sananda, he may be calling you, sit and listen.

Affirmation;- "My embrace of Change Creates my World."

Keywords to help in reading the cards;- Life Changes, Ancient Worlds, Atlantian Lives, Forward Movement, Intuition, The Right Shoulder, Genetic Evolution, Attachment, Trapped in the Past, Computers, Toxic Liver, Sananda (Jesus), Lord Osiris, Lady Isis, Serapis Bey.

Body Card Placement;- Zircon will work its magic on all Chakras and sites of Nerve pain or Stagnancy. Herkimer Diamond, Apatite, Ruby, Green Calcite and Labradorite are Zircon's best friends and work well in endless combinations and Trinities.

General Healing Trinity;- Energetically, Zircon has a sacred high frequency entry point at the Right shoulder that results in potent healing. This process is facilitated by Sapphire on the Left shoulder and Clear Quartz on the Crown Chakra.

Warrior of Light Trinity;- Ruby at the Right ankle, Labradorite at the Left ankle and Zircon at the Heart Chakra. Green Calcite at the Crown can also help this powerful releasing and healing process.

Chemical Composition;- Zirconium Silicate

Color Rays;- 31% Gold, 17% Silver, 13% Yellow, 13% Indigo, 13% Orange and 13% Blue

Animal Totem;- Spider

Essential Oil;- Juniper

Index of Crystal Trinities

(Sequence Title / Name and Primary Crystal)

Cause of Illness Trinity - Azurite
Chakra System Alignment, Balance and Healing Trinity (Total Healing, Quick Fix) - Kyanite
Channeling Trinity (Increases, Activates and Balances all the Needed Pathways for Spirit Communication) - Selenite
Children's Anger Trinity (Soothes, Heals, Increases Understanding and Expression) - Kyanite
Clear Communication Trinity (Good, Precise Word Choice and Delivery) - Aquamarine
Clear Ray Trinity - Clear Quartz
Clear Vision for Healing Action Trinity (Clear the pathway of Vision and allow control of Freewill) - Malachite
Crown Chakra Trinity (Most Holistic Activation of the Crown Chakra Available) - Diamond
Crystal Healing Enhancement Trinity - Clear Quartz
Crystal Pyramid Trinity (To Create, See and Play Within I.) - Apophyllite
Deneb Kaitos Trinity, Whale of a Star to Visit - Clear Quartz
Depression Healing Trinity - Turquoise
Depression Realization Trinity - Citrine
Devic Communication Trinity - Apatite
Discover Soul Family Members Trinity - Rhodochrosite
Discovering Paths of Service Trinity -Larimar
Dolphin Communication Trinity (Prepares a Person to Communicate with Dolphins and Translate their Song with the Heart for Healing and Growth) - Emerald
Dream State Mastery Trinity -Jade
Earth Breath Layout(Clears, Balances and Heals via the Earth's Energies) - Carnelian
Earth Record Keeper Trinities (Access records from ancient cultures around the world) - Boji Stone
Earth Star Activation Trinity (Amazing Grounding Retaining a Connection to Spirit) - Obsidian
Egyptian Goddess Sekhmet Trinity (Opens Clear communication regarding Power Mastery) - Topaz
Egyptian Past Lives Trinity (Realization and Integration of Egyptian Lives) - Lapis Lazuli
Egyptian Past Lives Trinity - Blue Lace Agate

Elemental Calling Trinities (Sequences of Contact for Earth (Gnomes), Air (Fairies), Fire (Salamanders) and Water (Undines)) - Lodestone
Enter the Phoenix Trinity (To burn in the fires of realization and be reborn) - Blue Lace Agate
Eye of Horus Trinity - Celestite
Eye of Ra Trinity - Gold
Father Issues Healing Trinity - Green Tourmaline
Feeling Healing Trinity (Emotional Detoxification, Embrace and Healing) - Lepidolite
Feline Communication Trinity (To speak Cat) - Sulphur
Female Hormone Balance Trinity - Chrysocolla
Feminine and Masculine Balance to View Life Purpose Trinity - Chrysoprase
General Healing Trinity - Zircon
Gentlest Healing Ever Trinity - Jasper
Grounded Heart Activation Trinity - Rhodonite
Healing Hidden Fears Trinity - Black Coral
Healing Power of the Goddess Trinity (Emotional Healing in the Goddess Space) - Opal
Heart Chakra Trinity (Most Holistic Healing of the Heart Chakra Available) - Pink Tourmaline
Igniting Passion Trinity - Ruby
Increasing Intelligence Trinity - Fluorite
Inner Child Mastery Trinity - Sugilite
Integration of the Three Fold Flame Trinity (Calls, Activates and Holds the Flames in Balance) - Pyrite
Joy and Happiness Trinity (Creates a Space around one for some down time) - Peridot
Kundalini Trinity (Raises the Kundalini Energy in a controlled manner.) - Apatite
Letting Go of Attachments Trinity - Pink Tourmaline
Life Purpose Discovery (This is especially potent with Star Children, helping them make the necessary decisions) - Lepidolite
Life Purpose Discovery and Related Decisions Trinity - Garnet
Light Quotient Expansion Trinity (Increases the level of light in the body cells at rest) - Selenite
Locate Missing Objects or People Trinity - Lodestone
Lymphatic System Balancing Trinity - Sodalite
Male and Female Balance Trinity (Balances on all levels with Self Love as the tool) - Rhodochrosite

Manifestation into the Physical Trinity - Citrine
Mantra Trinity (Explore the hidden effects and gifts of Sound and Music) - Rhodonite
Mayan Healing and Purification Trinity - Topaz
Messages from the Ancients Trinity - Sunstone
Migraine Headache Trinity - Green Tourmaline
Multiple Sclerosis Trinity (Supports, Protects and Facilitates movement in the direction of Health.) - Rhodonite
Music of the Spheres Trinity (The sound the planets make in the Universe) - Rhodonite
New Life Trinity (To open the doors to a new way of Life.) - Amber
Nightmare Trinity (Clears by offering the cause for healing in a less aggressive way) - Gold
Ocean Clearing (Calls the ocean to your aid, a potent healing exercise of Cleansing) - Aquamarine
Panic Attacks Trinity - Sodalite
Past Life Blocks Discovery Trinity - Azurite
Past Lives Trinities - Petrified Wood
Path of the Jackal Trinity (A Testing Pathway through Fears and Self Limitations) - Obsidian
Pathway to Isis Trinity (For the embodiment of the Goddess) - Moonstone
Personal Power Trinity (Mastery and Balance in Expression of Power) - Sulphur
Personalized Menopause and/or Hormone Balance Trinity - Pearl
Pleiadian Healing and Communication Trinity - Turquoise
Power Balancing Trinity for Star Children - Tanzanite
Purification of the Blood Trinity - Garnet
Release to Life Purpose Trinity - Green Calcite
Releasing the Ties Trinity - Lapis Lazuli
Restart Trinity (Creates a re-entry to life or any aspect of it, clearing the past, preparing for change and creating a new vision) - Sodalite
Sacral Chakra Trinity (Most Holistic Healing of the Sacral Chakra Available) - Ruby
Saint Germain Communication Trinity (1) (To potently align with his energy for healing and communication.) - Amethyst
Saint Germaine Communication Trinity (2) -Tanzanite
Sexual Discipline Trinity - Tigers Eye
Sexuality Trinity - Crocite

Sleep Deep and Peaceful Trinity - Howlite

Smoking Trinity (To give up smoking, recover the breath and lung health) - Botswana Agate

Soul Expansion Technique - Charoite

Soul Mates and Twin Soul Trinity (Calls and Draws them to you where needed or possible for Mutual Benefit) - Larimar

Soul Purpose Trinity - Rhodochrosite

Space of Emptiness Trinity (To place one on the middle road, the space between, for healing and spiritual growth) - Amazonite.

Space of Equality Trinity (Delivers one into the space of equality and offers insights on staying there) - Morganite

Space of Knowing Trinity - Celestite

Space of Silence Trinity and Exercise - Chrysocolla

Speak the Heart Trinity (Emotional Verbal Expression Helper) - Rose Quartz

Spirit into the Mind Trinity (Gently merges Spirit into the mind for Healing) - Kunzite

Spiritual Grounding Trinity (This will Powerfully call and hold the Spirit in the Body) - Hematite

Spiritual Growth and Stella Activation Trinity (Increases Light Quotient and Heals that which is not on our Path) - Obsidian

Spiritual Warrior Trinity - Ruby

Star Children Mental Balance Trinity - Sugilite

Star Races and Ascended Masters Communication Trinity - Labradorite

Star Travel Trinity (An amazing journey to your Soul's Stella Origin) - Moldavite

Starchild Activation Trinity (Balanced activation of the Path Forward) - Moldavite

Starchild Anchoring Trinity (Powerful Grounding, Activation and Healing for the Spirit) - Charoite

State of Knowing Trinity (Induces a High vibration into the sought after space of Knowing) - Sodalite

Stress and Worry Trinity - Charoite

Stress Release Trinity - Black Tourmaline

Super Clear, Pure and Real Trinity (The most Purifying Stones in one Place) - Malachite

Surrender to Fear Trinity (Places hidden fears into the hands of spirit) - Selenite

Tantric Mastery Trinity - Carnelian

Tantric Trinity (Opens all the necessary pathways, activates, heals and prepares) - Onyx

Telepathy Trinity (To facilitate and activate Telepathic ability) - Angelite

The Heart Trinity (The Most Potent Healing Sequence of the Heart from Atlantis) - Kunzite

The Initiation of the Star Denebola - Sunstone

The Lord of Time Trinity (Allows one to travel outside of time and space, discover and integrate past and future lifetimes and discover life paths) - Clear Calcite

The Mental Trinity (Mastering the Mental Body, The Third Initiation) - Pyrite

The Rose Quartz Fountain of Forgiveness - Rose Quartz

The Solar Plexus Trinity (Most Holistic Healing of the Solar Plexus Available) - Peach Calcite

The United Self Trinity (A Spiritual Trinity that Powerfully Paves the Path to Ascension) - Herkimer Diamond

Third Eye Chakra Trinity (Most Holistic Healing of the Third Eye Chakra Available) - Iolite

Third Eye Vision Activation Trinity - Iolite

Threefold Flame Balancing Trinity - Hemimorphite

Throat Chakra Trinity (Most Holistic Healing of the Throat Chakra Available) - Blue Lace Agate

Thymus Activation Trinity - Sapphire

Trinity of the Elders - Sapphire

True Self Realization Trinity (Caution; this Trinity is very aggressive in its action) - Opal

Understanding Current Life Circumstances Trinity - Tigers Eye

Uniting the Green Flames Trinity (A powerful Atlantian Sequence of Healing) - Emerald

Uniting the Heart and Mind Trinity - Fluorite

Uniting the Isis and Osiris Templates (Balances Male and Female sides and places one in the active Octahedron of Light) - Smoky Quartz

Vitality Boost Trinity - Citrine

Warrior of Light Trinity - Zircon

Whale Communication Trinity (Prepares a person to Communicate with Whales) - Diamond

Why I chose my Parents Trinity - Aventurine

Wicca Healing Manifestation Trinity (Powerfully manifests a chosen Healing Path) - Moonstone

Index of Masters, Angels and Other Important Beings of the Crystals

1) Agate Botswana - Kuthumi, God Shu, Goddess Tefnut
2) Amazonite - Lord Buddha, Goddess Maat, Krishna
3) Amber - Lord Buddha, Egyptian God Bes
4) Amethyst - Saint Germaine (Usually as Merlyn), Lady Portia, Archangel Zadkiel
5) Angelite - Archangel Mary, Archangel Raphael, Ascended Master Serapis Bey
6) Apatite - Pan (King of the Devic Kingdom), Master Kuthumi
7) Apophyllite - Pegasus, Lord Sirius, Ascended Master Aaron, God Nebo
8) Aquamarine - Ascended Master Saint Germaine, Nimue, Artemis, Ganesha, Archangel Raziel, Nun
9) Aventurine - Ascended Master Tut-Moses, Ascended Master Djwhal Khul
10) Azurite - Archangel Jophiel, Ascended Master Kuthumi, Khephera, Ashtar Command, Saint Germaine
11) Bloodstone - Egyptian goddess Maat, Ascended Master El Morya
12) Blue Lace Agate - Master Vywamus, Lord Maitreya, Archangel Mary, Shu, Brahma, The Phoenix
13) Boji Stone - Entire Devic Kingdom, Master Serapis Bey, Archangel Gabriel, God Geb and Goddess Nuit
14) Calcite (Clear) - Ascended Master Melchizedek, Lord Lanto, Archangel Metatron, Sirius Star System (The Great White Lodge)
15) Calcite (Green) - Lady Quan Yin, Lady Pallas Athena
16) Calcite (Peach) - Entire Angelic Kingdom, Goddess Sekhmet, Lord Maitreya, Lord Sai Baba
17) Carnelian - Ascended Master Serapis Bey, Prophet Samuel (Saint Germaine), Cleopatra, Goddess Sekhmet
18) Celestite - Archangel Raphael, Ascended Master Hilarion, Lord Maitreya, Ra
19) Charoite - Egyptian Goddess Maat, Ascended Master Paul the Venetian
20) Chrysocolla Archangel - Mary, Ascended Lady Nada, Goddesses Isis, Artemis, Mut
21) Chrysoprase - Ascended Master Djwhal Khul, Ascended Master Lanto
22) Citrine Quartz - Ascended Master Sananda (Usually as Jesus), Egyptian God Set

23) Coral (Black) - Lord Maitreya, Ascended Master Sananda (Jesus), Goddess Isis, Anubis
24) Crocite - The Lady of the Sun, Goddess Bast, Krishna, Rama
25) Diamond - Human Beings, Egyptian God Horus, Melchior (The Galactic Logos)
26) Dioptase - QuanYin, Isis, Sananda (Jesus), Akhenaten, The Lady Tara, Archangel Mary, Archangel Chamuel
27) Emerald - Ascended Master Paul the Venetian, The Lady Nada
28) Fluorite - Ascended Master Melchizedek, Archangel Zadkiel, Thoth
29) Garnet - El Morya, Sanat Kumara, Allah Gobi, Saint Germain (Merlyn)
30) Gold - Helios and Vesta (Solar Logos), Sai Baba, Lord Maitreya, Sun God Ra, Horus
31) Hematite - Ascended Master Saint Germain, El Morya
32) Hemimorphite - Kuthumi, Archangel Jophiel
33) Herkimer Diamond - Ascended Master Serapis Bey, Anubis, Lord of Sirius
34) Howlite - Lord Sirius (The Great White Lodge), Entire Brotherhood of Light
35) Iolite - Master Saint Germain, The Lady Portia, Isis, Lord Arcturus
36) Jade - Ascended Master Serapis Bey, Mayan Gods and Goddesses
37) Jasper - Ascended Master El Morya, Archangel Michael, Pan
38) Kunzite - Aphrodite, The Archangel Mary, The Lady of Rose Light
39) Kyanite - Anubis, Thoth, Ascended Master Kuthumi
40) Labradorite - Thoth, Melchizedek, Kuthumi, Saint Germaine, Master Osiris, Pleiadians, Arcturians, Sirians
41) Lapis Lazuli - Thoth, Lady Isis, Ascended Master Kuthumi, Archangel Jophiel, The 24 Elders that Surround the Throne of Grace
42) Larimar - Lady Isis, QuanYin, Lady Nada, Ascended Master Sananda, Archangel Uriel, Goddessess Artemis, Hathor and Nuit, Gods Poseidon and Anhur
43) Lepidolite - Master Hilarion, Archangel Raphael, Goddess Nun, Goddess Qetesh, Egyptian God Neheh
44) Lodestone - Lord Allah Gobi, Master El Morya, Master Osiris, Goddess Inanna, Goddess Anat, Lord Pan, Egyptian God Geb
45) Malachite - Sirius and the Great White Lodge, Goddess Het Heret (Hathor), Master Osiris, Goddess Tara
46) Moldavite - Ascended Master Kuthumi, Sirians, Arcturians, Pleiadians, All Stella Races, Lord Melchizedek
47) Moonstone - Lady Isis, Pallas Athena, Aphrodite
48) Morganite - Egyptian Goddess Maat, Ascended Master Paul the Venetian

49) Obsidian - Saint Germaine, Egyptian God Anubis, Ascended Master Osiris, Goddess Bast, Goddess Sekhmet
50) Onyx (Black) - Anubis, Bast, Ascended Master Osiris, Ascended Master El Morya
51) Opal - Lady Isis, The Lady of the Sun, Master Sanat Kumara, God Uenuku, Goddess Nuit
52) Pearl - Quan Yin, Goddess Artemis, Archangel Uriel, Sirians
53) Peridot - Paul the Venetian Master, Ascended Master Sananda, Lady Nada, Egyptian Goddess Maat
54) Petrified Wood - Ascended Master Serapis Bey, Ascended Master El Morya, Chronos, Dionysus, Neheh
55) Pyrite - Ascended Master Melchizedek, Helios, Vesta, Thoth of Egypt
56) Clear Quartz - The Lady Nada, Maitreya, Sai Baba, Ra, Khephera
57) Quartz Elestial - Ascended Master Melchizedek, Egyptian God Thoth, Archangel Michael
58) Rhodochrosite - Archangel Mary, All Female Masters
59) Rhodonite - Paul the Venetian Master, Archangel Chamuel, Hathor
60) Rose Quartz - Divine Archangel Mary, Lord Maitreya, Goddess Aphrodite, Lady Isis
61) Ruby - Paramahansa Yogananda, Master El Morya, Lord Osiris, Anubis, Bast
62) Sapphire - Lady Isis, Lady Nada, Lord Maitreya, Artemis, Poseidon, Nun
63) Selenite - The Pleiadians, Lady Portia, Vywamus
64) Silver - Lady Isis, Lady Nada, Goddess Hecate, Goddess Mut
65) Smoky Quartz - Ascended Master Osiris, Lord Sananda, The Rainbow Serpent, Geb and Anat of Egypt
66) Sodalite - Saint Germain, Ashtar Command, Egyptian God Horus
67) Sugilite - Saint Germaine, Lady Portia, Archangel Zadkiel, God Bes, God Horus
68) Sulphur - Lord Lanto, Helios, Vesta, Egyptian Deities Sekhmet and Shu
69) Sunstone - Ra, Akhenaten, Serapis Bey, Horus, Goddess Sekhmet
70) Tanzanite - Saint Germaine, Archangel Michael, Lady Portia, Lord Melchior, Angelic Kingdom
71) Tiger Eye - Lord Lanto, Sun God Ra, The Lady of the Sun
72) Topaz - Egyptian Goddess Sekhmet, Master Hilarion
73) Tourmaline (Black) - Master El Morya, Allah Gobi, Anubis, Osiris, Bast, Sekhmet
74) Tourmaline (Green) - Paul the Venetian Master, Sananda, Djwhal Khul, Arcturians, Delphic Oracle

75) Tourmaline (Pink) - Paramahansa Yogananda, Archangel Mary, Master Sananda (Jesus), Goddess Aphrodite, Lady Isis
76) Turquoise - Lord Maitreya, Lord Allah Gobi, Master El Morya, Master Osiris, Geb, Hathor, Estsanathehi
77) Zircon - Sananda (Jesus), Lord Osiris, Lady Isis, Ascended Master Serapis Bey, Archangel Metatron

Resources

Blavatsky, H. .P. *The Secret Doctrine Volume I, Cosmogenesis*. USA: The Theosophical Publishing House. 1978

Blavatsky, H. .P. *The Secret Doctrine,Volume II, Anthropogenesis*. USA: The Theosophical Publishing House. 1978

Blavatsky, H. .P. *The Secret Doctrine, Volume III, General Index and Bibliography*. USA: The Theosophical Publishing House. 1978

Crowley, A. *The Book of Thoth (Egyptian Tarot)*. USA: U.S. Games Systems Inc. 2002

Gurudas. *Gem Elixers and Vibrational Healing, Volume 1*. USA: Cassandra Press. 1985

Hurtak, J.J. *The Book of Knowledge: The Keys of Enoch*. USA: The Academy for Future Science. 1976.

Hurtak, J.J. *The Scrolls of Adam and Eve*. USA: The Academy for Future Science. 1973

Melody. *Love is in the Earth, A Kaleidoscope of Crystals.* USA: Earth-Love Publishing House. 1985

Raphaell, K. *Crystal Enlightenment, The Transforming Properties of Crystals and Healing Stones, Volume 1*. USA: Aurora Press. 1985

Raphaell, K. *Crystal Healing, Therapeutic Application of Crystals and Stones, Volume 2*. USA: Aurora Press. 1987

Raphaell, K. *The Crystalline Transmission, A synthesis of Light, Volume 3*. USA: Aurora Press. 1990

Satvic, G.T. *Know Thyself, Sathya Sai Baba's Messages in His Own Words*. India: Sai Towers Publishing, 1995

Schroyens, Dr F. *Synthesis, Repertorium Homeopathicum Symtheticum*. London: Homeopathic Book Publishers. 1990.

Whitcomb, B. *The Magician's Companion, A Practical and Encyclopedic Guide to Magical and Religious Symbolism*. USA: Llewellyn Publications. 1993.

Diagram:

The Current Sacred Cyclic Order of the Mineral Kingdom

Crystal Name.	Order	Crystal Name.	Order
Larimar	1	Peridot	40
Tanzanite	2	Jasper	41
Pyrite	3	Kunzite	42
Boji Stone	4	Crocoite	43
Clear Quartz	5	Silver	44
Diamond	6	Rose Quartz	45
Tourmaline (Pink)	7	Morganite	46
Charoite	8	Malachite	47
Lapis Lazuli	9	Carnelian	48
Sodalite	10	Bloodstone	49
Rhodochrosite	11	Blue Lace Agate	50
Selenite	12	Rhodonite	51
Hemimorphite	13	Azurite	52
Turquoise	14	Smoky Quartz	53
Sugilite	15	Aquamarine	54
Sapphire	16	Tiger Eye	55
Pearl	17	Opal	56
Coral (Black)	18	Moonstone	57
Tourmaline (Green)	19	Jade	58
Chrysocolla	20	Onyx (Black)	59
Herkimer Diamond	21	Apatite	60
Citrine Quartz	22	Apophyllite	61
Gold	23	Amber	62
Amethyst	24	Iolite	63
Angelite	25	Aventurine	64
Amazonite	26	Hematite	65
Fluorite	27	Sulphur	66
Lepidolite	28	Lodestone	67
Zircon	29	Petrified Wood	68
Ruby	30	Chrysoprase	69
Labradorite	31	Howlite	70
Calcite Green	32	Moldavite	71
Agate Botswana	33	Obsidian	72
Kyanite	34	Celestite	N/D73
Tourmaline (Black)	35	Quartz Elestial	N/D74
Topaz	36	Dioptase	N/D75
Emerald	37	Calcite Peach	N/D76
Sunstone	38	Garnet	N/D77
Calcite Clear	39	N/D=Next Dimension	

Please note this is a repeating Cycle, it has no true beginning or End.

Diagram:
The Liquid Crystals on the Tree of Life.

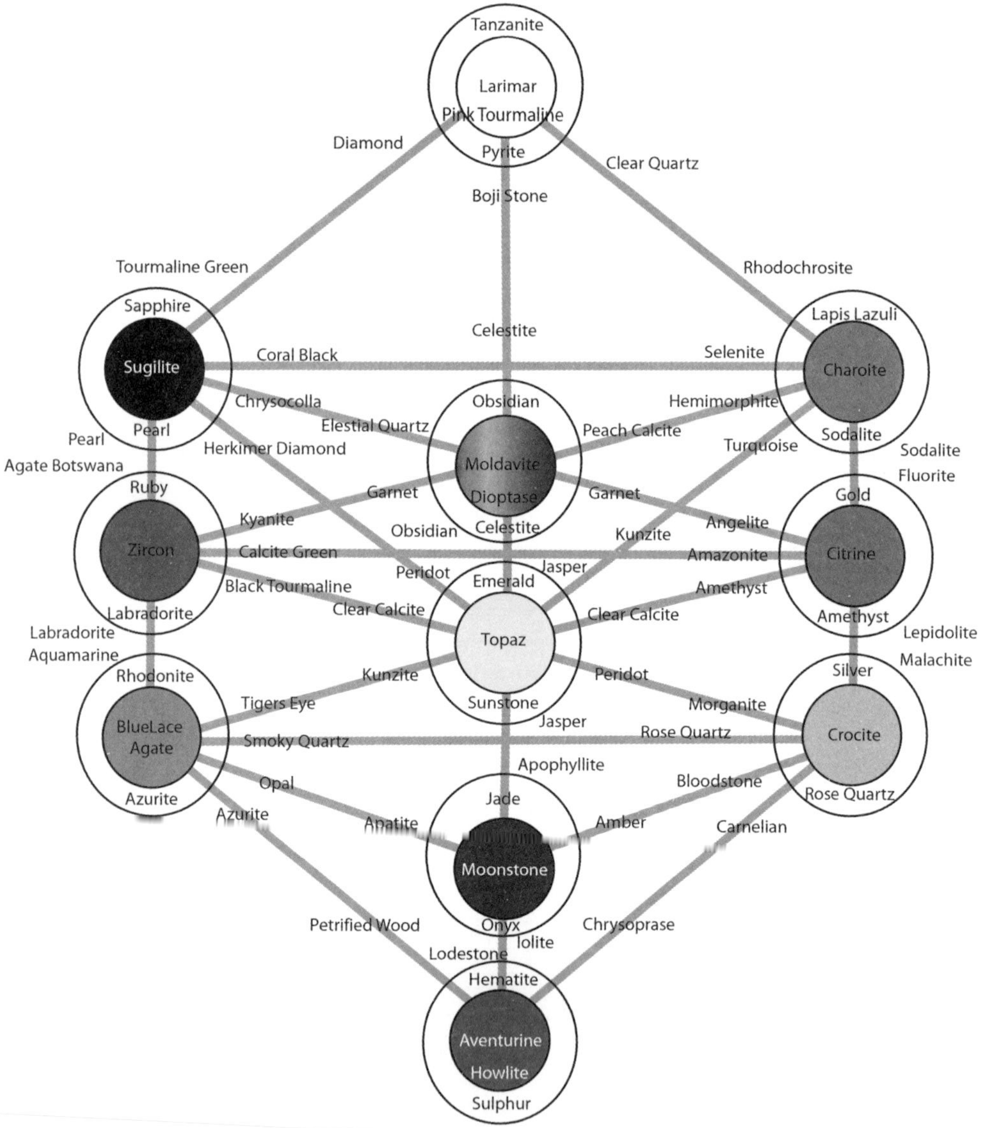

Diagram:
The TLC Crystalline Spine

Vertebrae	Crystal / Mineral Associations
C1	Obsidian
C2	Moldavite
C3	Celestite
C4	Tanzanite
C5	Larimar
C6	Pyrite
C7	Lapis Lazuli
T1	Charoite
T2	Sodalite
T3	Sapphire
T4	Sugilite
T5	Pearl
T6	Gold
T7	Citrine Quartz
T8	Amethyst
T9	Ruby
T10	Zircon
T11	Labradorite
T12	Sunstone
L1	Topaz
L2	Emerald
L3	Rose Quartz
L4	Crocite
L5	Silver
S1	Azurite
S2	Blue Lace Agate

Vertebrae	Crystal / Mineral Associations
S3	Rhodonite
S4	Onyx (Black)
S5	Moonstone
CX1	Jade
CX2	Sulphur
CX3	Aventurine
CX4	Hematite

About the Author

Justin Moikeha Asar grew up in the magical Pacific islands of Vanuatu. He views each day as a lifetime, seeing physicality as our ultimate gift and he encourages the embrace of Truth, Unity and Oneness through the natural cycles.

Teaching spirituality throughout Australia and around the world, Justin's firm physical grounding in Naturopathy, High Magic, the Druid principles, and Hawaiian, Egyptian and Atlantian spirituality is a balanced dance with his intimate embrace of the higher celestial realms as a keeper of the Pleiadian Liquid Light Technologies and an aspect of the Brotherhood of Light on Earth. Recently, Justin stepped into his known birth purpose as the seeding member of the Atlantian Hierarchy in preparation for its externalization to the world. Over the past 15 years, through the teachings of the 'Spirit of Geburah,' a master Ruby gifted from a Tibetan monastery, Justin has re-birthed the Liquid Crystals into the world, as an Atlantian Crystal Healing modality.

So far, Justin has become fluent in the Atlantian language both spoken and written, he has re-united the mineral kingdom, restoring its ancient sacred order. His work has led to the true recognition of the Master Crystal Devas by name and symbol and revealed the 11 ancient Atlantian cities. It has also assigned the Gods, Goddesses, Angels, Ascended Masters, Tarot, Tree of Life, Animals, Oils, Plants, and even the Stars back to the Crystals of Earth. The Liquid Crystals has quickly become the most advanced and holistic crystalline modality on Earth, offering the true Atlantian Way of Oneness.

Realized and guided from birth, Justin has deliberately withheld much of his work to avoid the inevitable classifications offered by the masses that would block his personal growth. However, he is now opening the doors and the Atlantian Way will become more available so we may live in harmony on our new Planet.

More information on Justin's work, meditations, courses and activations is available through the Liquid Crystals website: **www.TheLiquidCrystals.com**, or by visiting 'The Liquid Crystals' Facebook page where many crystalline souls gather.